My Heart Belongs

Peter Pan

MY HEART BELONGS

by Mary Martin

QUILL

New York 1984

Grateful acknowledgment is made to the following for permission to use their photographs:

© ABC-TV, page 88
Slim Aarons, page 187
Joseph Abeles Studios, pages 195, 201, 237
Zinn Arthur, page 184
Blumenfeld © 1946 renewed 1974 by The Condé Nast Publications, Inc., page 120
CBS-TV, page 141
The Central Press Photos Limited, page 280
Dallas News Staff Photo, page 219
John Engstead, Frontispiece, pages 227, 308, 309, 311, 312, 316
The Lynn Farnol Group, Inc., page 168
Jim Frank, page 335
Sy Friedman, page 13
Toni Frissell, Courtesy Frissell Collection, The Library of Congress, pages 192, 243
Mrs. Oscar Hammerstein's Collection, page 161
Wallace Litwin, page 109
Don Loomis, page 206
Los Angeles Civic Light Opera Association, page 204
Theatre Collection, The New York Public Library at Lincoln Center, Astor, Lenox and Tilden Foundations, pages 77, 198
Angus McBean, page 269
Roderick MacArthur, page 191
Gjon Mili, pages 111, 241
Bob Golby, Museum of the City of New York, page 162
NBC-TV, page 147
Jack Paar, page 256
Paramount Pictures Corporation, pages 86, 87, 90
Radio Times Hulton Picture Library, pages 139, 158
Otto Rothschild, Los Angeles, page 151
Jan-Michelle Sawyer, Kapiolani Children's Medical Center, page 321
Stork Club, page 67
Time/Life Picture Agency © Time, Inc.:
    Philippe Halsman, page 165
    Charles Moore/Black Star, page 275
    Mark Kaufman/Life, page 288
United Press International, page 76
Universal Pictures, Inc., pages 85, 88
The White House, page 339
Wide World Photos, Inc., page 272

To

the one who taught me the meaning of
the words *heart* and *belongs*—my husband,

Richard Halliday

I am enormously grateful to Dora Jane Hamblin, without whose help this book would not have been written.

My Heart Belongs . . .

I
"Will you crow for us?"

I certainly will.

I've been *on,* all my life, and "Will you crow?" has been one of my favorite questions for more than twenty years, since the first time I played Peter Pan.

Of all the exciting shows, the marvelous moments, the happy memories of what now seems a long, long life, Peter and Never Land loom largest in my mind. Partly because I love Peter so, partly because everyone else in the world loves Peter so. Mostly, I think, because Never Land is the way I would like real life to be: timeless, free, mischievous, filled with gaiety, tenderness and magic.

Most of my life has been spent in the magic make-believe world of the theater, where one tries to make people happy, make them forget their problems, wrap them for a few hours in beauty, music, laughter. For those of us privileged to be in show business there is a lot of very hard work and endless discipline, but I for one adored it. I'm still delighted to come back, as Wendy says, when "spring-cleaning time comes."

Peter's shadow, which always falls across the backdrop of a theater as he flies away, falls across my memories and the memories of friends I have never even met. When I go to big parties it seems to me there are ranks and ranks of people lined up, all saying, "The first show I ever saw was Peter Pan," or "The first time I ever saw you, you were Peter." All of them, generations of them. It makes me feel a bit like Rin Tin Tin, but I love it.

No doubt I crowed with a great many of them, sometime, somewhere. Crowing was often the only way to get children out of the theater. They simply would not go home; their mothers couldn't do a thing with them. So I would go down to the footlights and say, "Now, repeat after me."

Then I would crow. First softly, just a little *er-er*. The children would repeat it. Then I'd do *er-er-er*. They repeated. Finally a big loud *er-er-er-errrrrrrrrh* at the top of my lungs and oh! what joyous bedlam followed!

My final gesture was to blow fairy dust across the footlights. Then, at last, the children would leave, their voices crowing up the aisles, out of the theater, up and down Broadway. It was music to my ears but not necessarily to their mothers'. We got hundreds of letters saying, "Now that you've taught them to crow, how do we make them stop?"

I stripped all the gears in my throat, crowing. Not always for children. One day I was walking across Fifth Avenue in New York when suddenly a manhole cover rose up and out came a big, strong stevedore type with a hard hat on. He looked straight at me and said, "Peter, will you crow for me?"

"Certainly," I said. I stopped right in my tracks and crowed as loud as I could. The man smiled, said, "Thank you," and disappeared back down the manhole.

Peter Pan is full of circles for me. All my life is full of circles. Maybe everybody's life is this way, but mine is a circle and a circle and a circle, dissolving and expanding, touching other circles, closing again. Places and people who have been in my life always come back, sometimes years later. When one circle breaks, another starts. Then they merge.

The first person I ever taught to crow was our daughter, Heller. She was twelve years old, playing Liza, the little maid, in our first production of *Peter Pan*. She had just finished dancing her first ballet with the lion and the ostrich in Never Land, a ballet created by Jerome Robbins, whose billing on the program read—for the first time—"Entire Production Directed and Staged by Jerome Robbins."

A lot of thrilling firsts for all of us—and the beginning of a circle. Liza and Peter—Mary Heller Halliday and I—crowed on

Peter Pan teaching Liza (our daughter, Heller) how to crow.

Broadway at the top of our lungs in 1954, only to come full circle in May, 1975, when Mary Devon DeMeritt, Heller and Bromley DeMeritt's first baby girl, opened her beautiful dark eyes, waved her tiny expressive hands, and my granddaughter, the third Mary, crowed at *me*.

Heller's sons by a previous marriage, Timothy and Matthew Weir, looked pleased and proud and grown-up, though they were only ten and eight. The first time I crowed for them was in the spring of 1972, when my husband, Richard, and I came back from our farm in Brazil for a visit. The boys had never seen me in a show, but they knew my records. Matthew knew them so well, at age four, that he corrected me if I missed one single word while singing to them when they went to bed.

Richard and I had taught the boys to call us *vovó* and *vovô,* "grandmother" and "grandfather" in Portuguese, so when a knock came unexpectedly on my bedroom door at six o'clock one morning I wasn't surprised to hear Matthew calling me *vovó.*

"Vovó," he said, in one of those deep bass voices some little boys have, "may I bring some friends to meet you?"

Most of my life I have not been an early riser or, shall we say, at my best upon awakening. I was determined to be the world's best *vovó,* however, so I pried my eyes open, cleared my throat, and asked, in one of those deep bass voices some grandmothers have at 6 A.M., "When, darling?"

"Now," said Matthew. "They're here."

In marched a stair-step procession of little boys. None of them had ever laid eyes on me before. I sat up straight as I could, put on my best smile; Matthew graciously extended one arm in my direction and made the introduction:

"Meet my grandmother, Peter Pan."

It seems incredible even to me, but I never saw myself as Peter Pan until Christmas, 1974. I must have been one of the last people in the United States to see it. I remember at the time of our first television version, in 1955, the press reported that sixty-five million people watched it, a record at the time. I couldn't see it because it was live and it wasn't taped. Neither was the second television version in 1956. At that time the studios made what they call kinescope recordings of performances, and I finally saw one of those at Christmas. The third television *Peter,* which we performed in 1960, was taped. That is the one which is reshown occasionally, but I have never seen it.

When it was reshown in March, 1973, in the United States and Canada, hundreds, literally hundreds, of our friends sent cards, letters, cables that night to Brazil to tell Richard and me how thrilling it was to see the production again. The last thing they saw on their screens was "Produced by Richard Halliday." Next morning, on the early news, they heard that Richard had left us. He was fighting for his life in a hospital while they were watching the show.

Thus closed the most important circle.

I have been three people in my life, "I," "we," and "me." When I was young I was "I." Then for thirty-three years I was "we." That was the most important period. I would always have had a career, I suppose, but it would not have been the same one without Richard. He shaped it, directed it, guided, provided. Richard was the boss, always. He took care of everything, gave me the precious freedom to work, to perform, without all the irritating distractions and details. He dealt with those. Only now am I beginning to realize the millions of things he did for me every day, every hour, every minute of our lives together. It was *our* career.

If he were here, Richard would help me write this book. But now I am "me," alone. I can still hear his voice, kind and stern, saying, "Never apologize." Through all the years he insisted, "Don't be one of those performers who flutter and say to friends backstage, 'Oh, no! You weren't here *tonight?* I was in dreadful voice.' "

I remember, Richard. No apologies. Here goes on the circle of my life.

II
Curtain Up

I was born in Weatherford, Texas, on December 1, 1913. That was first Monday, horse-trading day. My father always insisted that they traded off a horse and got me.

Daddy wasn't a horse trader. He was a lawyer, and a pet. "Pet" was even his nickname, short for Preston Martin. My mother, Juanita Presley, was the musical one of the two. At the age of seventeen she had become a violin teacher at Weatherford Seminary, now Weatherford College.

She risked her life to have me. Doctors told her she could never safely have another baby, but she wanted a son so much that she just had to try once more. All the neighbors were waiting for the big event; the signal of my arrival was to be the raising of a curtain in Mother's bedroom window in the white frame house on West Lee Avenue.

It must have been a good omen—curtains have been going up for me ever since.

Weatherford was a wonderful place to grow up in. We had a big rambling house, a barn with a Shetland pony for me and a jumping horse for my sister, Geraldine, a small orchard in which every single tree was eventually climbed by Mary Virginia Martin, and a vegetable garden from which I loved to pull up new green onions, then wrap them in a cold biscuit to make the best sandwich I ever tasted.

There was also a square, with a courthouse in the middle.

My beautiful mother, the violin teacher, at the
Weatherford Seminary—now Weatherford *College!*

I thought the square was my own personal property, because I
loved it so and I knew everybody in every store all the way around.
On the first corner was my favorite grocery, owned by Mr. Sharp.
He gave me huge dill pickles from his big briny barrel. Just beyond was Mr. Richards' sporting-goods store. I always stopped
there to look at things I yearned for—boxing gloves, punching
bags, bicycles.

The barbershop was next. One of my special friends was
our barber, Zeddie Crow. Most of my life I have had bangs, in
one shape or another, and every week Zeddie cut my hair in a
Buster Brown bob. I was mad for Buster Brown; I even named
my dog Tige, after his. I was terribly disillusioned to find out
that Buster Brown was a midget, not a little boy. I was so eager
to be like him that I never consented to wear big girlish bows
on my hair until I found out the truth about Buster. One day
Zeddie gave me my own little scissors, which may have been a
mistake. I arrived home with a widow's peak, no bangs, and a
lifelong passion for cutting hair—my own or anybody else's. Dur-

Long before I sang "Daddy" in a Teddybare I had my own teddy bear and wore my first Teddybare.

ing the run of *South Pacific* the management and cast gave me a red-and-white striped barber's pole and a fake license because I spent the time between matinees and evening performances cutting the hair of the cast and crew. They used to line up outside my dressing room.

On the second corner of my square was Corcanges' drugstore. Jolly, round, black-haired, Greek Mr. Corcanges taught me how to make cherry phosphates and chocolate sundaes. His tall blond wife introduced me to reading. She had a rental library in the shop and I was one of her best customers. In those days I chose books more by weight than by content. I read *The Well of Loneliness* and *The Life of Isadora Duncan* at age eleven. I didn't have the remotest idea what they were all about, but they certainly were *big* books, and I did think that Mme. Isadora had an exciting and dramatic ending, breaking her neck with that scarf and all.

Baker-Poston's dry-goods store was between Corcanges' and the motion-picture house. There wasn't a week that I didn't go through Baker-Poston's from one end to the other. What I liked best was their system of making change; to me it was like the beginning of space travel. You made a purchase, gave the money to a dear little lady with gray hair. She put the money and the bill in a steel capsule about the size of a large cucumber, pulled a handle on a chain, and up it would go, *zip* to the ceiling and then on an elaborate wire system to some cage in a mysterious office at the back of the building. There another gray-haired lady would make the change and send the cucumber and the receipt back to you. Even if I had only ten cents, I would buy something for five, just to watch this miracle happen.

The next corner was the bank. I didn't have any business with them, so I passed by to Daddy's office on the second floor of a building he owned, with a butcher's shop underneath. Daddy had about four rooms overlooking the square. I am sure he saw me making my rounds, knowing that he would be next. He was a terribly busy man but always had time to see me. Daddy had time for everyone. I have seldom known anyone who had the depth of feeling for other human beings that my father had. No problem was ever too small to bother with, no problem so big that he wouldn't tackle it.

He was tall, good-looking, silver-haired, with the kindest brown eyes. Mother was the disciplinarian, but it was Daddy who could turn me into an angel with just one look.

One of the most vivid memories of my childhood is the first time I heard Daddy in a courtroom. I was terrified. I was standing out in the hall, waiting to go in, when suddenly I heard my Daddy's voice as I had never heard it before. He was ripping into his best friend, Mr. Sam Shadle. That Mr. Sam was on the other side of the case didn't mean anything to me. I just thought, "In one more minute he's going to sock Daddy because of all that loud talk and the awful things he's saying."

When they broke for lunch, out came Daddy and Mr. Sam with their arms around each other's shoulders, laughing like lunatics. So help me, Mr. Sam came home with us for lunch, and then back they both went to out-yell each other some more. I decided then and there that I would never understand the law.

Right outside the courtroom, on the lawn, was a bandstand where the town band played every Saturday night. I used to sing there, in a trio of little girls dressed up in bellhop uniforms, doing things like "Moonlight and Roses," or "When the Red, Red Robin Comes Bob, Bob, Bobbin' Along." Even in those days without microphones my high piping voice carried all over the square. I have always thought that I inherited my carrying voice from my father. Also, his sense of timing.

On the opposite side of the lawn from the bandstand was a huge plaster watermelon. Weatherford, or more properly Parker County, Texas, is famous for its tremendous Tom Watkins watermelons. They grow—or used to—up to one hundred pounds. I find my friends skeptical about this, but I have pictures to prove it. On Fridays and Saturdays I remember horses and wagons tied up all the way around the courthouse, filled with these huge watermelons. The smell of them, and of horses, dill pickles, ice cream, and leather boxing gloves, is with me still.

Years later somebody put up a big sign on the courthouse lawn: "Weatherford, Texas, home of watermelons and Mary Martin." I never got top billing in my beloved hometown.

Perhaps to compensate for her disappointment in not having a son, Mother tried to make me into the most feminine thing you ever saw. She could design and sew anything, and she made me the most beautiful clothes—"all on her fingers," as we say in Texas. Every Christmas she gave me a doll with a fabulous handmade wardrobe.

I must have known that she really wanted a boy, because all the time she was trying so hard to make me feminine, I wanted to be a boy. I climbed trees, hung by my heels from the trapeze, ruined all my lacy dresses, and lovingly *un*dressed all my beautiful dolls on Christmas morning, never to play with them again.

Like all children I was sure I could fly. One day I tried it, from the roof of our garage, and landed with a broken collarbone. It was years before I found out that I *could* fly, but only with the help of a beautiful idea and a very strong wire.

Never, never, never can I say I had a frustrating childhood. It was all joy. Mother used to say she never had seen such a happy child—that I awakened each morning with a smile. I don't remember that. I do remember that I never wanted to go to bed, to go to sleep, for fear I'd miss something.

Mother was strict about manners. To this day I can't walk out of an elevator or into a building, if I'm with someone, without waiting for them to go first. I must confess that I wasn't always that polite to Sister, christened Geraldine, called Jerry by her friends, and always known to me as just Sister. She was eleven years old when I was born, and she had the most terrifying medical diagnosis that I have ever heard—"leakage of the heart." Nowadays, thanks to science and miraculous operations, it can be cured, but in those days she was a semi-invalid. I used to watch, furtively, to see if her heart really leaked, but I never saw anything.

I remember carrying trays upstairs for her meals. My poor darling sister is lucky she didn't die of malnutrition because I usually sat down midway on the steps to enjoy the best of each of her breakfasts, lunches, and dinners. Fortunately she had wanted a baby sister as much as Mother wanted a baby boy, so she put up with me. It must have been trying for her to accept a baby who grew into a healthy demon of a tomboy, but she was forever rushing to my rescue, getting me out of scrapes which might have brought down the wrath of Mother or Daddy.

Mother wanted me to go to school as soon as possible, and to learn to play the violin. Rather reluctantly, I started both at age five. Neither was a big success. Mother delivered me to kindergarten on the first day, but by the time she got back home I was there to greet her. I knew a shortcut across the meadow.

This ritual delivery-and-escape went on for about a week, until Mother had a brilliant idea: she took my little green-wicker rocking chair over to kindergarten. As soon as I got out of that dull, hard seat at my desk I was happy as a lark, rocking back and forth and occasionally putting my feet on the desk. I've always been happier with my feet up in the air. The teacher must have been balmy to allow it, but at least I stayed in school.

Violin lessons were somewhat the same thing. My ear was much better than my reading, so I simply memorized the music, by ear. Only in later years have I learned the treble clef enough to pick out melodies with one finger. But from the time I was born I could *hear* notes, and reproduce them.

Until this day if a violin in the orchestra is a fraction under or over the note, it drives me wild. That doesn't mean I can play one! I still bow a violin today exactly as I did at age five. I even did it onstage, for more than two years, in *I Do! I Do!* but every night the same sounds came out, the same ghastly sounds I made at five.

One of the important circles of my life is the fact that every single solitary thing I learned in Weatherford, Texas, every experience, every little trick or skill or game or joke, was useful to me sometime, somewhere, later on.

I'm sure this is true of most people, but it is uncanny to me how many long-ago things come back, repeat themselves. There were the cartwheels, for example. I don't even remember who taught me to do cartwheels, but I loved them. When I went to the Third Ward School, which was just up on West Lee Hill,

I would come home from school by starting at the top of the hill and doing cartwheels all the way down, two blocks, without stopping.

All the mothers would see me and run to call my mother and say, "She's doing it again!"

I never got hurt doing cartwheels in Weatherford, but more than twenty-five years later I knocked out a conductor, an accompanist, and myself doing them across stage during rehearsals in New York. It was the "Wonderful Guy" number in *South Pacific*. At one point I had to do a crossover, get from one side of the stage to the other, and Josh Logan, our director, was trying to think of some bit of business I could do on the crossover. He asked if there was something I could do, something I would like to do.

"Sure," I said, "I can do cartwheels across the stage."

"And sing at the same time?" he asked.

"Why not?" I replied. "I did them from the Third Ward School clear down to my house in Weatherford."

So we put them in. I would sing "I'm in love" . . . cartwheel . . . "I'm in love" . . . cartwheel . . . "I'm in love" . . . cartwheel, etc., "with a WONDERFUL GUY!" Clear across the stage.

That was fine. I had done it a thousand times in rehearsals, and I was having a ball. Until one of the last days before we went to New Haven to open. Josh wanted more light on the stage instead of just the dim rehearsal bulbs, so he could sit in the theater and judge the whole show. They brought in big spotlights and put them on either side of the stage. I started off and everything was going normally until I came up from a cartwheel and caught one of the spots right in my eyes. Instantly I was blinded. I didn't know where I was, where the floor was. But given the momentum . . . I went over again, flipped, went flying up into the air and off into the orchestra pit.

I landed first, briefly, on conductor Salvatore Dell'Isola's head. I bounced off that, hit the piano, crashed onto Trude Rittman's head—she was playing the piano at the time—and then onto the floor of the pit. The last thing I heard was Trude's voice saying, "Oh, God, my neck is broken." Out front all anybody heard was a big loud, thump, thump, thump. Then silence. The conductor was out like a light; Trude was out like a light; I was out like a light. They all thought I had been killed.

Fortunately nobody's neck was broken, least of all mine, though one whole side of my body just turned into jelly. I had to play for weeks with the black-and-blue half of me frozen by one of those spray things, so I couldn't feel all that battered flesh. When we opened in New Haven there were no cartwheels. That night I sent a football helmet full of flowers to Dell'Isola, and another to Trude Rittman.

One thing my mother never had to make me do was learn songs. I sang from morning till night. I also danced, and learned "pieces." My first elocution teacher was Auntie Flo Hutchinson. She wasn't really my aunt, but everybody in Texas is Cousin, or Uncle, or something. She had little red books with impressive titles like *Evolution of Expression* which all her pupils had to memorize. They were full of things by Wordsworth, Browning, Longfellow. My favorite was Robert Browning's "The Laboratory." Auntie Flo's method was that you read the poem aloud, looked for the key word which expressed the thought, and then underlined the word and stressed it as you read. In "The Laboratory," for example:

> Now that I, tying thy glass mask *tightly,*
> May gaze through these faint smokes *curling* whitely,
> As thou pliest thy trade in this *devil's*-smithy—
> Which is the poison to poison *her,* prithee?

For ages I thought "prithee" was somebody's name, but I adored doing the piece, in which I could be a little dancer in the king's court. The king was looking at a new dancer, and I got to poison my rival. Delicious. I also got to dance.

I could memorize very quickly when I was a girl, and even today I have an almost photographic memory for words, dialogue, scenes. Always I see and remember the key word, usually an adjective or a word that reminds me of something, which makes the subject matter *spring* to mind, makes it move, have impulse. This is still, I'm sure, because of what Auntie Flo taught me.

My first voice teacher, when I was twelve years old, was a

wonderful lady by the name of Helen Fouts Cahoon. She had
been a friend of my parents from their high-school days. Later
she married and went to Chicago to study, then came back to
head the voice department at Texas Christian University at Fort
Worth, the nearest city to Weatherford. I thought she was the
most beautiful woman I had ever seen. She was a coloratura
soprano so naturally I wanted to be a coloratura soprano. I
begged my parents to let me take voice lessons, and I begged
Miss Helen to take me.

Years later she confessed that she hadn't known quite
what to do with me. I sang all the time—nobody could make me
stop—but I was too young to study voice seriously. She made me
promise never, never, never to push my voice in any serious, classical repertoire except when I went to her for lessons, twice a
week. Probably she saved my voice by this rule that I thought was
so terrible. She also taught me breath control, which was a very
good thing. I have needed every breath I could get onstage these
many years. It takes breath to fly and sing, to ride horses and
sing, to do cartwheels and sing.

Again, the circles: when I first went to New York to try
to make it on Broadway, my friend Mildred Woods and I found
an apartment on Fifty-seventh Street. We rented a penthouse
from Mary Anita Loos, the niece of Anita Loos and also a
writer. She was moving out, but before she left she said, "There's
someone in this building who says she knows you. Her name is
Helen Fouts Cahoon." I couldn't believe it. Miss Helen had been
teaching music in New York for years and there she was, one
floor below me.

I ran down the back stairs and rang her bell. We started
working together again, and I never stopped taking lessons from
Miss Helen all the rest of her life. Whenever she had time and
I had time, I ran down the stairs and worked. There wasn't
any air conditioning in New York in those days, and the more
I vocalized, the hotter I got. One day I had stripped off practically
everything, down to my slip, when I noticed a man in the building across the street peering toward Miss Helen's windows with
binoculars. I ran to the window and hollered, "That's all right
for now, but someday it will cost you four dollars and forty cents
to see me." Nowadays I'm less astonished by my sassiness than
by the price of a seat on Broadway in the late 1930s.

Long before I met Miss Helen, or any other singing teacher, I had made my debut before a real audience—not just my doting parents or some captive playmates. The occasion was a firemen's ball in Weatherford. I was five. I sang with my first beau, Ford White, about seven. Our number was "When the Apples Grow on the Lilac Tree." We were a hit, but my biggest passion that great night was not Ford White. It was the fire trucks and the big brass pole in the station. I longed, yearned, to slide down that beautiful glowing pole. That ambition wasn't to be realized until years later, when Richard and Jerome Robbins put a fireman's pole into Peter Pan's house in Never Land. They had it made, smuggled it onto the set, and Jerry gleefully showed it to me, shouting "Surprise!" I got to slide down it hundreds of times.

The year I was twelve, I put on a two-hour recital with my best friend, Bessie Mae Sue Ella Yaeger, playing the violin. Bessie Mae lived in Mineral Wells, Texas, about twenty miles away. Her parents and my parents had been friends before they were married. Bessie Mae and I were practically raised together. We studied all the same things outside of school. She learned to play the violin, she sang, she recited. But I danced better.

On the night of my recital I sang, danced, "spoke pieces," and performed a one-act play in which I was all five characters. The following week Bessie Mae did her own recital in Mineral Wells and I danced. I remember part of her performance was that she sang *Madame Butterfly,* in English, in costume, and in key. She still has her costume, and at the drop of a hat she will get up and perform *Madame Butterfly,* in English, in hysterics, and only slightly in key.

Bessie Mae and I were very much alike. We came from the same environment; we had the same talents. We even looked alike—brown eyes, reddish hair, though hers was darker. We were both exhibitionists. She had personality, charm, warmth—all qualities which have been attributed to me, rightly or wrongly, through the years. So why did I have the career and not Bessie Mae? Or why Mary Martin instead of *Jerry* Martin?—she certainly has the same genes and loves people as much as I do.

Now after all these years I think I know part of the answer. I react to an audience. Give me four people and I'm *on.* Give me four hundred and I'm a hundred times more on. Bessie

On the night of my elocution recital. Bessie Mae Sue Ella Yaeger was guest violinist.

Bessie's recital. I was guest dancer. She *certainly* got a lot of flowers.

Mae and Sister prefer to perform for smaller groups, individuals, their immediate families. Sometimes I think that I cheated my own family and my closest friends by giving to audiences so much of the love I might have kept for them. But that's the way I was made; I truly don't think I could help it.

In the same year that Bessie Mae and I did our recitals, I discovered the Episcopal church. Mother was marvelous about religion. She thought that people should know all sects and then decide what was best for them, what helped them the most. She and Sister became Methodists. Daddy I'm not sure ever made up his mind, but he went with them to the Methodist church every Sunday. I attended every church in town.

I loved Sunday school at the Methodist church because of Miss Price, a wonderful teacher who made Bible stories so exciting, so stimulating. I went to the Baptist church on Sunday night, for B.Y.P.U., the young people's organization, and I went to the Presbyterian church for choir practice on Wednesday nights. I was a little afraid to go to Mass at Weatherford's Catholic church because I didn't know what they were saying, or even if it was proper for me to be there. But I loved Father Burns because he played baseball. I never could get over a priest playing baseball with me, his flying skirts and my gangly legs, and cookies and cream soda at his house afterward.

There wasn't a synagogue in Weatherford, but we had a Jewish family, the Haases, next door. I practically lived in their kitchen, so I probably learned more about their philosophy than any other.

Now that I think back on it, food had a lot to do with my churchgoing. Very often there was a birthday cake at the Methodist Sunday school. There were punch and cookies at B.Y.P.U., tea and cake at choir practice with the Presbyterians. Best of all was the Negro church where I went with my darling nurse, Billie, who practically brought me up. *Her* church had fried chicken.

It was the Episcopal church which finally had everything I was looking for: beauty, formality, pageantry, singing, and a great minister, Reverend Barlow, who gave a sermon on talent which I have never forgotten and never will. Mr. Barlow read from the Scriptures about talents, and I understood that God gives them and that He will take them away if we don't use them properly. I never forgot that lesson. All my life I have felt guilty if I didn't use any talent I have, as fully as I could.

All this time I sang in any church that would turn me loose. I also sang for the ladies of the Garden Club, the Music Club, the DAR, and the Eastern Star. Then I graduated to the men's clubs: Lions, Rotarians, Elks, Shriners, and the Knights of Pythias.

I also played dress-up at the drop of anybody's hat. By this time Sister, who had been told that the leaking valve in her heart might close by the age of sixteen, had completely recovered. The valve had closed, and she was well. At age eighteen she went off to a girls' school in Denton, Texas. We still didn't know each other very well, because an age difference of eleven years seems a lot when one is eighteen and the other is seven. But I certainly did get to know her wardrobe. We had a cedar closet where Mother stored winter clothes, including Sister's. I found the key. Those clothes thereafter got much more wear off season than in season.

The worst thing I ever did to her was to wear her Persian Princess costume before she did. The organizers of something called the Cotton Bowl Pageant in Waco, Texas, had chosen Sister to represent Persia. The Persian Princess of West Texas, I guess, though why Persian, I'll never know. Sister hadn't gotten home from school, but I had. I found the most beautiful jeweled turban with egret feathers flying straight up, the most fascinating baggy silk pants, the craziest gold, turned-up shoes. It would have been downright sinful not to put them all on. I did. Just then Sister walked in. Mother spanked me, hard, with the wooden side of the hairbrush.

Most times Mother and Sister let me get away with murder, really, though I can still hear my Mother's voice saying, *"Now what have you done?"* Whenever she brought herself to whack me with the hairbrush I would refuse, stubbornly, to cry. She would say, "Heartless child, why won't you cry? Anybody else would cry."

All she had to do, and she knew it, was say, "I'm *sad* because of the way you behave," and I would burst into tears and cry and cry and cry. All my life I have acted first and thought later. Physical punishment didn't impress me much, but to admit that I have hurt someone's feelings, or failed them in what they expected of me . . . well, that is the end.

Anyway, that was the first but not the last time I ever played a Persian Princess.

In my heart and in my dreams, though, I was everything else. I was everything I ever saw on what we called "the silver screen." When I was young there was only one motion-picture house in Weatherford, the Palace. I was its best customer. The owner was Mr. Kindel, who was another of my "kissin' cousins," though we were no kin. Daddy was Mr. Kindel's lawyer, so our family had a pass. Mother would not have allowed me to go to every single movie that ever came to Weatherford if it hadn't been for that pass.

I sat there in the magic darkness, eating bags and bags of popcorn, gulping down chocolate ice cream cones, and saw practically everybody who ever performed in silent movies. Then the first talkies. When Al Jolson sang "Mammy," I cried for three weeks. Even now if I hear that song, I cry.

My ambition to be part of the world of make-believe was born right there. Strangely enough it wasn't for the movies that I yearned, but for the stage—for Broadway, though then I probably hadn't even heard its name. Certainly I never had seen a live performance, but I didn't know the difference. To me those people on the screen were live.

Most actors and actresses learn their craft in school, or in summer stock. I learned mine at the movies. After weeks and months and years of stumbling out of that enchanted Palace Theater, blinking in the light of everyday Weatherford, I had become an accomplished mimic. I won prizes for looking, acting, and dancing like Ruby Keeler. For singing *exactly* like Bing Crosby. For fluttering my hands like Zasu Pitts. I learned every Busby Berkeley routine I ever saw. It may not have been the best training, but I'm grateful for every single thing I learned.

I even learned stagecraft—and a little more—from one of those inspired public-school teachers who turn up, praise be, every now and again. Mine was Mrs. Alvis, in junior high school. She looked like a Dresden figure and to me she was a saint. One afternoon soon after I went into junior high she called all the girls into her room for assembly. She read to us "My Creed" by H. A. Walter. It is a very inspirational poem and it was never forgotten by Mary Virginia Martin. The words are still what I have tried to live by.

> I would be true, for there are those that trust me;
> I would be pure, for there are those who care;
> I would be strong, for there is much to suffer;
> I would be brave, for there is much to dare.
> I would be friend to all—the foe, the friendless;
> I would be giving and forget the gift;
> I would be humble, for I know my weakness;
> I would look up—and laugh—and love—and lift.

Even more than that creed, Mrs. Alvis' voice and presence made an impression on me. From the moment she began to speak, I felt that wonderful thing which can happen in the theater: chemistry. Between teacher and pupils, performer and audience. It is the most exciting experience in the world. It is the secret of all successful communication, the magic of expressing what you believe and holding those who hear.

Unfortunately for me, this was rarely true in my classes. I never thought I was learning very much. My teachers didn't think so either. Singing, dancing, reciting were my three R's. Other things I tried to learn by instant application and recall. Mother and Daddy never tried to interfere with all my outside activities, but they had a rule in our house which I knew very well: I *had* to pass in school. To do so, I used my quick memory to "photograph" every chapter of every subject, at the very last moment, before an exam. This usually worked, but after the exam was finished I couldn't remember a thing. And yet today I can still sing songs in phonetic French, or Italian, or Spanish, that I learned at the age of twelve.

My quick study failed me utterly once. It was my senior year in high school. I had the lead in the senior play, a song in the baccalaureate service. On the side I was in love with the captain of the football team. I also had to pass geometry. Poor Mr. Craddock, the geometry teacher, was also the football coach. Perhaps he understood me because for him teaching was only a sideline to coaching, and for me geometry was a bore because I cared only for "the arts"—except, of course, for the boy who was the captain of Mr. Craddock's team. There we were, two people staring at each other across an empty classroom and a world. We might as well have been speaking Greek. After my third futile attempt to pass the exam he sighed, tore up my paper, and said, "I could keep you here until you're fifty, and you won't understand geometry any better than you do now. You have talent for other things. I suggest you work hard cultivating it for the rest of your life. You'll need to."

I did graduate, which was fortunate for all the family. Daddy was president of the school board, and it would have looked awfully odd if he had handed me my diploma when I was fifty.

My graduation was odd enough as it was, because I had just

had another of my impetuous accidents. That one, I always thought, was because I was both *too* conscientious and not conscientious enough. Mother always said, "Let your conscience be your guide." I wish she had never said it, because to this day if I ever go against that inner voice of mine, I get into trouble. But I keep trying to go both with it and against it. I hope that doesn't indicate that I have a shifty character.

My accident happened on the important day of the senior-class picnic at Lake Mineral Wells. Mother made me promise not to go swimming, because it was early in the season and I had too many responsibilities in the class affairs to follow. I must not catch cold and lose my voice.

I agreed with her completely, but I also took my bathing suit. I did not plan to go *in* the water, just *on* it, in a boat. Six of us were having a divine time rocking the boat while the rest of the class went swimming. Suddenly the boat tipped over. Now my conscience, rather belatedly, became my guide: I had promised not to go in the water, so I leaped as fast as I could toward the embankment. And landed on a broken Mentholatum bottle which promptly cut my right foot almost half in two.

My friends, those who hadn't fainted at the sight, took me to Bessie Mae Sue Ella Yaeger's father, who was a doctor in Mineral Wells. He took one look and said, "Well, Boy [he always called me Boy], we'll have to sew that up very quickly. It will hurt."

It did. They didn't give Novocain in those days.

I played the lead in the senior play on crutches. I sang "O Divine Redeemer" at baccalaureate on crutches. And poor Daddy, who had bought a new white suit especially for the occasion, had to hand me my diploma as I lurched by on crutches.

III
Even Tomboys Grow Up

Shortly after I fell off the trapeze at about age five and bled all over my best white organdy dress, my mother put me into what she called rompers. I adored them, until I discovered the opposite sex. There was a very short interval between these two events. Everything starts early and happens fast in Texas—at least to me.

When I was very young I found boys' games a lot more interesting than girls' games, and then when I got a little older, I found boys more interesting than girls. The first man in my life was my darling daddy. But there were also Cub and Howard. They came along with Billie, who was their aunt. They were *all* my family. Billie did everything but breathe for me. I have a brown birthmark high on the calf of my left leg, and for years and years I thought Billie had touched me there, with her finger. Every time I asked her if it was her fingerprint, she said, "Yes, Baby, yes." I was so proud, I loved her so.

Cub was our handyman for everything. Howard was my playmate. Cub always got me out of trouble with higher-ups like Mother and Daddy, and Howard practically let me kill him with my wild schemes. He was two years older than I, but he always got the worst of any deal I cooked up. I always wanted to play the villain, so he had to be the victim, burned at the stake or scalped, or anything else my mind invented.

He did best me once in a watermelon-eating contest, and

then he washed my face in the rind. He was right. Howard Young grew up to be a leading citizen of Houston.

Then there was James Porter McFarland. He was the best fighter in the second grade, one of my favorite boyfriends. One Christmas I wanted boxing gloves, and Santa Claus, who may have been a little worn down by my incessant requests, gave them to me. I trained harder than Jack Dempsey ever did, and then I took on James Porter McFarland. I knocked out his two front baby teeth.

James Porter was pretty nice about it. He later invited me to swing with him in our new "glider," a swing that can seat four people. We swang and we swang and we swang and somehow the glider hit something and knocked out *my* two front teeth. But I can say with pride that he never laid a glove on me.

Later on, I got less combative. I became a southern belle. I think every girl baby is born knowing how to flirt . . . first with her father, then with any other male in sight. From the time I was very young I went to dances, chaperoned by my mother and all the other mothers in all the towns I went to—Forth Worth, Mineral Wells, Dallas. I had my share of beaux: Georges, Ralphs, Bobs, Toms, and one—I can't remember his name—who told me that I had such big brown eyes that you could drop little kittens into them. Well!

My first true love came when I was twelve. That sounds silly, but I guess people can fall in love at age twelve. His name was Gus Cranz, and he was the freshman yell leader at Rice Institute in Houston, He was seventeen, or maybe eighteen, and he had a kind of Gary Cooper face, with bright blue eyes. I loved him, and I always will. He invited me to attend the big freshman weekend at Rice, and my understanding parents drove me more than three hundred miles to have this exciting experience. They both thought I was suffering from puppy love, but *I* knew that Gus was the most handsome, most intelligent, dearest, kindest junior cheerleader on any varsity team in the whole world.

I had a passion for purple, I thought it was so sophisticated, so Mother made me a purple suit for the occasion, then we both got carried away and added a purple hat and coat.

I even had real silk stockings. Never had I felt so terribly grown-up—until we arrived at the hotel. Gus met us. Daddy inquired about our reservations, we got into an elevator, we arrived at our room. Just in time to see a baby's crib being moved into it. My darling daddy had written from Weatherford requesting reservations for "Mr. Preston Martin, wife and baby."

Every time my father entered our front door he shouted "Wife!" and in all the years of their marriage, my mother never got over the embarrassment of it. She thought it was undignified. I thought it was funny. I thought his calling me Baby was funny, too, until that day in Houston. But he called me Baby until the day he died.

I had a blissful weekend, and I met a new friend named Lynn Foster who invited me to stay with her. She and Gus were friends; their mothers were friends. Gus sent me a red rose on my breakfast tray every morning, and one day Lynn said, "If only I could meet a man who would send me a rose on my tray . . ." She had already met him—Gus. He married her.

Then there was Ben. Benjamin Jackson Hagman. Ben's grandparents had emigrated from Sweden, where the family had been silversmiths and jewelers, and settled down in Racine, Wisconsin. Eventually they owned lumber mills near Grand Rapids. In 1906 they moved again—to Texas. Ben's father, William Louis Hagman, named Ben for the two Americans he admired most—Benjamin Franklin and Andrew Jackson.

Unfortunately I only knew Ben's father the last year of his life, and I never met his mother, Hannah. She was a practitioner in the Christian Science church for almost twenty years and died, tragically, of cancer, before I met Ben.

I always regretted not knowing the complete family because they were very devoted and all three sons—William Jr., Carl, and Ben—were big, handsome, vital young men who had inherited a warm joy of life from their parents.

I met Ben when I was fourteen, but I didn't go with him until my last year of high school. We tried to make up for it all during summer vacation. That may have been one reason why my parents packed me off to Ward Belmont, a young ladies' finishing school in Nashville, Tennessee. I went at sixteen and I finished it all right—in two and one-half months.

Before I went, I was looking forward to it. Bessie Mae had gone there the year before and she was eager to share her own excitement about the school with me. At first I adored it, too. I made a lot of friends, and I sang at every club function anybody ever gave. My club was Penta Tau, a local sorority. There were no nationals at Ward Belmont. To this very day I never do a show, anywhere in the country, without some Ward Belmont girl coming backstage to say, "Well, I never . . . I remember little ole Mary Martin sittin' on top of an upright piano, singing just like Fanny Brice, or Ruth Etting."

That part is fun; I love seeing my old classmates. It was joy, too, when years later I worked on Fannie Brice's radio show, and sang for her one of her great numbers, "I'm Cooking Breakfast for the Man I Love." I could still imitate her, in a version I had sung from the top of the upright piano at Ward Belmont.

But apart from the singing and my friends, school was dull.

I wasn't accustomed to strict rules about makeup, to limited dating, hours on campus, chaperons all over the place. I did love the head of the music department, Dr. Stetson Humphrey, and his wife, Irene. They were the first "northern couple" I had ever met. I thought "Doc" was fabulous, and Irene had sung opera at La Scala in Milan, almost unheard-of for a young American singer in that day and age.

Other lessons were less than fascinating. Once in English class the teacher asked us to write a theme on our favorite historical personality. The first one that came to my mind—maybe because of my Ben—was Benjamin Franklin. In my dormitory room I read everything I could find about him. It was so interesting, and I learned so much, that I just copied down every word. And added a few dramatic variations and embellishments of my own, of course. Later, in class, the teacher gave a lecture on plagiarism and read out my name as an example of a plagiarist. I didn't even know what the word meant until Bessie Mae explained it to me.

Then came the day when I had to write the midterm theme. I don't remember what the subject was, but it must have been serious, because I was terrified. I didn't want to write it. I couldn't write it, I thought.

The truth was, I was homesick. For Weatherford, for Mother. I had never been away from Mother for such a long time before, I never realized how close I was to her, what an integral part of my life she was. I was genuinely sick. Homesickness can be that strong.

As always, Mother came to the rescue. She got Ben and the two of them drove all the way to Nashville. To comfort a homesick teenager.

Only now do I realize that perhaps Mother was troubled, too. If there was one thing she loved more than anything in the world, one way she could work out her problems, it was driving a car. She always drove as fast as the car would go, for miles. When she got home, she always felt better. So she got in the car with Ben and she *drove*.

When they got there, Mother helped me get consent to escape from the stately cage of Ward Belmont for two or three days in town. None of the students could get out without parental consent.

Then Ben and I talked Mother into letting us get married. Through the years, I never stopped wondering why she gave her consent. She could have prevented it, but she didn't. No doubt she had her reasons. She loved me so much that she could seldom bear to say no, for one thing. Perhaps one part of her said that if she let me marry young she would always have me as a daughter, and she would also have Ben as the son she wanted so much.

I used to blame Mother for my early marriage. Even when I started to write about it, I blamed her. As I wrote it all down, the blame faded away. Now that I have a son and daughter of my own, now that I have watched them go through physical and emotional problems, I realize that Mother just plain didn't know what on earth to do about me. Although I had always had beaux, I insisted that I was in love with Ben. Mother knew that in my silly head was a dream of a "cottage small," with picket fence and roses and babies. She probably was terrified that I would go and have an *affair*, a word unthinkable in those days.

Also, I must be frank: I wanted to get out of Ward Belmont, and I did *not* want to write that term paper. I never did, as it turned out. While I'm confessing I might as well admit that I have always wanted to have my cake and eat it, too. It has never worked.

Anyway, Ben and Mother and I went off to Hopkinsville, Kentucky, and I got married at the age of sixteen. How hillbilly can you get? In Hopkinsville it didn't matter if you were fourteen, fifteen, sixteen, they handed out the license anyway. Ben was twenty-one, so that was all right, he didn't need his parents' con-

Benjamin Jackson Hagman—
Ben—and me.

sent. I don't remember whether Mother went with us to get the license, but I remember she was in the Episcopal church when we walked down the aisle. I hummed a little bit, because I knew somebody should be singing "Oh, Promise Me" or "Because," or one of those things. It was November 3, 1930.

I had forgotten completely that I was supposed to sing "O Divine Redeemer" at church at Ward Belmont that very weekend. Doc Humphrey and I had rehearsed it for days. Right out of my head it went. Ben and Mother and I drove straight from the wedding back to the gates of Ward Belmont. I kissed Ben and Mother good-bye and went back to my room in the freshman girls' quarters.

Maybe if Ben and I had gone from the ceremony to our home, to our marriage . . . I don't know. Our plan was that I would go home to Weatherford for Christmas holidays, we would announce our marriage, and I would live happily forever after with Ben, free of scholastic discipline and free of parental supervision.

That was the plan.

Soon after my marriage, Bessie Mae became desperately ill from an infected foot and had to go home. I was so envious I could have died. How could she go to blessed Texas if I, a married woman, ahem, had to stay at school until Christmas? I broke down and told her all about Hopkinsville. Never in all her life, before or since, has she been speechless, but she was that night. We finally decided to tell just a few dozen of our closest friends, and let nature take its course.

It did. Within a few hours I was called to the dean's office. Never before had I been honored by such a summons. The dean was a dear man, a southern gentleman, and I am sure he was far more embarrassed than I was. We stared at each other for a long time and then he said, "Miss Mary, I understand that you have broken the rules of the school."

That I had, but I thought I'd just wait until he got to the main event. He said, "Ah, it has been called to my attention that you have . . . ah . . . um . . . married the young man who came from Texas to visit you."

I said, "Yes, sir."

"Miss Mary," he asked, "has this marriage been . . . ah . . . um . . . consummated?"

I didn't know the word, so we stared at each other for another long time. When he asked if I had ever "lived" with this young man, I could say firmly, "No."

"Good!" said the dean. "Then it can be annulled."

Annulled? There went my freedom, there went my plans. There went my cottage small and there came that midterm theme.

After some fast talk from me, and a telephone call which confirmed my mother's consent to the marriage, there was nothing the poor man could do but send me home. I wasn't exactly kicked out, it was just that married ladies don't belong in finishing schools. Or didn't then.

I was ecstatic. Bessie Mae and I could go home together on the train. It was only the second time in my life I'd been on a train. The first time was going *to* Ward Belmont.

At the Fort Worth station there was a whole committee to meet us. Ben jumped on the train first and slipped a wedding ring on my finger. Then we got off to greet his family, Bessie Mae's family, and my family—all but Daddy. Ben had told Daddy of our marriage but I had never heard a word from him afterward. I never knew what he thought. As we walked in the front door of our house, Daddy said only, "Hi, Baby, glad you're home."

We spent our honeymoon at my house, our first "wedding night" in my old bedroom. None of it made any sense. We were too young. I was hardly prepared for the physical aspects of marriage. In those days, one rarely spoke to mothers about sex. I didn't know enough to talk to a doctor, a minister. It's difficult to believe, now, how ignorant we were.

Our marriage was not consummated for a week or so, but almost from the moment it was, I was pregnant. Boom. I had morning sickness the whole time. There I was, right back where I had started, but pregnant, with no little white house with roses. Ben liked to hunt and fish and play cards. I tried to keep up, to be the little Texas housewife. I played bridge in the afternoons, when I wasn't throwing up, and I played poker at night with Ben and his friends. But I never really liked games.

On September 21, 1931, our son was born. We christened him Larry Martin Hagman. He weighed eight and a half pounds and was the image of his father. I weighed ninety pounds and was terrified by the baby. I did all the things I longed to do—breast-feeding him for three months, making formula, learning to give him a bath without drowning him, and singing him to sleep.

It was all role playing. I felt that Larry was my little brother, Ben my big brother. Role playing was something I had known since I was born, but it wasn't a good basis for a marriage.

Ben had a job as an accountant but those were Depression years and it was difficult to make ends meet. He could pay the daily bills, that was about all. Mother and Daddy had given us a house, a car, our furniture. Right away Ben decided to become an attorney-at-law, like Daddy, whom he always worshiped. He started studying at night. Eventually he had to devote hours and hours to study, and he had to go to Austin, Texas, to take the bar exams, so he left his job and we all moved to Weatherford again to live with my parents.

It was a practical decision, but it left me deep in the heart of—a vacuum. Back home, Mother took over Larry, Billie took over me, and Daddy paid the bills, looking after us and loving us. I was allowed to take Larry out sometimes, but every time I did, something happened. Other children could ride around a ring on a little Shetland pony with an attendant leading it, but when Larry did it, he fell off and broke his collarbone. He fell from slides. He got stung by bees.

All these childish disasters had happened to me, too, but Larry was different. He was Mother's son. She changed her accusation from "What have you done now?" to "What have you done to *him* now?"

I was seventeen years old, a married woman without real responsibilities, miserable about my mixed-up emotions, afraid there was something awful wrong with me because I didn't much enjoy being a wife. Worst of all, I didn't have enough to do.

Everything happened so fast that I had to wear my graduation dress for this first formal picture of me with my baby, Larry Hagman.

At this point Sister, as always, came to my rescue. Several years before she had married a man from "up north," Robert Andrews. Very sensibly, they had waited awhile to have a baby, so when my Larry was born, their son Bob was only nine months old. Suddenly, Sister and I had everything in common—our babies, domesticity, time on our hands for laughing and talking together. We spent hours, days together and grew closer than we had ever been before.

Sister has complete, unselfish love. Far from being even a tiny bit jealous, she was proud of me before I ever did a thing. Every time I performed anywhere, she wrote five hundred thousand letters to five hundred thousand of her closest friends. They must consider me the poor man's Frank Sinatra in Texas because Sister wants to charter buses, trains, airplanes, anything she can lay her hands on, to bring *everybody* if there is a chance I will perform anywhere inside Texas or even near it.

In the months while we were laughing together and playing with our babies, Sister knew something was wrong. She would

look at me in a particular way she has, with her steady brown
eyes, all the wheels running around like crazy inside her head.
One day she asked, as casually as she could make believe, "Have
you ever thought about teaching dancing?"

How that thought ever occurred to her, I will never know.
But she was perceptive enough to see that I desperately needed
something to do. Throughout my young life people kept describing me as "just a natural-born dancer," but the truth was that I
didn't know one single step, not one loving thing about dance
routines. I had picked up some imitations of tap dancing from
watching Ruby Keeler and Eleanor Powell at the Palace Theater,
and I knew Ginger Rogers when we were little girls. Ginger lived
on Cooper Street in Fort Worth and was a member of the very
select Cooper Street Gang. I was taken into that giddy company
as the only out-of-towner because I could do the Charleston so
well. Not as well as Ginger could, of course: she later won the
West Texas Charleston contest and was on her way to fame.

Sister helped me on my way by teaching me my first real

That's Sister on the left when
she taught me the waltz clog.
I'm the other one.

dance step, something called a waltz clog that she had learned as a physical education major at Columbia University. She explained it to me, demonstrated it, and I wrote it down in my own semi-literate dance language:

1. Step—Brush—Brush—Ball—Change
2. Step—Brush—Brush—Ball—Change
3. Step—Brush—Hop
4. Step—Brush—Hop

When I had mastered this, in about ten minutes flat, it dawned on me that I could teach it to others. Had I ever thought about teaching dancing? I just *had*, at that very moment; I tasted the first true happiness I had known in two long years.

To Sister, Fanchon, and Billy Rose

IV
A Funny Split
and a Sad One

I opened my first dancing school when I was eighteen in what had been my uncle Luke's grain-storage loft. Uncle Luke was one of Daddy's brothers, and he gave me the space free. It was enormous and drafty, but it was on my beloved square. We swept out the remains of corn and wheat which Uncle Luke had stored there, managed to get a piano up the steep, shaky stairs, put up a barre for ballet training, and I was in business.

Oh the nerve of me! My first pupils were three very bright little girls who learned "Sister's Waltz Clog" at their very first lesson. I began to make up ballet steps, becoming a choreographer before I had ever heard the word. At night I drove about twenty-five miles to Fort Worth to learn as many routines as I could from a young man there. He taught me the Shim Sham, the Shuffle Off to Buffalo, and a triple time-step with break.

Within a month I had thirty pupils. I was running hard, giving lessons all day, studying every night. I loved every minute of it and I had a virtuous feeling that I was contributing to our nonexistent "financial state." Just how much I contributed is another question. I charged two dollars a month for two lessons a week in a group class, four dollars for private lessons.

Many families couldn't afford even that, or didn't want to, because tap dancing, which everybody considered just a fad, was hardly in a class with piano lessons or violin. But in all small towns the moment one child starts something all the others want to do it, too. The children were clamoring to take lessons, and their parents and I settled on that good old Depression barter system called "taking it out in trade." The grocer would give me four dollars' credit for his little Jackie's lessons, the filling-station man gasoline in return for his son's instruction.

It would have made an accountant shudder to look at my accounting books, but it didn't matter because there were no books. In addition to gas and groceries, there were clothes for Larry in return for the department store owner's daughter's lessons. Ben and the family were proud of me but they didn't take it very seriously. Neither did I. That first year I never dreamed of having my school become a business. Anything was better than playing cards, and I was doing something I wanted to do—creating.

Soon, by rushing back and forth to Fort Worth to keep one step—literally—ahead of my pupils, I had expanded to teaching tap, ballet, acrobatic, ballroom dancing. I still had only one big room, so it had to be blocked off with imaginary partitions to separate all the activities. It also had to serve as reception room and audience hall where mothers could sit and wait for their children, or watch the lessons.

This led to one of the funniest encounters I ever had with a mother. She came up our rickety old stairs holding by the hand a little daughter who was just champing at the bit to learn to tap-dance. Daughter was all bright-eyed and a little shy, but Mother looked stern and—*scared*. She explained that their family was rock-ribbed Baptist and didn't believe in dancing, but that her daughter would give her no peace until she had looked into this new thing called tapping.

Thank goodness I have always been quick on the trigger, so I allowed as how her daughter was absolutely right. Tap was really a form of exercise which was very good for healthy young bodies, I said, something like gymnastics. That mother was just as eager to please her daughter as was any other mother, so she said she would stay and watch a demonstration lesson.

How she ever came to terms with her soul I don't know, but from that moment on she brought her eager little beaver to every lesson. If I was giving ballroom lessons, she would turn her back to the part of the room where this sinful activity was taking place, and would only do an about-face when the tap lessons began. Her daughter became one of my very best pupils—"exercise" pupils, that is.

I guess the next funniest one was an oilman from Oklahoma, about sixty years old, who walked in one day and demanded to take private ballroom lessons. I was a little dubious, but because he could pay hard cash for his lessons, I accepted him happily. He was a good ballroom dancer and took to his lessons like a natural. Finally he broke down and admitted what he had really come for. He wanted to learn to tap-dance. So help me, he solemnly learned Sister's waltz clog!

After the first school season, I decided I had to learn an awful lot more—enough material to take those quick little pupils of mine through another year of instruction. I looked into schools for dancing teachers and found one that sounded divine: the Fanchon and Marco School of the Theatre. The list of courses made my head spin and my feet tingle: Standard and Ultra-Modern Tap, Acrobatics, Ballet, Toe, Spanish, Character, Adagio, Baby Work, and Production Routines. As if that weren't enough, also Costuming, Staging, Lighting, Production Effects, and Expression.

This was for me. But it was in Hollywood, California, and how was I ever going to get there? Again, my wonderful father came through. He was so surprised and delighted that I was ever going to make anything of my life that he advanced me money for both the trip and the tuition.

Mother, as always, wanted me to have anything I desired. She was delighted to keep Larry. Ben, happy with his new career as a lawyer in Daddy's office, with his hunting and fishing, was agreeable. Off I went, happy as a lark, with friends who were driving to California.

The first thing I learned was how little I knew. There were about fifty teachers, from all over the world, in that class and most of them had been in the business for years. Because I was young and "kinda Texas cute," every instructor at Fanchon and Marco wanted to put me in the front row. Then they would start calling out combinations of steps and I hadn't the remotest idea what they were talking about. Sometimes the instruction was in French, sometimes in Spanish, but even when it was in English, I might just as well have been back in geometry class.

Years later I learned that the secret of success in show business was to work your way from the back row of the chorus to the front. Not me, not then. I spent most of my time trying to work my way furtively from the front to the back, where I could see and not be seen.

Out of all those fifty teachers, I got the most for my money. I didn't waste one waking moment. I studied eight hours a day and then practiced for hours anywhere I could find an empty room in the school, until they locked it up for the night.

I also volunteered for everything. One day in acrobatic class the instructor asked for a volunteer to try a new machine they had rigged up to teach pupils how to do the split. There were two boxes on a trolley, on the floor, and a rope hanging in the center from the ceiling. The idea was to put one foot on each box, hold on to the rope, and gradually let the boxes slide in opposite directions. This was to be a daily, gradual procedure, with each pupil learning just how far down into a split he or she could comfortably go. Until finally, after days of it, the pupil could do a perfect split on the floor.

Given my past history, everyone is probably ahead of my story. I not only volunteered, I also grabbed that rope and shoved out with both feet and went into an instant split. Well past a split: my legs were at a slight angle and my—there is no other word for it—crotch was on the floor. Then, of course, I couldn't move. When they finally got me out of this precarious position, they took me to a doctor to coax my legs back into their hip sockets. For days I walked as if I had one foot on the curb.

At Fanchon and Marco came another of those wonderful men in my life, and another circle. The man was Nico Charisse, who taught modern and Spanish dancing, also castanets. He was wonderful to me. His sister Nanette taught me ballet years later in New York, and his sister's child, Ian Tucker, was the smallest of the Lost Boys in *Peter Pan*. Nico used to come through Texas to see me, and there on one trip he stopped in Amarillo and met a Texas ballet student named Cyd. They were married and she became the beautiful Cyd Charisse.

When I got back to Weatherford after that first stint at Fanchon and Marco, everybody looked me over to see if Hollywood had changed me. On the outside it hadn't. Inside I think it had. I was hooked on the excitement of show business.

My school had changed more than I had. While I was away Mother and Daddy had *built* me a studio as a surprise. It was a jewel of a red-brick building which looked like a one-story home, just a block from our house, directly across from the high school. It had a wood-paneled reception room, a stone floor, a fireplace. French doors opened onto a paneled studio with windows on three sides. Mother, who had designed it all, found an antique mirror from some old saloon in Fort Worth and it covered one entire wall. There were ballet barres, a dressing room with bath and showers for students. There were tumbling mats, medicine balls, a piano, even—wonder of wonders—a Victrola just for the school.

Classes, immediately, were enormous. Everybody in Weatherford wanted to find out what I'd learned in Hollywood. I had learned more than dancing. My first ads in the Weatherford *Daily Herald* and *Democrat* were pretty grand:

> Mary Hagman School of the Dance
> Mary Hagman .... Director
> Aileene Newell .... Assistant
> Nona Ruth Potter .... Accompanist
> Estelle Holloway .... Business Manager

Aileene was a beautiful teen-ager who was an extraordinarily quick learner. Nona Ruth could play any type of music on the piano—classical, jazz, combinations. Estelle was one of the most fun, liveliest grandmothers I have ever known. She kept the books and made up schedules, rode herd on the mothers, tried to make us all eat—especially me. There was a little kitchen in the studio —right away we got fancy enough to call it a studio instead of just a school—but somehow I never had time to get in there.

In addition to these helpers, I also by this time had my dear Mildred Woods, who was to be friend, companion, chaperon, boss, secretary for years to come. At first she helped out with Larry. I had become so busy that I couldn't help Mother handle the house and "our" little boy. Mildred was two years older than I, with the fattest, roundest little five-foot body, a tremendous amount of freckles, and the most glorious red, curly hair I have ever seen. She came from a little town called Peaster, near Poolville. I love funny names like that; I collect them. Well, Mildred thought Weatherford was a city, by comparison with Peaster, and she loved our big house. From the beginning we felt like sisters. All my time and energy could go into the school.

And did it go! I designed costumes for the pupils, worked up a total class of one hundred, started a reducing class for young and middle-aged matrons, planned a gala spring recital, opened another Mary Hagman School in Mineral Wells, twenty miles away.

Mineral Wells was a resort town. People came from all over the world to drink the waters; remember Crazy Water Crystals? I had so many Mineral Wells pupils that my "staff" decided I should go there once a week. Uncle Luke didn't own any lofts in Mineral Wells, and I could hardly ask Daddy to build me another studio, so one day I went over to talk to the manager of the Crazy Hotel. He talked to the president of the Crazy Water Crystals company, Hal Collins, and we made a deal. They would give me the rooftop ballroom for my dancing classes. In return I would sing in the lobby, with the hotel orchestra, every Saturday.

This was my first singing job, though no money changed hands. I didn't know it, but that was to be the pattern of my singing career for some years to come. From that day until I finally left Texas, I sang each week on the radio from the lobby of the hotel with Jack Amlong and his band. I was known as "Mary Hagman, the Crazy Girl." No comment.

More of the men in my life: Jack Amlong taught me how to sing into a microphone; his pianist, Frank, taught me how to phrase blues songs. As "the Crazy Girl," I sang everything from hillbilly, "Hand Me Down My Walkin' Cane," to "Stormy Weather."

I also whistled. Now if there is one thing I really am proud of, it's my whistle. Dancing and singing, I'm not so sure, but I can whistle up a storm. Loud or soft, high or low, sexy or sweet. I whistle while I learn my lines. I whistle in taxis. My family insists that I do it all the time, whether I'm aware of it or not. It must be maddening.

During our second year, the Mary Hagman School had recitals in both Weatherford and Mineral Wells. They were something to behold. I had one routine, using "The Blue Danube Waltz," that just about knocked everybody's eyes out. Dozens and dozens of little girls tapped, in complete precision, to "The Blue

Danube" in every conceivable rhythm—waltz, tango, march, four-four. That routine would still be good today.

So would my Martinettes. That's a pretty corny name, I admit, but I got the idea from the Fanchonettes, twenty-four perfectly matched dancers, all beautiful girls, who did production numbers at the Paramount Theater in Los Angeles and the Fox Theater in San Francisco. I just had to have something like that for my school. I compromised with twelve instead of twenty-four, and I selected them from high-school girls aged fourteen to seventeen. They had three things in common: beauty, overdevelopment for their age, and total lack of any knowledge of dancing.

Training the Martinettes was a labor of love, because none of them could afford to pay for lessons. We worked in my spare time, usually lunch hour or at night after the ballroom classes had finished.

They performed in public for the first time at the Weatherford spring recital. It almost killed us all, including my mother, me, and a tall, lanky girl with a lovely voice by the name of Eileen. Mother got involved because we had to perform in the gymnasium of Weatherford College and I insisted that I had to have a sky to hide all those ugly gymnasium rafters. My mother would tackle anything, even the roof of a gymnasium, so she tie-dyed several thousand yards of cheese cloth and stitched them together to make a blue sky. It was beautiful, truly better than many things I have seen in professional theaters. Mother could have been a great designer or costumer. Once when I was a little girl she made me a butterfly costume, of many shades of silk and lamé, that would stand up to the best of Mme. Karinska's or Irene Sharaff's. She also constructed a cocoon of burlap from which I emerged, became a butterfly, and then died. It was very touching.

Into Mother's blue sky went a half-moon large enough to conceal willowy Eileen. She was to be the surprise ending of the extravaganza. The lights would go out, the moon light up, the high-school orchestra begin "Beautiful Moonlight Madonna." Eileen would descend in the moon, carefully suspended from the highest rafters by concealed ropes, and sing.

On the big night the moon swayed, the band played, the audience waited and little old impresario me went into a frenzy. There was *no* Eileen. Three hours of waiting inside that moon, with the heat and the strong smell of oil paint in the tie-dyed cheesecloth, had knocked her out cold. She had fainted.

Even Ben got swept away from his law practice and onto the stage of that first recital. I persuaded him to do an adagio dance with me and he took it all in dead earnest. But no matter how hard he tried to look like a god, no matter how hard I tried to look like a nymph, he looked like the big hunter he was and I looked like his gun, I was so skinny. Our dance was supposed to be a thing of lyrical beauty. It *was,* I'll admit, a howling success. People laughed until they cried as he slung me all over the place, up, around, over his shoulder.

When that season ended we were all exhausted, but unfortunately I had again run clean out of new routines. I packed up to go back to Fanchon and Marco. This time Mother drove us. She, Mildred, Larry, and I took a funny-looking house in the foothills and I went back to studying all day, practicing all night.

Then fate intervened. I think all people in show business are fatalists. They almost have to be. I don't believe in just leaving things up to fate, but when it happens, I don't buck it. So on the day that I wandered into an audition and didn't know it, I stayed there. I was in my practice clothes, leotard and tights, and I went absent-mindedly into the wrong room, which was full of about fifty girls dressed to the hilt and even below it. There was also a beat-up piano, a beat-up-looking accompanist, and a beautiful girl singing in the middle of the room. I knew immediately that I had made a mistake, that I should leave. But fate had directed me to the room. I stayed.

One by one the girls went up and sang "So Red the Rose." Some only got to sing a few bars and were dismissed. Some got to sing it all. I didn't know the song, but after about twenty girls had had a crack at it, I did. It was time to stop enjoying myself and get back to work. I got up to tiptoe out when I heard a voice say, "Hey, you in the tights! Aren't you going to sing?"

Well, action first and thought later, as always. I reversed directions and walked to the piano. The beat-up accompanist said, "What key?"

Key? I didn't know then, and I don't know now, what key I sing in. Through the years my key gets lower and lower, but at that moment it made no difference to me one way or another.

"Oh, any key," I said, grandly as I could. It was no trouble,

after hearing all those other girls do it. I sang it letter perfect;
the man said, "Thank you, next," and I walked out of the room.
I felt like the priest who made a hole in one on Sunday morning.
I was pleased as punch to have had my first audition, but who
could I tell?

Later that day, during tango class, I was summoned to Miss
Fanchon's office. I had never had the pleasure of even seeing Miss
Fanchon, and I assumed that somehow word had gotten to her
that I had crashed an audition. It was like Gabriel blowing his
horn; one audacious Texas gal was going to be thrown outside
the Pearly Gates. I thought I was about to be asked to leave still
another school.

I walked into her room with my eyes cast down. She said,
briskly, "You will leave at seven A.M. tomorrow, all expenses paid,
and seventy-five dollars a week." Then she added, "With costume." I thought the woman had lost her ever-loving mind. Why
did I have to be expelled in costume, with seventy-five dollars
thrown in? I tried to explain about getting into the wrong room.
Then I lifted my eyes and focused on her and realized that the
woman sitting behind that big desk was Miss Fanchon. She had
been *in* that room, listening to the auditions. She hadn't heard
about me, she had heard *me*. I had won the audition.

Well, bliss. Mother, Mildred, even little Larry, I think, were
dumbfounded. I was to sing "So Red the Rose" at the Fox Theater
in San Francisco while the Fanchonettes danced one of their production numbers in costume in every shade of rose from deep red
to delicate pink. I made that seven o'clock train and all the way
to San Francisco I tried to find out, discreetly, what would happen
when we got there. I learned that the wardrobe mistress would be
in charge of my costume, that we would rehearse with the orchestra and lights as soon as we arrived, that we would perform that
night.

Oh, the innocence of ignorance: I wasn't even scared, I
just couldn't wait to get *on*. I was fitted to a gorgeous rose-chiffon
evening gown, heard the orchestra rehearsing "my song," and saw
a man setting up a mike in the wings. Then somebody called my
name and I stepped out.

"Please take your place at the mike and we'll begin," the
voice said.

That has to be the quickest entrance and exit anybody

ever made in the theater. I was to sing in the *wings,* offstage. My costume was only to permit me to take a bow with the Fanchonettes at the end of each show. For a week we did six shows a day, seven on Saturday and Sunday.

I was completely on my own for the first time in my life, making an unheard-of amount of money, seventy-five dollars a week. I even had my own makeup room. The only problem was that I didn't have any makeup. Finally, I worked up enough courage to ask the Chinese acrobatic dancer in the room next to mine if I might borrow hers. My makeup kit, I explained, had been lost in transit. She was a darling girl, and I'm sure she caught on to my fib, but she gave no sign of it. I watched every move she made, copied it, and came out for the first bows the most Chinese Texan you ever saw.

Nobody had told me how cold San Francisco can be in July, so I had brought no warm clothes. Everybody in that company loaned me something, and everybody helped me select the makings of a proper kit. There are, truly, *no* people like show people.

Each night as I walked up the hill from the Fox Theater to my hotel, an adorable little shoeshine boy about seven years old asked to carry my makeup kit. He was so dear, and so cold. At the end of that week when I got my check I paid my hotel bill and then went out and spent every cent on my shoeshine boy. I figured that never in a million years would I have made that much money except for an act of God, so the money didn't really belong to me. I had had a fabulous experience, and anyway, I had my return ticket to Los Angeles.

Then I lost the ticket.

And then also I came to truly know those two wonderful show people, Fanchon and Marco. Mr. Marco, Fanchon's brother, was in charge of all their activities, from his office in San Francisco. I decided nobody would understand how stupid I was and how grateful, if I didn't go right to the top. I don't know how I talked my way into Mr. Marco's office, but I did. I told him the whole saga, from blundering into the audition to losing my train ticket back to Los Angeles. That blessed man not only bought me another ticket, but he also personally took me to the train and put me on it. To this day I don't know if he was

touched by my story, touched in the head, or just anxious to get
me out of his hair and safely back to Los Angeles.

By this time I was kind of well known around the school.
Miss Fanchon called me to her office for the second time. She was
a strong, beautiful woman with Grecian features and huge black
eyes. This time I wasn't too scared to notice them. She asked
me what I wanted to do with my life and I blurted out, "Stay on
the stage." I guess I should have said, "Stay in the wings and
sing," because that's all I had really done. But she offered me
the same job, at the same salary, to sing "So Red the Rose" in
the wings of the Paramount Theater in Los Angeles.

At the end of my brief career in theater wings, Mother,
Larry, Mildred, and I drove back to Weatherford for another
year of dancing school. I had three hundred pupils and added
a third school in Cisco, Texas, in one of Conrad Hilton's first
hotels. All this necessitated driving hundreds of miles a week,

In front of Fanchon and Marco; show biz
already buzzing in my ears.

singing in hotel lobbies to pay the rent, dealing with mothers—
an art in itself—and putting on recitals.

Then my beautiful studio burned. The firemen, who had
always been my friends, discovered later that a crank had done
it, a man who thought dancing was a sin. He poured kerosene
all over everything and set fire to it. We rebuilt the studio, but
I learned a lesson that night—never care too much for posses-
sions. They can vanish into thin air.

Some of my joy in teaching went up in the smoke of the
studio. I didn't know it, but I was on the ragged edge of a small
breakdown. I adored the children, but I began to think, "If I
see one more child use one more of my mannerisms—sing as I
do, or dance as I do—I'll *scalp* it." And I couldn't stop crying.
I, who had never cried. It was an odd kind of crying, with no
special emotion to trigger it and no warning—just all of a sudden
tears pouring out of my eyes and down my face.

There was strain at school, strain at home. Ben and I had
both grown up—and grown apart. We both loved what we were
doing, but we didn't do much together. I felt that if we could get
into our own home, together, be real parents to Larry, we could
save our marriage. But there were too many emotions. Mother
was devoted to Larry. Every time Ben and I suggested taking
him away she would become genuinely ill.

Ben was kinder than I was. Each time I urged, hard, for
us to move he would say, "You can't do that to your mother."

Clearly it was time for me to stop, or slow down. Perhaps
I would have, if it hadn't been for Billy Rose. The Fort Worth
Star-Telegram announced that the great showman was coming
all the way from New York to put on a "Super Colossal Extravaganza" at the Casa Mañana in Fort Worth. That was like a man
from Mars landing on Texas soil. The star attraction would
come out from New York but Mr. Rose wanted to audition local
talent for a chorus. That meant *us*. We sure were local, and we
were loaded with talent. I rehearsed those overdeveloped Martinettes until even they looked haggard. I designed and helped
make new costumes for them: black horsehair hats trimmed in
rhinestones, long black-satin dresses split to the knees with black
tulle ruffles sewn on the inside; long white gloves with rhine-
stone bracelets, long black cigarette holders with real cigarettes.
These were my sophisticated ladies of the evening. I got myself

done up like Fred Astaire with white tie, top hat, tails, and a cane tailor-made in Weatherford by Joe Gilbert, who had a store on the square.

My sophisticated ladies and I were all speechless when we arrived in the ballroom on top of the Texas Hotel in Fort Worth for our audition. It was midnight and it was pandemonium: acrobats, midgets, dog acts, adagio dancers. I looked all over for the great Billy Rose. All I could see in a huge chair was a felt hat, a cigar, and beautifully shod small feet.

Our number was announced; the Martinettes lit up their cigarettes; I belted out, "Evening, ladies of the Evening, I can hear you calling me . . ." The girls made formations with cigarette holders, hats, gloved arms. I flew around like a Mexican jumping bean doing "wings," taps with the cane, standing toe taps. I wound up with a nip-up and a whirling dervish finale.

"What else can you do?" asked a voice from under the hat.

After I got my breath I said, "I sing blues."

"Then sing!" commanded the master showman.

What did I choose? "Gloomy Sunday," for heaven's sake, a song so blue that people were committing suicide all over the place that year and leaving notes saying, "It was 'Gloomy Sunday' that did it."

No comment after that one. We all traipsed off home again and waited. Days later the phone rang. Billy Rose's office asked if I would please report the following day. Would I! Mother drove me to Fort Worth; I was too nervous to drive. This time I really saw the great man's face. It was attractive, very young, and had New York written all over it.

"Are you that kid with the good-looking girls who fooled me the other night at the auditions?"

I didn't know what he was talking about but I said I guessed I probably was. He said he had thought we were a professional act from some local nightclub. Professional? My heart leaped. We were *in*. He said he intended to hire the Martinettes. My ears began to ring as they always do when I'm excited. All the blood rushes to my head and sounds like surf.

Then from far away, silencing the surf, came his next remark: he was hiring the Martinettes, but not *me*.

"Young lady," he said. "I've found out all about you. You're a dancing teacher in some place called Weatherford. You are married, have a little boy, a good family, a respected father who has given you every advantage. My advice to you is to tend to them. Tend to the family, the diapers. Stay out of show business."

I can hardly remember the few days after that. All my life I have tended to block out things that hurt. All I remember is that the conflicts boiled up again, all the tuggings inside me. Yet I'll never stop being grateful to Billy Rose. His advice to stay out crystallized my desire to go in—into show business.

One hot summer night right after that, Daddy was sit-

My daddy, Judge Preston "Pet" Martin, in Weatherford.

ting alone in the garden. I went out to ask if I could talk to him—about my marriage, about my dreams. He listened and then he took me in his arms and said, "Baby, you were too young to get married. Now you are beginning to grow up. Do you think deep in your heart you could ever be a real wife and mother? Could you forget about entertainment, even stop teaching?"

I told him no. I was miserable to think of the unhappiness I had caused him, Mother, Ben. Heartsick at the thought of separation from my little Larry. But something stubborn in me said that the only way I could repay all their love was to be what I had to be. To the very best of my strength and ability.

There had never been a divorce in our family. Daddy asked me to wait a year before making a final decision. I agreed, but I had to go. Ben, bless his kind heart, saw me off for Hollywood one more time. He kissed me "so long," not "good-bye."

I was never to return to Weatherford again as Mary Hagman.

V
What a Difference
a Kiss Makes

Once again Mildred Woods went with me—this time as my companion. Even though I was married and a mother, my parents would not allow me to go unchaperoned. We found a one-room kitchenette with a Murphy bed, back at Fanchon and Marco's, and I began two long years of frantic, discouraging, sometimes comic efforts to get into show business. I tried so hard that people in Hollywood nicknamed me "Audition Mary."

Thanks to Fanchon and Marco, and a man by the name of Murray Pennock who worked with them and was always very nice to me, I had my first professional audition, my first job, and my first time on a national radio network—all within ten days. On the same night that Billy Rose's Casa Mañana opened—without me—in Fort Worth, my parents heard me sing a song on the Don Lee Network from Los Angeles.

The program on which I sang was *Gateway to Hollywood.* When they told me I was "sustaining," I was enchanted. I didn't know that "sustaining" meant "no pay." The conductor was David Broekman, a white-haired, brilliant German.

He didn't know that I couldn't read music, and I wasn't about to tell him. He found out, on the day I didn't get to the studio in time for rehearsal because I was caught in a traffic jam. Mr. Broekman didn't bawl me out. He just said gently—too gently, when I looked back on it—that the orchestra had already rehearsed and that we would go on the air immediately.

We went. The orchestra played a beautiful introduction. I stood there with the music in my hands, mute. They played a recitative, then another recitative. Total silence from me. It ended with the orchestra all alone: I was supposed to sing a song I had never heard, and I couldn't read a note. I was never late to a Broekman rehearsal again.

Having a sustaining program was fine at first. I had another one later, for NBC, in which I was the "Singer of a Thousand Love Songs," five minutes every evening. The only trouble was that "sustaining" didn't sustain much.

Among the first auditions I had in Hollywood was one arranged by one of my agents, Colton Cronin. At that time I even had two other agents, Ken Dolan and James Doan, and I ended up later with more agents and managers than you could shake a stick at. Colton took me to a beautiful home in Beverly Hills. I had never been in Beverly Hills, so I wasn't prepared for such grandeur, such taste. I was ushered into a drawing room where a lady and several gentlemen were having tea. The lady was elegant, attractive, cool, the personification of everything I ever dreamed of in a Noël Coward movie. The gentlemen were gentlemen. I hadn't met their kind since I left Texas.

I was determined to give them a sample of everything I could do. I began with a fast rhythm number. Then a ballad. Then a low-down "Oh, Rock It for Me." Finally I announced I would like to sing "in my soprano voice, a song you probably don't know, 'Indian Love Call.'"

When I had finished my last "Yooo-hoo-hoo-hoo-hoo-hoooooo," there was a polite murmur. A tall, craggy man who looked like a mountain escorted me to the door and thanked me for coming. He said, "Young lady, I think you have something. I would like to work with you, on lines and phrasing, if you could come to my house every week."

I said, "Oh, yes, yes, yes, thank you."

And then with that twinkle in his eyes that I learned to know so well, he added, "Oh, and by the way, I know that song. I wrote it."

He was Oscar Hammerstein II!

He and his gracious wife, Dorothy, who presided over the tea table, have been among my closest friends since that day. Oscar kept his word. He worked with me, and within days after our first meeting he arranged for me to sing for Jerome Kern. Once more I was ushered into a home of grandeur, simplicity, taste. I was met at the door by a butler—a *real* one, as in English movies—and shown into the drawing room.

Adorable is a word not often used in describing a man, but adorable is what Jerome Kern looked to me when he walked in: the tiniest, most birdlike man I ever met. He was like a spirit, like a bird "one day old," as Sir James Barrie once described his own creation, Peter Pan.

I went through my routine of songs. This time I left out "Indian Love Call," but I did something far more intricate, "Les Filles de Cadiz," with high trills. It was one of Lily Pons's numbers. I guess I just got carried away, meeting Jerome Kern: now I was not only a soprano, I was a coloratura soprano.

Mr. Kern didn't comment for a moment. Then he gave me some of the best advice I ever received—and I have had enough advice to fill this book and another besides. He said, "Miss Martin, why do you want to be a prima donna? They are a dime a dozen, and most of them have better voices than yours. Why don't you find your own *métier,* your own style, and perfect it? Learn to be you."

I still had a long way to go before I was ready to do the type of show these men were to write, but armed with their advice I auditioned for everything, day and night. Sometimes I truly did ten auditions a day. If I heard somebody wanted a blues singer, I'd rush off. If they wanted a soprano, off I'd go. Or maybe somebody wanted a dancer? I auditioned for dancing. Nothing went right. When I auditioned for dancing I was sure I should be a singer. When I auditioned for singing, I thought dancing was my real talent. If I sang blues, the auditioners really wanted a soprano. If I sang soprano . . . well, you get the idea.

Even though being a motion-picture actress didn't appeal to me, I also auditioned for the studios. Paramount made a silent test. So did Twentieth Century-Fox, Universal, MGM. Everybody but Republic. Republic made westerns and they wouldn't even audition me. Why, I will never know, because if there was one thing I could have done in those days it was play a western. I could ride a horse, shoot a gun. I had a genuine Texas accent. I still have, except when I'm onstage. If I start telling a story, or talking to some good old Texas kin, kissin' or otherwise, it comes out. I never had a chance to use my drawl, or a gun, or a horse, until I played *Annie Get Your Gun* years later. By that time I had picked up the English pronunciation of "either." When I let go with "eye-ther" and "y'all" in the same sentence, it can be pretty confusing.

Hollywood studios kept trying to make me into a glamour girl. So did booking agents, and nightclubs where I auditioned. People were forever "seeing something" in me. I must have been discovered more times than the entire coastline of the eastern United States. I had vitality, some singing talent, good legs, big brown eyes, tremendous enthusiasm. What more could anybody want? A lot, it turned out.

In my first audition at the Trocadero, Hollywood's best nightclub, I did a dance number standing on one foot with the other beating out a "nerve tap," something I had learned from watching Eleanor Powell. I also sang "Sweetheart, Sweetheart," at the top of my lungs. It was a disaster. When I got a second chance at the Trocadero I changed my hair, wore the sexiest evening dress I could afford, and sang the low-downest song I knew. I didn't dance. So naturally I looked and sounded like everyone else who ever sang in a nightclub. I wasn't hired.

It was the same at the studios. I would arrive for a test, be made up, and be put on a swivel stool to show my right profile, left profile, full face, back of the head. *Smile.* The consensus was always the same: neck too long, cheeks too thin, nose too round, hair wrong color. Smile okay, except that I photographed like a chipmunk. The two front teeth James Porter McFarland had knocked out in the glider grew back in big and shiny. They dominated all the others.

I was also too fat, I who had always been so skinny. I remember once, when I was about twelve, all the strings came out of my tennis racket and, just actin' silly, I put it over my head. It fell straight to the ground. No more. In Hollywood I discovered drive-ins where I could eat chocolate sundaes day and night. I shot from one hundred to one hundred and thirty pounds in six weeks.

Every pound showed in the only screen test I ever made which gave me a chance to do a little scene and to sing. Buddy DeSylva, head of studio production at Universal, arranged it for me. He was convinced that I had talent, and he was determined to help me. For this test I wore a white bias-cut evening dress which photographed *fat*. My hair was dark auburn, shoulder-length, which photographed black. The makeup department gave me such long eyelashes I could hardly get my eyes open. That test is the only one I have ever seen, and it is so ghastly I have never permitted even my own children to look at it.

Failure at Universal was just about the last straw. There were no studios left. I was still "sustaining" on radio; Daddy was still sending me money from Weatherford. Then one day I got a phone call offering me forty dollars a week to sing at the Cinegrille, a bar in the Hollywood Roosevelt Hotel. Would I take it? Would I! Telling the family was another thing. I called home to report the good news, and Mother and Larry arrived as fast as Mother could drive the car.

Preston Martin's daughter singing in a bar? What if some inebriated man had the audacity to tip me? I rather hoped one would—it would help pay the rent. I emphasized to Mother the part of the job which involved singing, in my semicultured soprano, to nice elderly ladies at teatime in the hotel lobby. Mother met the hotel manager and his sister, who were exceedingly proper people. She was appeased.

Maybe it's true that heaven will protect the working girl. Singing in the Cinegrille bar was one of the most rewarding experiences of my entire life. I didn't drink or smoke, and nobody who worked for that hotel was about to let me start. Everybody—the bartenders, the waiters, the owners—conspired and cooperated to keep me protected and pure.

Also at the Cinegrille were Charlie Bourne and Bill Hoffman, two of the greatest and wackiest musicians in the world, who taught me a skill and routine which I have used all through the years. They were masters of the piano, and we would start out on a song together. Zany Charlie, if he felt like it, would all of a sudden play "Stormy Weather" while I was singing "Tea for Two." Not to be outdone, Bill would change to "Isn't It Romantic?" while Charlie went back to "Tea." This happened night after night, until I decided that if they could do it I could, too. While Bill played "Tea" and Charlie played "Stormy Weather," I would start singing "I've Got Rhythm." So help me, it works. Years later Ethel Merman and I did that same old counterpoint singing on a television show which was a huge success, the Ford Special on June 15, 1953.

Much as I loved working at the Cinegrille, I was still stuck with that forty dollars a week, less the agent's 10 percent. When the Casanova nightclub offered me two hundred, I went. There I saw for the first time one of my dream men, Bing Crosby, in person. He was making a lot of movies in those days, and he came to the club late with his friends. I had an arrangement of "Shoe Shine Boy" which I adored. Bing liked it, too. Every time I would get ready to go home, at four or five in the morning, in would come Bing and group, and he would say, "Get that girl to sing 'Shoe Shine Boy.' " He never knew my name, but he kept "that girl" singing until six or seven in the morning.

From the Casanova I went back to another bar, Gordon's, which offered me four hundred dollars a week. I thought I was so rich I enrolled Larry in a private school, the first of about eleven that poor boy went to. I was so afraid he would grow up a sissy, surrounded by women, that I put him in a military school. He loathed it. I should never have had any fears— Larry Hagman has always been all man, like his father.

In the middle of my two years as Audition Mary, my private life changed. Daddy had found it was possible to get a divorce by proxy. Very reluctantly, he arranged it. Ben agreed gallantly, and agreed also to my custody of Larry. By this time he had his own law office and a secretary. His secretary was a lovely young woman named Juanita, whom he later married, and who is a dear friend to me today.

Then two more marvelous women came into my life. One was Dema Harshbarger, head of the talent department at NBC. She liked me even though I had flunked an audition there, and she arranged an interview for me with the president of NBC, John P. Royal. Nothing came of that, either, though through the years John has been one of my biggest boosters. He has done more to put me on NBC-TV than anyone I know. He won't even remember, unless and until he reads this, that I sat in his office umpteen years ago to receive the most pleasant "Sorry, nothing at the moment . . ." turndown that I've ever had.

Through Dema I also met my second mother—Hedda

Hopper. That busy lady did everything in the world to create success for me. I cannot for the life of me remember how or when we met. Suddenly she was just there, like a fairy godmother, advising me, writing things about me in her column before I had done anything to deserve it, encouraging me with advice and counsel. She even baby-sat with Larry while I rushed from one audition to another. Little Larry Hagman at one moment in his life had the highest-priced baby-sitter in Hollywood for free. If I had known her as well then as I did later, I would have had the audacity to print up a business card for her: "Have Hat, Will Sit."

All that time another circle had been hovering around in the background, looking for a good place to light. All through my life, when things seemed at lowest ebb, something good was waiting. I was driving listlessly along one desolate Hollywood morning, wondering what would ever become of me, when I practically collided with a huge open touring car. The driver, who looked like a tremendous, very stern owl, began telling me in some choice Back Bay Boston words what he thought of my driving. I listened automatically for a while, then I looked at him and interrupted his yelling.

"Doc!" I shouted. "Irene!" There they were, Dr. Stetson Humphrey and Irene, from the Ward Belmont music department. They had decamped from Nashville with two children and two dogs, and they were in California to start their own school. They were the tonic, the knowing, loving help, I had needed. They took me into their home and they took me over. I was never to lose them again until Doc died in 1962. I still have Irene, as friend and teacher.

When we found each other in Hollywood my voice was in dreadful shape. I had pushed it too high, too low, all over the place, trying to make it match just one audition somewhere, somehow, sometime. For months Doc and Irene worked with me, hours a day. Doc gave me a daily voice lesson free. Irene taught me to sing in Italian, German, French, Spanish. It was a turning point at a crucial period. That I was able later to contribute a scholarship to their school was some compensation on my debt, but I could not and can never repay their friendship and faith in me.

All through the Hollywood years people helped and jobs

trickled in. Even Mary Pickford tried to help me. By that time I had gotten a thirteen-week job as a summer replacement on Buddy Rogers'—her husband-to-be—radio program. Mary tried so hard that I got to be known as Mary's Mary instead of Audition Mary. I dubbed a song for Margaret Sullavan in some movie I can't even remember, at MGM. I sang "Pack up Your Troubles in Your Old Kit Bag," and earned two hundred dollars. To help pay for Larry's military-school uniforms, I dubbed "I'm the Daughter of Mademoiselle, Mademoiselle You Remember So Well," for Gypsy Rose Lee.

Buddy DeSylva got me another job, as a dancing teacher, for two hundred a week. I was hired to teach French actress Danielle Darrieux how to sing and dance a number entitled—would you believe?—"It's a Dog's Life if You Don't Weaken, Baby."

I was so excited to have a job that I choreographed and memorized the whole number in one hour. Then I sat, waiting to meet my pupil. Days passed. Buddy told me to relax. After all, I was being paid by the week, so why didn't I just walk around the studio, meet people, stop being such an eager beaver? The attitude was new to me. I was used to getting things done.

One afternoon I took Buddy's advice and wandered into the studio music department. Several men were writing orchestrations. One was sitting at a piano. He looked at me and asked, "Kid, think you can sing this?" I looked at the music and, wonders never cease, I knew it—and in Italian. It was Arditi's "Il Bacio" ("The Kiss"), a number I had learned from Doc and Irene. The men were orchestrating it for Deanna Durbin's first motion picture. If I had known that day what "Il Bacio" was going to do for me, and her, I might have choked on it. At the time I was only pleased to be able to sing it.

While I was giving out at top voice, a man walked into the room. He said he was Joe Pasternak, the man who had discovered Deanna Durbin. He asked me to come see him the next day. Joe Pasternak, like Bing Crosby, might have "discovered" me right then, but I never did go back to see him. By the next day I had been fired from Danielle Darrieux's production and I couldn't get back on the set.

Downfall came that afternoon. I was summoned to Miss Darrieux's dressing room. She took one look at me and started batting out French a mile a minute. I couldn't speak French. She left her room with her maid, her manager, her wardrobe woman, her makeup man, and her husband. There I sat. It was a dog's life, all right.

Then Buddy DeSylva intervened. He told me to perform the song and dance, in English, for the entire company on the sound stage. I couldn't wait to show him how much the job meant. I knocked myself out doing the dog number. There was spontaneous applause from the cast and the co-star, Douglas Fairbanks, Jr.—all except Mlle. Darrieux. She burst into tears, into French, and I never saw her again. I was banned. Apparently she was humiliated to have a dancing teacher perform her number for the entire company. Now I know that she was right. I learned a great deal from that, about what not to do. And it wasn't a total loss—I still have the rather tattered pass issued to Mary Martin, dancing teacher, by Universal Studios.

In the late summer of my second year as Audition Mary, I got one more chance: to sing on a Sunday night talent show at the Trocadero nightclub. It wasn't Major Bowes's amateur hour, but it was almost as important, almost as big a springboard.

This time none of my agents, and none of the men with pinstripe suits and white neckties, got into the act. Doc and Irene and Mildred and I made all the decisions about what I would wear and what I would sing. I didn't have many clothes. Mildred and I shared wardrobes. We had both lost weight by now.

We decided that I would go on in a short, full black taffeta skirt, a white blouse, a red velvet cummerbund, and a black velvet beanie which I borrowed from Irene. With my last five dollars I bought a white bolero jacket. The song we selected for openers was "The Weekend of a Private Secretary." The music was written by Bernie Hanighen, who later wrote the lyrics for a show in which I starred on Broadway, *Lute Song*, and the lyrics were written by Johnny Mercer. For this secretary number I went on in horn-rimmed glasses and a dazed, eager look. The song was a rumba all about a secretary on a forty-nine-dollar vacation cruise to Havana. She met a Cuban gent, took off her glasses, and . . . the song was a little bit risqué.

For my second number I was determined to sing "Il Bacio."

I had learned to sing it purely, beautifully, in very high soprano. But always in the middle of it, because it was so grand, I got the giggles. Partly to hide giggles, partly because it was fun, I began to change it into a jazzed-up, syncopated version, a little bit of the Charlie Bourne-Billy Hoffman-Mary Martin treatment. Later it became a fad to swing the classics, which did some of the classics a lot of good. I like to think that maybe I helped lead the way with my swinging "The Kiss."

The Trocadero was jam-packed that Sunday night. Doc and Irene whispered to me, "This time you can do it. You're ready." On I went.

Mildred told me later that my secretary number went well, maybe because I really looked like a secretary instead of a nightclub singer. Then I started "Il Bacio." You could have heard a pin drop. From there I began to swing the be-daylights out of it. Just let them have it, trumpet noises coming from that refined soprano throat.

When I finished the number I thought everybody was

At the Stork Club with my "angel," the man who believed in me and took me to Broadway, Lawrence Schwab.

leaving. People were getting up, scraping their chairs. Then it started: shouting, whistling, calls of *bravo,* people standing on chairs, on tables. In all that madhouse of noise and yelling, I knew I had made it. In ten minutes my life had changed.

The late Jack Benny, who was in the audience, once told me it was one of the most exciting moments he could remember. He invited me to a table where I met one of the most important men in my whole life—Lawrence Schwab. I had never heard of him, though he was one of the most important producers on Broadway, and he was to become a friend for life.

Lawrence that night offered me a part in a new musical comedy he was planning, *Ring Out the News.* He said he would pay my way and Mildred's to New York. Almost as an afterthought, he told me to have my teeth capped.

All through the years young people have asked me what makes the big break happen. I have always answered the same: *work.* Work and work and work, be ready when the break comes. It could be one break, or forty, or a hundred and forty. I had hundreds of auditions, but I was not ready until that fateful Sunday night.

Finding a Lawrence Schwab in your life doesn't hurt either.

To Daddy

VI
How to Striptease
and Not Know It

Sweet, swinging "Il Bacio" took me to Broadway, but it was Cole Porter's "My Heart Belongs to Daddy" that kept me there.

When I first sang "Daddy" it never entered my mind that this was a risqué song. It entered a lot of other people's minds, though, or I would never have got the part. Right in the middle of rehearsals for a show called *Leave It to Me,* June Knight, the girl who was supposed to sing "Daddy," ran off and married a Texas oilman. He didn't want her to sing such suggestive lyrics, so he put his husbandly foot down. June left the show. That's how I found myself onstage, hayseeds and all, doing a striptease before I had ever heard the expression.

This certainly wasn't the show Lawrence Schwab had signed me for, *Ring Out the News.* It did have something to do with news, though, and it did have to do with what I've always called my "inner voice." That's the voice that gives fate a little help, now and then.

Fate and I both needed help, in the late summer of 1937. Lawrence had given me a contract for one hundred and fifty dollars a week, for fifty-two weeks; three hundred dollars a week if I had a leading role. Mildred and I were to report to him in New York in the autumn. He made it clear that I would have to support myself for a few more months, between signing the contract and beginning rehearsals. I signed with never a backward glance. I would have written "Mary Martin" all over the Magna Carta to get to Broadway.

In the meantime, Hollywood had become fun. After my big night at the Trocadero, and Lawrence's invitation to Broadway, every studio in town discovered me. I, who had trudged back and forth all over every lot around, found myself picked up one day by a big black Cadillac and deposited at the entrance gate of Twentieth Century-Fox. There, they said, I should wait until a famous producer's personal big black Cadillac called for me—to be driven to his office exactly one block away!

I also got a short engagement as featured singer at the Trocadero, sharing the bill with Joe E. Lewis, whom I consider the most fabulous nightclub entertainer in the business. Mildred and I couldn't believe any of it.

The blow fell on the last night of the Trocadero job. Mildred and I had said good-bye to Doc and Irene, to all the friends we had made in two frustrating years. We had bought our train tickets for a triumphal return to Weatherford on our way to New York. We had packed. Then came a special delivery from Lawrence. He was not going to do *Ring Out the News.* The show he was currently trying on the road was not a success. Until the backers were paid, he had to abandon plans for *Ring Out.*

That last night at the Troc there were flowers, presents, toasts, dear notes from the hatcheck girls and the parking lot attendants, and from our burly bosses. I couldn't bear to tell anyone anything. I left in a blaze of glory, and in unbearable despair.

It was even worse in Weatherford. Half the town met us at the railway station, there was even a brass band to welcome the hometown girl on her way to Broadway. I could have crawled under that train and died, but old freckle-faced Millie turned to me and said, "Okay, honey, let's see you start acting."

For two weeks I really acted. I acted for my family, for my friends across the street, Virginia Mae Milmo and Ralph Kindel, for Jack Gordon of the Forth Worth *Press,* for Fairfax Nisbet, who had always been so nice to me, for John Rosenfield, the critic of the Dallas *Morning News,* for Bessie Mae Sue Ella Yaeger, and for a new boyfriend, John Astin Perkins, who sent me a huge horseshoe filled with red roses. All the time I felt like a criminal. Lawrence had already sent Mildred and me travel

money, under the terms of our contract, and I decided there was
only one thing to do—get to New York right away, stop this al-
most-lying to the people of Texas. Maybe I could get a job in
another show; if I couldn't, I'd just have to go back to Weatherford again and face the music. Lawrence didn't expect us for
weeks, but that inner voice said, "Let's go."

We went on a cattle boat. I had always wanted to go
somewhere on a boat. It took longer from Texas to New York by
boat than by train, but there wasn't any hurry, after all. Lawrence
didn't expect us for weeks. Years later there was a story that
Richard always reserved every room on a freighter just so he and
I and our family could travel in solitary bliss. That isn't true,
but it is true that we always took freighter trips when we could
afford the time, and it is true that by luck we often had them all
to ourselves.

Mildred and I, the cattle, the crew embarked on a bright
sunny day. Daddy drove us from Weatherford to Galveston; I
longed so to tell Mother and Daddy everything: that I didn't
have a job, that I didn't know what would happen, that I owed
them things I could never repay. I could find no words for any
of it. I just told them I loved them both with all my heart. Daddy
stood on the dock like a strong, handsome rock, waving us out
of sight. I didn't know that I was never to see him like that again.

Mildred and I had a perfect trip, in Stateroom 13. When
we got to New York I looked up hotels in a phone book and
selected the St. Moritz, just because it sounded so grand. We
arrived on the thirteenth day of the month and they gave us a
room on the thirteenth floor. It seems too much, but it is true.
Lawrence Schwab was out of town so we went sight-seeing in
Central Park, saw the zoo, called at Colton Cronin's mother's
theatrical boardinghouse. She didn't have a room available but
she let us eat at her big round table, where we met real show-
business people. This was living. Within three days I was a
goner for New York.

A lady named Radie Harris, who wrote for the *Hollywood
Reporter,* will never know how much she contributed to my
general euphoria. I had never met her, but she had been darling
to a friend of mine, another singer by the name of Joy Hodges.
When Joy heard I was going to New York, she gave me Radie's
name. I telephoned and she invited me to lunch at the Algonquin

Hotel. Miss Hay-in-her-Hair, me, had never heard of the Algonquin, didn't know it was famous, but fell in love with Radie because she was so warm and friendly. She wrote a story about me before I had even been cast in a show, saying, "This kid from Texas is going to be great. . . ." She was the very first person to interview me in New York. I was sure that I had *arrived.*

When Lawrence Schwab got back to New York he issued two orders. One, move out of the St. Moritz, which at this time housed quite a few well-kept ladies. Second, find an accompanist and start doing auditions. Again. He found Mildred and me an apartment on Fifty-fifth Street where the phone rang day and night with men asking for Mabel or Ruby. We must have moved into the former apartment of rather less well-kept ladies. Our luck with an accompanist was better. Lawrence knew of a fabulous girl, Rosa Rio, who was willing to work with me. All my life I have had a thing about accompanists. If they follow and don't lead, if they can change keys at the drop of a hat, if they can play wonderful chords which tickle my imagination, I am happy. I can sing for hours. If they can't, I can't sing. Rosa had all that I wanted and more.

Within days Lawrence sent us to the Ritz Towers to an audition. He was too busy to go himself, but he had found another agent for me, Dorothy Vernon, a beautiful woman who was also a marvelous agent. Dorothy and Rosa and I went up in an elevator halfway to heaven, into a huge living room with people sitting around in a circle like an Indian powwow. I marched in and announced, "I would like to sing four numbers. If I can't sing all four, I'd rather not sing." Get me! I was so accustomed to being stopped after one song that I was prepared to fight.

A man reclining on a couch said, very mildly, "Carry on, on all fours."

Thus encouraged, I sang every style I knew, straight through. One of my numbers was "Il Bacio." As I finished I could tell by their faces it was a success. Then they introduced themselves. The little lady with the beady eyes was Bella Spewack, coauthor with her husband, Sam, of *Leave It to Me.* Sam was also the director. There were producer Vinton Freedley, Sophie Tucker, Victor Moore, William Gaxton. The man on the couch who had said "Carry on" was Cole Porter.

Bella Spewack asked me if I had ever been on the New York stage. I knew nobody could fool this intelligent lady so I said, "No, ma'am, but I can . . ."

She replied, "What makes you think you can?"

All I could answer was "Try me."

They did. That same night at eight o'clock I walked into my first Broadway theater. It was pitch black except for one blazing white light in the middle of the stage. It seemed dusty, echoing, ominous, the Black Hole of Calcutta with a torture light at the ready. I couldn't believe this was what I had been waiting for all my life.

A figure emerged from the shadows to shove a little book into my hands. "These are your sides," the figure said. "Read the part marked 'Dolly.'"

I looked at the booklet. There were printed words, then a lot of dots and dashes, then a single word, then some more lines. Another figure emerged from the gloom, a man with an overcoat on his shoulders and a felt hat pulled down over his eyes.

"It doesn't make any difference how you say your lines, kid," he said. "Just say them loud, straight to the balcony."

Then he read a line. I looked and saw that his last word was my cue. I stepped forward and shouted, "I'd like to renew my subscription." It came out so loud that the bright light dimmed a bit. Billy Gaxton, the man in the overcoat and hat, laughed so long I thought it must be a funny line. It wasn't; he was laughing at me.

Later Sam Spewack came over to say, "If you get the part, young lady, don't ever change your reading of the subscription line, no matter what anyone tells you. I've never heard a line read like that in my life."

That was how I got into *Leave It to Me,* a musical remake of Sam and Bella's *Clear All Wires.* I was Dolly, the dumb blonde who was being kept by one big wheel on the newspaper and in love with another one. If I hadn't listened to my inner voice, if I hadn't gone to New York weeks before Lawrence Schwab expected me, I wouldn't have been there in time to get the part.

In my mind, it was a part. To all the marvelous people in the cast I *was* the part. I wasn't blond, but I was dumb. I certainly proved it to them on the day of my very first rehearsal with the cast. I was so excited I got up about an hour too early, got into a taxi, and told the driver, "Imperial Theatre." What with my Texas voice, and his New York ears, he understood "Pier Something-or-other," 46 I think, and that's where he took me. Straight to the piers where I had come in on that cattle boat only a few days before.

By the time we got all that sorted out, I was forty-five minutes late to my first rehearsal. I walked in so scared my knees knocked, explaining to everybody that I had started out in plenty of time. Nobody bawled me out. They just stood there, in a long silence, looking at me. It was quite clear they thought they had a hick on their hands, an innocent kid from Texas, probably a virgin, obviously in need of protection. Billy Gaxton, who had quite a vocabulary, never used a bad word when I was around. Mildred, my chaperon, never left my warm side. There was a conspiracy, just as there had been in Hollywood nightclubs, to keep me lily white.

I didn't know the whole plot of the show for weeks. I didn't know for sure whose mistress I was. To this day I'm a little hazy about it all. I was so busy trying to learn my "sides," and the songs, the dances. When I was hired we had only ten more days of rehearsal before New Haven tryouts.

Sophie Tucker used to watch me all the time in the wings. Once after I had sung "Daddy" in rehearsal she came over and said, "Kid, do you know what you're singing? Do you know what the words mean?"

I said, "Of course," but she persisted.

"Do you know that 'Daddy' is not your father?"

"Of course I do," I insisted. "I know that he's a man who takes care of me."

Sophie—I adored this woman—shook her head and kept on at me. "But do you *know* what you're singing?"

I wasn't all that sure. I didn't have any idea what finnan haddie was, for example, until somebody told me it was fish. Finally Sophie explained, "It is a naughty song, a risqué song. There's one thing I want you to do. Each time you sing a lyric you don't understand, don't know exactly what you're singing, tell it to your audience. I mean like, 'If I invite a boy some night to dine on my fine finnan haddie, I just adore his asking for more,' but, on the last line, *never* look at the audience. Look straight up to heaven, fold your hands, and sing '*but* my heart belongs to Daddy.'"

That's the exact, straight way I sang it, every time. I couldn't really understand why Sophie was so interested in those lyrics, because *I* knew my big number was to be "Il Bacio," in the first act. "Daddy" was in the second. Cole hadn't written a song yet for the first act, and he liked my rendition of "Il Bacio" so much that he decided I could do it until he had time to write a number of his own for that spot. Unfortunately, "The Kiss" stopped the show in New Haven and stopped it again in Boston.

Cole Porter never meant it that way. Nobody meant it that way. Tamara, the star, who had made "Smoke Gets in Your Eyes" famous, was not too happy. Neither was anyone else. In the profession, an upstart is an upstart. Somebody who had never been on the stage before was stopping the show in both acts. Nobody minded about "Daddy"—that was Cole's song, after all, and a great one. But to stop the show in the first act, with a trick song which wasn't even Cole's—that was a bit much.

They all—Sophie, Billy, Victor—had the same agent, Louie Shurr. They went to him and said something had to go. Louie came to my dressing room one matinee in Boston. He hemmed and hawed and finally said, "I'm the one to tell you that we're taking out 'Il Bacio' because it is not Mr. Porter's number. Everything else in the show is his."

I was devastated. I was also furious. I was convinced that was the song which was going to make me famous. I said, "No, you can't take it out, I'm sorry."

"Young lady," he continued, "that's too bad. I'm sorry, too, but you're not going to sing that song."

I seldom get angry, but that day I did something I had never done before—and have never done since. I picked up a Pond's cold cream jar and slung it across the room at him. I missed, which was lucky. It might have killed him.

That was the first shock in Boston. The second was the headlines in the Boston papers: "New Striptease Artist Mary Martin." Well, now, Mary Martin doing a striptease? I'd never seen one and I didn't know what they were talking about but the worst problem was how to explain to my family in Weatherford. Mildred, who was a lot more capable in that department than I was, sent off a letter quickly to say, "Mary is doing a kind of a strip, that is, she has to take off some of her clothes, her hat, her gloves, etc. They call it a striptease but it really isn't. . . ."

It really wasn't but it really was, I guess. I simply never

Mother came to see what a striptease was and found me
in my same old Teddybare.

thought about it. It came about by accident. At one part in the
show Dolly, me, had become an embarrassment to somebody or
other; it was all mixed up with a story line about politics. Anyway, dumb cluck Dolly had to be shipped out of town. All the
way to Siberia. Literally. Onstage I arrived in Siberia dressed to
the teeth, even a fur hat. There were six boys, dancers, who met
me in Eskimo suits, and we did a number in which there were
a lot of lifts. The boys would pick me up, sling me around, pass
me from hand to hand.

One of the Eskimos was Gene Kelly. He was just a kid
then on his first Broadway job, but I liked him from the first day.
He was so talented, had so much drive. I've never known anybody who worked so hard perfecting his art. Of all the boys, he
was the one who came into the theater every day of his life to
work, for hours and hours and hours, on the stage. From the
beginning I knew he was going to be somebody great. I couldn't
anticipate, then, that he was going to change the whole look and
spirit of Hollywood musical films—but I knew his drive and his
determination were boundless. He's still at it, he still dances
with the verve of the young man I first knew.

In "Siberia" in *Leave It to Me*. The cutest Eskimo, the one *not* looking at me, is Gene Kelly.

Gene and the other boys had no trouble with the lifts so long as I was in rehearsal clothes, simple leotards. But after choreographer Robert Alton saw the designs for the actual costume I would be wearing in performance, he had a premonition. He asked designer Raoul Pène duBois to make facsimiles of every single thing in muslin—the fur cap, the coat, the gloves, the dress.

Sure enough, as he had guessed, with all those clothes on I kept sliding right out of the boys' hands during the lifts.

Bob Alton had the most delicious, wicked wit. He kept saying, "Well, *that* will have to come off . . ." and he conceived the striptease. In the final production there we all were, Dolly Winslow in freezing Siberia, dancing up a storm to a hot rumba, singing her heart out to six mute Eskimos, and taking things off. One by one I removed the gloves, the lynx coat, the lynx cap, the baby-blue velvet jacket covered with silver bugle beads, the skirt that matched, the pink chiffon petticoat, and last but not least—because it stayed on, the *pièce de résistance*—the pink satin, chiffon, and lace chemise. Some people called this garment "teddy bears."

That was as "bear" as I ever got, but it was enough for me to have overnight acclaim as a stripteaser.

I was the Melba-Martin toast of Boston, wined and dined at the Hasty Pudding Club. The Harvard *Crimson* kidnapped me for a party; the social Back Bay Bostonians, who included our producer Vinton Freedley, took me in. One of them gave a big party and Vinton arranged that Lucius Beebe would be my escort. Ye gods, I didn't even know his name. We became friends years later, but that night I think he could have shot Vinton for landing him with a dim-witted Texas girl: Mr. Beebe never said a word to me all night.

Then New York. Earl Wilson, who didn't have his column then but who was already writing for the New York *Post,* came to do my first real show-business interview. Mildred showed him into our apartment after I had washed my hair and rolled it up. Earl came in, saw me with my head in the oven, and screamed, "What are you doing?"

"Drying my hair," I said.

He wrote a long story about me which took up about half page in the *Post.* Below the fold. He still writes about me—and my children, and my grandchildren.

Everybody was nervous on our Broadway opening night but me. All I wanted to do was get out onto that stage. Afterward there was a party at El Morocco. I said I couldn't go because I didn't have the right dress. Vinton said I had to go, and he gave me as a present the gorgeous dress they had made for my "Il Bacio" number. It was gold lamé with brown velvet ribbons, grand, grand, grand. Again Vinton arranged an escort for me, his friend Jules Glaenzer, who had often attended our rehearsals. He was such a nice man but I thought he was old enough to be my father. Later I found out he was president of Cartier's!

By the time I had removed my makeup, showered, dressed in my new ball gown, the party was in full swing. When we walked into El Morocco the orchestra was playing "My Heart Belongs to Daddy." There was applause, everybody was standing up, I got so excited that I applauded, too. Finally I whispered, "Who's coming in, Jules?"

He said, "You."

It may sound a put-on now, but it wasn't. Everything had happened so quickly. At that moment I was much more embarrassed than thrilled.

Then the buildup began. The show was a hit, and so was I. Walter Winchell closed his Sunday night broadcast with one of those excited FLASH FLASH FLASH things of his about "Texas girl hits New York with a storm . . ."

It became a snowball. Everybody was taking my picture, but when friends called up to say, "You're on the cover of *Life!*" I didn't believe it. Not *Life.* In those days they never had people on the cover. They had animals.

I was too superstitious even to buy a copy of the magazine. But on the way to the theater the taxi stopped for a light, right at a newsstand. I said to Mildred, "You go, buy *Life.*"

"No," she said. "You go."

Finally I went. I said *"Life"* to the man and he handed it to me, sort of rolled up. I didn't dare look. Back in the taxi I unrolled it and the cover was—a dog, a Labrador retriever.

Right away I thought everybody had been putting me on, and I didn't think it was funny. I was always sensitive about my nose. Later it turned out that the man had sold me the previous week's issue. I really was on the cover of *Life,* on December 19, 1938. That was the first; I was to be on *Life*'s cover four more times afterward.

After that they put my name in lights for the first time. The marquee was kind of skimpy so they had room only for "M. Martin," but it looked good to me. I also had some pretty glamorous boyfriends. Winthrop Rockefeller was the main one. He hadn't met Bobo yet. Then there was Richard Kollmar, who hadn't met Dorothy Kilgallen yet. Dick was a young actor then playing the juvenile lead in *Knickerbocker Holiday,* right next door to *Leave It to Me.* We often met as we came out our respective stage doors. One night he asked if I would like to see a Sunday benefit performance of their show. Of course I said yes, please. Two events that night made Dick seem very exciting. First, I had never seen a Broadway show from the audience, and everybody onstage at his show looked utterly gorgeous to me. I always thought Dick was attractive, but onstage, with the lights and make-up—I was impressed.

Second, he introduced me to that wonderful man Walter Huston, the star of *Knickerbocker Holiday.* Mr. Huston amazed me by giving me a kiss on the cheek and then saying, "I probably am the only person in New York City who knows where Weatherford, Texas, is. I even know which water pipes go to your house."

When he was young and struggling, he had been an engineer and he had installed the whole waterworks for Weatherford! I nearly fainted when he asked, "How's old Cub Young?" Cub, *my* Cub, the family handyman. I all but floated out of the theater that night, on the arm of Dick Kollmar. Later Walter and Nan Huston became close friends of mine. One of my great regrets is that I never got to play with that wonderful man, a show we both wanted to do, *They Knew What They Wanted.*

Through all these exciting times I kept being interviewed. People asked me the usual questions and I gave them the usual answers—about Weatherford, my father the judge, my mother, Sister, everything. Nobody ever asked me if I was married, so I never told them. Finally one young man—I can't remember his name and I am sorry, because I liked him—went to Weatherford, all on his own. He got the whole report about Ben, Larry, my marriage, everything. His story wasn't sensationalized at all, but I certainly did suffer a sudden verbal loss of virginity, if there is such a thing.

The cast, plus Bella and Sam and Vinton, had been protecting me all this time. Their reaction to the "exposé" was to laugh, uproariously. They took it as a spoof on my part, which it truly never was. Billy Gaxton, who had a fabulous sense of humor, found the whole situation funnier than anyone else did.

He said, "You've been pulling the wool over our eyes, and I'm going to fix you."

He did, too. The next night onstage we were doing a scene in which I had to ask him a question. I've forgotten what it was, but that night he answered, very clearly, "You go offstage and down the hall to the right. You'll find it."

I thought, "Uh-oh, he's acting as if I wanted to go to the john, in front of all these people." I turned purple and went up to him to whisper, "I don't want to go to the bathroom, I'm just giving you my line."

He looked me straight in the eye and practically shouted, "Listen, Dolly, I'm telling you—go off down the hall, turn right . . ."

It went on and on. The audience was in hysterics. I could have brained Billy. From that moment on, he had a ball using all the words he had so carefully avoided using before. He and Madeleine, his wife, were my friends forever after.

The journalistic revelation that made Billy want to tease me didn't bother me at all. It was all true. I never had considered it a secret; it was just that nobody ever asked me.

I was hurt badly by the press once, during my "Daddy" days, but it wasn't really their fault. Almost always they were marvelous, including the critics, whom my daughter, Heller, referred to as "crickets" when she was little. Perhaps it is because the press has been kind to me that I don't understand people in show business who resent reporters. If I decide to be a public figure, that is my business. It is the reporter's business to write about public figures, among other things. Most of them are interested in getting as honest a story as they can. So why not tell the truth?

My Texas newspaper friends, Jack Gordon and Fairfax Nisbet, taught me that. While I was still singing in nightclubs in California, a young man named John Chapman wrote about me— long before he went to New York to become one of the most important "crickets." Hedda Hopper was heaven, and Radie, and Earl Wilson and Walter Winchell in New York. *Time* magazine once followed me around for weeks. If I did one interview with them, I did a million; then, of course, something as important as the Second World War happened so I never got on the cover.

Jimmy Fidler on the air made me furious one time being cynical about Hollywood marriages, including mine, and once Claudia Cassidy in Chicago made me so mad I didn't want to play Chicago anymore. She wrote a big story about how I must not like the city because I was only staying a week or so. Despite the fact that she knew perfectly well it was a tour, that we had ongoing engagements and couldn't just stop. Years later we made up. But almost always the press was nice—the newspapers, *Harper's*, *Vogue*, *Newsweek*.

There was a darling young man in Cincinnati who came to interview me when I was doing *Hello Dolly!* He was a sportswriter and he resented having to talk to some dame about the theater. He ended up interviewing me about all the things I *didn't* know about baseball. It made quite a good story and I learned a lot about baseball.

The bad time came in my first year in New York. After three or four months of *Leave It to Me,* I got a call from Mother saying Daddy had had a cerebral stroke. It was a Saturday morning, so I had to do two shows before I could catch a plane and fly home to Texas.

Daddy had been in a coma, but he opened his eyes when

I walked in. He said, "Baby, you're here." Then he told me how happy he was that I was a success on Broadway. Just before I left, he said, "You sing a song for me, don't you?"

I wanted to cry, but I didn't. I just said, "Yes. I sing about Daddy."

Then it was time to leave again. I had to fly back to New York for the Monday night performance. Planes weren't all that fast or frequent in those days. To make matters worse, a blizzard grounded me in Washington. I telephoned to New York and the production arranged for a police car to take me to the train. I missed the first act but got there in time to do the "Daddy" number. That night and the next day I telephoned to Weatherford about every two hours. Daddy seemed to be getting on well. By Wednesday morning, with two shows to do, I was exhausted. When I got up that morning I asked Mildred for the paper, but she said it hadn't come.

At matinee time, she suggested I eat in my dressing room, to rest. She said she had talked to Mother, everything was all right. I stayed in my dressing room between shows, so when it was time for the evening performance I hadn't seen anyone but the show people, I hadn't seen a newspaper all day. When I finished "Daddy," I had a strange feeling. The song hadn't really gone over as it usually did; something was wrong in the theater. I went off, into the wings. Sophie Tucker was waiting for me.

"I'm sorry, kid," she said, "we can't do a thing about this. There are photographers in the hall there waiting for you. Your father has died; New York City has known about it all day long."

Everyone tried to shield me, but there was nothing to do. The photographers burst through, everybody was shouting, flashbulbs were going off. I tried to get away but they followed me, clear to the dressing room, inside. I was hounded. Finally, after the show Dorothy Vernon maneuvered my escape from the theater, in a wig and disguise, and took me to her apartment at the New Weston Hotel.

Next day there were headlines: "Daddy Girl Sings About Daddy as Daddy Dies." It was horrible. Daddy was dead, dead, dead. I couldn't even get home for the funeral. This experience left a lifelong scar.

Most of my memories of and associations with my own daddy and with "Daddy" the song are not somber ones, however. He was a great daddy; "Daddy" was a great song in a marvelous show. What a launching for a new girl on Broadway! I recorded "Daddy" many times, in many different versions. The first was with Eddy Duchin's orchestra, in the key I had used onstage. That recording is very high, sweet, the way I sang it then. Over the years, versions changed. I even made one sort of low-down, but I never sang it raunchy.

The show led to the first of some absolute deluges of flowers from unknown admirers. During the entire run in New York I kept getting masses of flowers, always with a little note in poetry, signed, "Daddy." I hadn't any idea who was sending them, but my dressing room looked as if I were about to be laid out. I even tried calling the florist, but he wouldn't tell me who my mysterious "Daddy" was.

At this time I had so much energy, and I was trying so hard to live up to my success, that I sang one show a night at the Rainbow Room, in Rockefeller Center, after I had finished the theater performance.

One night I got a note with my flowers which said, "I'll be watching you tonight. Daddy." I never went out into the room after I sang, but that night Mildred said, "We've got to find out who Daddy is."

During the performance the headwaiter came to say, "Afterward, I want to escort you to a table." We went out into that gorgeous room and walked and walked and walked through the audience and the tables, and way over in the corner there was a table and a little head sticking up, just barely over the top. It was Daddy. He was old, and in a wheelchair. Mildred and I started thanking him for all the flowers. He said he should thank us for the joy I had given him singing "Daddy." Then he offered to take us home to our apartment, in the longest, blackest limousine you ever saw in your life. There was a chauffeur, and rugs over our legs in the back seat. Finally, I just had to ask him, so I said, "I'd love to know your name." He was Mr. Guggenheim, the tycoon, and he sent me flowers until the day he died. Every time the note was signed, "Daddy."

VII
My Pastel Life
on the Silver Screen

While *Leave It to Me* was still going strong, Paramount Pictures offered me a contract in Hollywood. What on earth possessed me to accept it, I don't know. Just plain stubbornness, I guess. Having been tested and rejected so many times by so many studios, I couldn't wait to get back out there and show them all.

A whole series of Paramount executives had come to hear me sing "Daddy." Most of the same ones turned up at the Rainbow Room to see me in a different setting. And there they heard me sing in a different range of voice, and I finally got to sing "Il Bacio." That did it! They offered me a contract. If they noticed how "bear" I was in the famous striptease, they didn't show it: the first thing they cast me in was *The Great Victor Herbert,* to co-star with Allan Jones, absolutely covered in clothes—hoopskirt, ruffles, pearls, feathers, fans. They even put me into long white gloves—I never did find out just what was the matter with my arms.

Then for months the makeup men had a field day. Using my same face they made me up to look exactly like Jeanne Parker . . . and Jean Arthur . . . Claudette Colbert . . . and Rosalind Russell . . . kinda. They even tried to make me look sexy. But most of the time, I just looked sick.

It was the style in those days—1939, 1940—to make up every new girl to look like whoever was the reigning star of the moment. They did such a good job of making me look like Clau-

My first film, *covered with clothes in The Great Victor Herbert.*

dette Colbert that I spent a whole evening sitting beside her husband at a dinner party and until I opened my mouth he didn't seem to notice that I wasn't his wife.

After *Victor Herbert,* I made *Rhythm on the River* with Bing Crosby. We were fooling around on the set one day and Harry Barris, one of the Rhythm Boys, Bing's first singing group, was doodling "Shoe Shine Boy" on the piano. Bing walked over and said, "I used to hear a girl sing that in a nightclub. I went out every night to hear her. Then all of a sudden she disappeared. I never found out where she went."

I walked straight over to Bing and said, "You like that song? Sit down and I'll sing it for you." I still knew my old arrangement. All the time I sang he stared at me, his eyes getting wider and his smile happier.

When I finished he said, "That's the way that girl sang it."

"Well, Bing Crosby," I told him, "I'm that girl."

Maybe if Bing had "discovered" me two years before, my break would have come sooner. I doubt it, though, because I

Jean Arthur,

Jeanne Parker,
Rosalind Russell,

Claudette Colbert,

and, well, kinda sexy.

But mostly I just looked sick.

wasn't ready yet. Bing and I always had "Shoe Shine Boy" as a bond, and I still love the song. It makes a great lullaby for grandchildren.

Making movies with Bing almost made Hollywood worthwhile. He is the most relaxed, comfortable, comforting man. No matter what happens he can ad-lib, cover up, carry on. He can even sing with gum in his mouth, he just parks it over on one side. While we were making films we also sang together on the *Kraft Music Hall* on radio. I've seen him a hundred times drop his entire script in midshow and go right on singing. He'd just lean over,

With Bing Crosby
in Hollywood.

In *New York Town* with Fred MacMurray and Robert Preston.

grope around with his hand to find the script, pick it up, and find his place instantly. He never missed a note.

Every time I looked at him I thought to myself again, "Be careful what you wish, it might come true." For years now I've said it to my friends. Back in my popcorn-eating Palace Theater days in Weatherford, I wished and wished and wished that some day I could meet and work with my three dream men—Bing Crosby, Maurice Chevalier, and Noël Coward. I still don't understand how I came to choose Noël Coward. This marvelous, sophisticated, chic Englishman was about as far from Texas corny me as a man could get. But I thought he was the most exciting thing I'd ever seen. Years later he actually wrote a musical comedy for me. I never did get to play with Maurice Chevalier, but once he sent me three dozen red roses, and he wrote about me in his autobiography. The first time I met him I was so flustered that I kissed his hand. It shouldn't happen to a Frenchman.

After *Rhythm on the River,* I made *Love Thy Neighbor* with Jack Benny and Fred Allen, *Kiss the Boys Good-bye* with Don Ameche and Oscar Levant, *New York Town* with Fred Mac-Murray and Robert Preston, *Happy Go Lucky* with Dick Powell and Rudy Vallee, and I don't know what all else. I think I made eleven pictures in about three years. I cried after every single preview, I thought I was so awful.

Some of them I actually never saw, ever. One morning last year, in my new home in Palm Springs, I woke up early and tried to turn on the *Today* show. Something was wrong with the channel so I switched, and got an old movie. Suddenly I sat up straight in bed, stunned—there I was, on the little screen. I had missed the credits and I didn't recognize the story line, but I watched. I was bouncing around in a chic little dress looking cute—kinda. Then came a close-up of "me" and it was—Janet Gaynor. My dearest friend in all the world. I guess they must have tried to make me look like Janet Gaynor, too, in the Hollywood days. I leaped out of bed and telephoned Janet, but by the time she got her set turned on the film was off. Neither of us will ever know what "we" starred in that time.

It's rather typical of Hollywood, that story. We were all interchangeable, everything was canned, processed. Actors were hardly even part of it. We never did a story in sequence, sometimes didn't even know what the story was. Directors shot bits and snatches, the end first, maybe, then something in the middle, then a stock shot.

Mostly the actors just waited around. I would go out at six o'clock in the morning to have my hair done and my makeup put on. Then I sat, until six o'clock in the evening. Sometimes around midday they'd do a long shot, or maybe a close-up, one never knew. It was all so boring, so wasteful, so enervating. Even if you were ready to work, eager to work, by six o'clock at night you didn't care anymore. At least I didn't.

Some actresses are brilliant at it—Ingrid Bergman was, for example. Once I used to see Ingrid every day, strolling around the lot with Gary Cooper. They were making *For Whom the Bell Tolls,* and they looked like tall blond gods to me. They *were* Hollywood magic, but there wasn't any of it for me.

The movies at least paid me enough so that I could send for Mother and Larry to come and share a home with me. Larry went to Black Fox, another military school, and I hardly ever saw him. I

My greatest gift.

was up and out before dawn most days, home at about his bath time before bed. All the intervening hours seemed to be full of people telling me "Stand here," "Stand there," "Don't move," "Come speak to the press," "I need just a moment of your time."

By now I had also collected the typical movie-studio entourage: makeup man, makeup girl, wardrobe woman, voice coach, diction coach, hairdresser, secretary, and a man whose only job was to powder my nose. A whole man, just for that. My nose was so sore all the time that I used to think, "If that man comes near me one more time, I'll scream."

My Hollywood period is now almost nonexistent in my memory. I still owe Paramount six more pictures on that old contract, but it has surely run out by now. Hollywood was just an interlude. A very, very important interlude to me, however, because it was there that I received my greatest gift: I met my life-long leading man—Richard Halliday.

VIII
How to Carry Friendship
Too Far

I love to wear a gold-colored chain my granddaughter Heidi Hagman found for me, made of a series of small clasped hands. There are stuffed fabric clasped hands on the couch in my sitting room, a present from my son and his wife, and a very delicate version of them, made lovingly by me for my husband in tiny stitches on fine gauze, framed in the living room. Richard and I used the hands as our family symbol at our Brazilian farm, and I used them as the trademark of a boutique I started there.

The real ones are on my left hand, third finger.

Our attachment to hands started in 1940, when Richard gave me a ring he had ordered especially made. It was a man's hand clasping a woman's hand, in two tones of gold. The hands could be unclasped, to show a ruby heart in the palm of the man. Over the years people have said, "But you can't see the heart, you wouldn't know it was there." We knew.

When he gave it to me, Richard described it as a "friendship ring." When we decided to get married and use it as a wedding ring, I remember telling him, "I think this is carrying friendship too far."

A year before I ever laid eyes on him, or even knew his name, Richard knew who I was. He wasn't madly impressed. He was at the opening night of *Leave It to Me,* with his mother, his grandmother, and his aunt. They later told me he slept through

the whole thing, "Daddy" and all. He denied it, but I believe the
ladies, because Richard had the flu at the time and felt awful.

At that time he was a story editor for Paramount Pictures,
in their New York office. While all the other executives were
coming to catch the show and offer me a contract, Richard was off
in Florida with his sister, Didi, recuperating from the flu. When
Paramount did a test, he was the only executive to turn it down.

In spite of him I was hired, and in spite of himself he was
sent out to Hollywood, at almost the same time, to become West
Coast story editor. The first day I arrived on the Paramount lot I
found reporters and photographers waiting to do the new "star."
I also found a man with a huge bear on a chain. The studio publicity head asked if I would shake hands with the bear. The very
last thing Lawrence Schwab had said to me before I left New York
was *"Don't* pose for any silly publicity pictures." I remembered
that, and I wasn't very eager to get close to the bear. But, after
all, it was my first day. I wanted to be agreeable.

I put out my hand. The bear grabbed me, and down we
both went in a big bear hug on the green grass. At this precise
moment Richard Halliday walked past us with another man. I
didn't see him—how could I, from under that huge bear? Everyone
was screaming, "Get the bear off that girl!" which seemed a good
idea to me. Richard recalls that he looked down at this untidy
scene and said to his companion, "There is nothing that girl won't
do for publicity."

Shortly after that, a man who wanted to be my agent invited me to a small dinner party. He coaxed me there by saying
I could meet Jean Arthur, one of my idols, and her husband,
Frank Ross. There would be an extra man for me, he said, a story
editor by the name of Richard Halliday.

Well, the moment I had one good look at Richard I
thought he was the most handsome, divine man I had ever seen.
He was very tall, thin, with black eyes, black curly hair, impeccable clothes. He sat across from me but he spent the entire evening talking to Jean Arthur. He never addressed one word to me.
Every now and again I'd say something so he had to look at me
and listen, to be polite. Then he'd turn back to Jean. After dinner
he went out on the balcony with her and they talked and talked
and talked. I thought they would never come in.

Just as I announced that I had to go home, he and Jean

walked in from the balcony. My host offered to call his car for me but Richard said, "Never mind, I'll drop her off."

Drop her off! As if I were a parcel, or a load of freight. I protested, but he asked where I lived and he took me home. We sat outside my house and talked for hours. All about careers—his, mine, how important they were. A dozen times I said I had to go in; then we would start talking again. I don't remember how late it was, but far too late for a girl with a 6 A.M. call at Paramount.

We had no formal dates after that, but our paths crossed at the studio and at parties. Then I went off with Allan Jones on a publicity tour, personal appearances in theaters, for *The Great Victor Herbert*. Richard wrote to me occasionally, saying intimate things like "Wish you were here to make a fourth at bridge"—but *all* his letters were written by his secretary. He just dictated them and signed them. It made me so mad that I persuaded Mildred to type my letters back to him.

Mildred said, "If you ever marry again, it's going to be that man."

I said, "Are you out of your mind? Marry a man who has his secretary write to me?" Besides, I knew Richard was going out with some of the most glamorous ladies in Hollywood— Rosalind Russell, Madeleine Carroll, Patricia Morison.

I had a man or two on my own string. Winnie Rockefeller was still around, and a man to whom I was officially, if not emotionally, engaged. He was Frederick Drake, publisher of *Harper's Bazaar*. I had met Fred in New York, and I had seldom known anyone like him—so attentive, so thoughtful. He sent me violets every day and he introduced me to Joy perfume, the only one I have ever liked—an expensive taste. Fred was much older than I, had been married twice, had a son near my age. Perhaps he was a father figure, I don't know, but I found him fascinating, magnetic.

Fred wanted to marry me, but I couldn't agree. I had had that, once and for all. One day while we were lunching at "21" he gave me an engagement ring. I didn't want to accept it. I kept saying, "No, I can't marry you." Finally, because he looked so unhappy, I suggested a compromise.

"How about having an affair?"

Poor Fred almost choked. It surely was a switch, I guess, but I wanted to find out a lot of things, mostly about myself. I wouldn't be breaking the Commandment because I wasn't married anymore. Today the trend is far more relaxed about things like that. In those days my suggestion was daring.

After the *Victor Herbert* tour I visited Lawrence and Mildred Schwab in Florida, to relax. Both Winnie Rockefeller and Fred Drake came down to court me, and I went off on a holiday to Nassau with Fred. All the time I kept thinking of Richard's letters, secretary or no.

Once I was back in the film factory, Paramount was eager for me to be seen. I was invited to studio parties, premieres, dinners. Often my hosts and hostesses would invite Richard, too, because he was a new face in Hollywood. Oh, how ingrown societies long for a new face! Also, Richard was a bachelor. I was delighted, but there was no romance. Because of our working hours, I usually drove to the parties by myself. Richard also often drove to the same parties alone, and inevitably we would be dinner partners, then separately we would each drive to our own homes.

Within weeks Fred began reading in the papers about Mary Martin and Richard Halliday at this affair, or that dinner, or some big "do" or another. Each time he called he asked, "What is all this?" I told him the truth: studio publicity. There were a couple of other Hollywood suitors around this time. One of them had a Rolls-Royce with real zebra upholstery. Larry adored him because of his car. There was another who wanted to give me an emerald the size of a bottle cap. Of course, I didn't accept it; I had enough troubles without that.

Finally, Fred got so upset about the publicity that he decided to come to California. I told Richard that for ten days I could accept no dinner parties. I asked him not to call me or see me at the studio, because I was engaged to Fred and he was coming out. Richard didn't seem particularly shattered by this, but every day afterward delivery trucks brought enormous packages to my house, huge boxes of soap, bath salts, cologne. Each had a note about "keeping it clean," and each was signed "Unsigned."

Fred met me for lunch every day at the studio, took me home at night after work. Naturally, he saw those stacks of packages, and he kept wanting to know what they were. All I could say was, "I don't know. Some nut who keeps sending me things . . ."

After ten days, Fred had to leave. I went back to the studio to find a huge box of ballerina orchids with a card signed, "Richard": "This is the day . . . he's gone . . . when can I see you?"

I couldn't wait. We started going to parties again, with a difference—now he picked me up in his car. One party I'll never forget. It was an Elsa Maxwell spectacular, a progressive party on a bus. She hired the bus, complete with orchestra and bar.

We all drove to Pickfair, Mary Pickford's house, got on the bus, and started a round of glamorous houses—one for cocktails and hors d'oeuvres, another for the next course, and so on. It was all to end back at Pickfair, with buckets of champagne and a breakfast to end the evening.

That night I wore my first fur jacket, a short silver fox which I adored. They called them "chubbies," I think. Somewhere about the middle of the party Richard said, "Let's get out of here and go for a drive." We drove and talked, and talked, and talked. Suddenly I noticed I didn't have my jacket. There was nothing to do but go back to Pickfair and upstairs to find where they had put the coats. I went up, grabbed what I thought was my coat, and we drove away in the dawn. It was all *very* Hollywood.

In the car I felt nice, warm, happy. Then I looked down, and here was this coat clear to the floor. I thought, "My gosh, it's been a long night. I knew this coat when it was a pup and now it's a Newfoundland dog." Next morning I telephoned Pickfair. They said Norma Shearer was a little bit cold because she'd had to wear such a short coat going home. What I remember best of all was that that night was the first time Richard kissed me.

He still had never invited me to his house. I invited myself one day because I wanted to meet his mother, Hope Hammond, who was a famous interior decorator, and I loved her at sight. Richard was out in the garden, reading scripts. He didn't come in.

I was to learn this was his pattern of life, his kind of complete discipline while working. When he finally invited me to dinner I thought hopefully, "Maybe this is it, a nice quiet dinner with Richard, his mother, and me as guest of honor." I wore a divine cashmere jacket, plaid, and a skirt and hat I had bought in Nassau. Afterward Richard always said the skirt was plaid, too, but it wasn't. I put on my new outfit, climbed into my car—and got lost. We lived on the same street, but it was one of those winding ones and everything looks different at night, in the dark.

I was so upset about being lost and late that I didn't give a thought to my clothes until I walked into his living room and saw all the beautiful people. Everybody else was in evening clothes. Madeleine Carroll, who turned out to be the guest of honor, was standing at his fireplace with her arms out on the mantel, wearing the most gorgeous cream-colored satin evening dress and what looked to me like all the crown jewels of Russia.

Maybe that did it. Richard probably decided he had never come across anybody like me, who couldn't find her way from one house to another on the same street and who turned up in plaid cashmere. He started to call me more often. Everyone we knew took credit for getting us together, and they all had a part —Elsa Maxwell, Edith Head, Myrna Loy.

Myrna and her husband, Arthur Hornblow, invited us to a beach party at their place one night, with William Powell. I was shooting until about eleven o'clock so by the time we got there, everybody was in the water without a stitch on. They told us to take off our clothes and join them. I wasn't about to take off my clothes right there on the beach in front of strangers. Richard solved it. He said he would go behind a rock, undress, run straight into the water. Then I should follow, and he would stare straight out to sea.

After my mad dash into the ocean, Arthur Hornblow started to swim toward me. I was so embarrassed because of our Garden of Eden condition that I kept warding him off by splashing water all over the place, saying, "Ooooh, look at the phosphorus!" To this day Arthur teases me about that night, about a twenty-five-year-old gal who had stripped on Broadway for a year and then was terrified by bathing nude for the first time, at absolute pitch-dark midnight.

That night, like all the others, Richard and I spent in company. We never had been truly alone together. Even the evening he gave me the clasped-hands ring, he did it with Edith Head and other people around.

At last came the great night when he invited me to dinner alone with him at his house. When I arrived he was sitting outside in a new black convertible, pushing the buttons so the top

went up uuuup and down, uuuup and down. It was a private
joke. Both of us had convertibles but mine was newer than his
and had an automatic top. He had to get out and manipulate his
top by hand, and he never wanted to close it. I insisted that if
he was really a friend he would put the top up so I wouldn't get
all windblown and catch cold. I also told him that I had another
beau who had a convertible with an automatic top *and* zebra
seats. So there he sat triumphantly in a convertible, showing off.

We had a marvelous dinner. Again we talked and talked.
This time we told each other everything. There were no secrets
left. The logical thing seemed to be to go to Las Vegas and get
married. We got straight up from the table, went to Mother's
house, and woke her up to say we were going to marry. Then we
called Richard's mother in New York and told her. We tried
desperately to reach Fred, because technically he and I were
still engaged. I couldn't reach him at his home or his office.
Finally, I sent him a telegram to say I had tried to reach him, that
I was sending back his ring. I have never been proud of my
conduct toward him. I didn't see Fred again until years later
when we met on the street in New York. He took me to tea at the
Plaza Hotel. All he asked was "Are you happy?" When I said
yes, he smiled and said, "I'm glad."

Richard and I drove the rest of the night to Las Vegas,
went to a motel to change, then to the courthouse. We had to
stand in line at the registry office. I signed my name; Richard
signed his. When I saw him write "Richard Halliday" I asked,
"Why did you write that?"

"Because it's my name," he said patiently.

"Really? I always thought it was Holiday."

The man in the registry office began to look at us strangely.
Perhaps I did go on a bit about it, but I was so surprised. From
the beginning I had thought it was Holiday. The registry man
brought me back to reality. "Don't you even know his name?" he
inquired.

The man probably would have thrown both of us out of
his office had he known that Richard's original name was neither
Halliday nor Holiday. He had been christened John Hope Ham-
mond. His father was a well-known newspaper man named Jack
Hammond, and his mother was Hope Harvey, daughter of "Coin"
Harvey. Richard's grandfather Coin was quite a fellow. His

given name was William—William Hope Harvey—but practically everybody in the world called him Coin because of a raft of books he wrote about money management, trusts, free silver, world financial affairs. He was once William Jennings Bryan's campaign manager, and he was a candidate for President of the United States on the Liberty Party ticket in 1931.

Coin died in 1936. Long before that, his daughter Hope and Jack Hammond had separated. When Richard's sister, also named Mary—another circle—but she is called Didi, decided to become an actress she changed her name from Hammond to Halliday—Halliday was the maiden name of their grandmother—and Richard decided to change his name, too. He made it legal when he was fifteen. Why he chose to change John to Richard I never knew. Perhaps he just liked the sound better.

He became so completely Richard Halliday that I didn't know when we were married that he had ever been John Hope Hammond. Neither did the man in the registry office, fortunately. His cold stare, all the waiting in line, my doubts about marriage in general, came over me again. We had to stand in line again for the civil ceremony. There was a window nearby, and I seriously considered jumping out of it. What was I doing getting married again after ten years? I looked at Richard and wondered how much I really knew this man, even though we had talked out our entire lives in one evening.

Then we were at the head of the line, saying "I do." Richard put the clasped-hands ring on my finger—again—we got back to the car, drove home to Hollywood. By the time we got back it was dark, about six or seven in the evening. I went straight home to see Larry and tell him. It had been too late to wake him the night before, when we drove away.

Again Larry was sitting in the bathtub, scrubbing up for bed. I walked in and said, "Luke, I just got married." Luke was my pet name for him; he called me "Mimi."

"Which one, Mimi?" he asked. "The one with the zebras?"

"No," I said. "I married Richard Halliday."

Larry just said, "Oh."

In retrospect, this dialogue seems very cryptic. But my son and I were more like brother and sister, or perhaps very close friends who sometimes got to play together. We didn't have mother–son discussions.

Anyway, his "Oh" meant that he wasn't very impressed. Richard had been courting me, not Larry.

When I went off to Richard's house to begin my married life with him, Larry was sitting solemnly scraping at one foot with a washcloth, saying to himself, "Daddy Dick . . . Dick old boy . . . Richard," trying to decide what to call him.

It was all sooooo Hollywood. Even the cars. Suddenly we were stuck with three Buick convertibles: mine, Richard's, and the one he had borrowed from a dealer for a joke, the night of our first dinner date alone—could it truly have been only thirty-six hours before?—just so he could sit outside and run the top up and down. In all the excitement of running away to get married he had left his own car in the garage and driven the borrowed one. Now it had more than a thousand miles on it. The Buick people were not amused, so he had to buy it.

We never had time for a honeymoon. I left my house to have dinner with him, drove away to get married, drove home the very next night, had to be at Paramount at six o'clock in the morning. After I had broken the news to Larry, I just packed up a few clothes from my house and carried them over to Richard's.

The first night we began our love life together I didn't even have a wedding nightgown. I always slept in pajamas. Richard said, "Don't worry," and began pulling out of his closet a pile of boxes all beautifully wrapped for Christmas. This was May. He explained that he bought nightgowns and negligees for his sister, his mother, his aunt, every time he saw one he liked. He always had them wrapped for future Christmas presents.

It was quite a scene, Richard taking down the brightly wrapped boxes and me opening them, until finally we found the most beautiful white negligee which was just right. That was my wedding gown and my wedding nightie.

The next thing Richard did was throw out all my clothes. He didn't like anything I owned, certainly not the great plaid cashmere from Nassau. He took me to I. Magnin's and bought me everything. He made me over, a whole new image. Even my hair was done differently. I wondered why on earth this man had married me, if I needed so much redoing.

He had a whole staff of servants to look after us at his house, while we both worked like fiends. I think I made five movies in one year. Fortunately Richard was an early riser so we could at least have breakfast together, in bed. Then we'd go off to work. When I had night rehearsals or shooting, he had story sessions. We were usually too busy even to have lunch together. When we got home at night we were so tired we just went to bed and ate dinner there.

About two months after we were married, a top executive of Paramount, Russell Holman, Richard's boss and longtime friend, and the man who had pushed harder than anyone else to get me the Paramount contract, came out from New York. We invited him for dinner alone, just the three of us.

Richard got the menu together, gave the orders, organized everything. It was his house, his staff. When we went into the dining room the first course came. The servants cleared it away. We talked, sipped wine, which we never had, and I thought, "What fun." Nothing more happened.

I noticed Richard making odd gestures and I thought, "My goodness, he's developing a tic." Suddenly he hissed at me, "The bell." I understood "bell" all right, but I didn't know where it was. Finally he had to explain, "In front of you, under the carpet, to the right." I found it, and the servants brought in the second course.

As if that wasn't bad enough, I noticed a beautiful cabinet against the wall and commented on it. Then, when the plates came in for dessert, I said, "I'm *mad* about your plates."

Russell and Richard were getting paler and paler. Finally Russell said, "You don't often dine at home?"

I said, "We've never been in the dining room."

"Where have you been?" he asked politely.

And I said, "We dine in bed."

It was the first time I had been in that dining room since the evening I saw Madeleine Carroll draped gorgeously over the mantelpiece.

Shortly after that, Richard and I began looking for a house to buy. I guess he thought I would pay more attention to the surroundings if they were our very own. We found a French provincial house in Bel Air with a beautiful garden. It had once been Jeanette MacDonald and Gene Raymond's house.

Richard had his own furniture in New York, which he could ship out to furnish our home. I couldn't contribute anything, because I had always lived in hotels. I couldn't even contribute ideas, except one, which I delivered in a loud voice: "I hate antiques."

Richard said, "Oh?" That's all. Just "Oh?" Then he was very quiet.

As we were driving along one day I saw a shopwindow full of fabulous furniture. I asked him to stop. I gazed and gazed at it, and told him, "I like that."

Richard said, "Well, you know, Mary, those are antiques."

"They are not," I said. "Antiques are all heavy black things with slippery horsehair covers. We didn't have any of that in Weatherford."

He gave a sigh of relief. "Now I feel better, Mary, because all of my furniture coming from New York is antique. What you dislike is Victorian. I don't own any."

At that moment I began to learn about Richard and his taste. He thought it would be so much fun for me to do my own home, the first real one all my own. It wasn't fun. I was paralyzed, immobilized by panic. I didn't know a thing about homes, furniture, curtains. Richard, though he had never married before, had had homes all his life. He had lived in an environment of lovely antiques and exquisite taste since he was a little boy. Sometimes he and his mother had gone without new clothes to save up and buy some piece of furniture they both loved.

While we were waiting for his things to come from New York, Richard bought me the first present for our new home, a beautiful Blüthner grand piano. This was to be the story of our life—beauty before practicality. Having no bed, we took bedrolls to our empty house and slept under the new piano.

Then vans of chests, chairs, silver, crystal, books, records began to arrive. I was ecstatic, and terrified. How to put this all together? Richard left it to his dear little wife, Miss Idiot of 1940. Every night we went home and moved furniture around, but I never got it settled.

Then came our first fight. Richard, coming home tired from his busy day at the studio, I coming home utterly exhausted from shooting since six in the morning, both faced a home upside down with furniture. I heard my darling husband shouting for the first time—and at me. I heard myself shouting right back.

"How can I make these stupid movies and also do this huge house? Besides, I don't know how."

Things really were very tense.

On one wild day I had to go to a radio rehearsal with Bing Crosby, then back to the studio at night to shoot a mob scene. The movie was *New York Town,* a night scene of a parade of Nazis down Fifth Avenue. I was to be caught up in it and knocked down. We shot it on a studio set but under real rain, in the real dark. Somebody made a misstep and suddenly it felt as if everybody in the whole parade had either walked on me or fallen over me.

When it was over I started to drive home. I thought I was all right, but just outside the Beverly Hills Hotel a car stopped quickly in front of me. I slammed on my brakes and spun around about six times. By the time I got home, shaking, Richard was worried to death and therefore furious.

"Why didn't you call me?" he demanded.

"I couldn't," I said. Then I had hysterics. Complete hysterics, never having had them before in my life.

He picked me up and took me into the bathroom and started pouring cold water on my head. I screamed, "How dare you, how dare you?" but he had read somewhere that cold water made people stop having hysterics. I did stop, at least long enough to tell him what a son-of-a-bear he was. I also thought this was the end. Nobody could love me and pour cold water all over me. Besides, this marvelous, intelligent man had made a mistake when he chose me in the first place. I couldn't do the house, I didn't know anything about taste. I didn't even know what to tell the servants to order for meals.

It's a strange thing to look back upon, but all the time before we were married, even for a short time after, we never said "love" to each other. I think we were both afraid, it's such a big word. I couldn't say it because I loved him so much; I couldn't possibly believe that he loved me that much. When he gave me the clasped-hands ring he had engraved on the inside, on my hand, "To MM from RH with ?" Later, when we were married, he went back to the jeweler and had engraved on his hand, inside, "Love!! May 5, 1940."

After my bathroom hysterics there was a tentative truce.

Richard said I was never to drive again while working. He hired our first couple, the man to drive, the woman to help with the house. The first thing I did was make the poor chauffeur help me run away from home. In one of our happier beginnings, Richard and I had spent a long weekend at a ranch near Victorville, California, where there were no telephones, total peace. When I decided to run away I took my studio maid, Pearl, with me, asked the new driver if he knew where the ranch was, and ordered him to take me there. I made him promise not to tell anyone where I was. Then I wrote a letter for him to take back to Richard.

I don't remember what all the letter said. It was a total outpouring about how I could never make him happy because I didn't know enough. I would love him forever and ever but I couldn't be what he wanted; he shouldn't try to find me. P.S. Tell Paramount I might never come back. They could fire me if they wanted to.

I didn't know it, but I was very ill—from the rain, the cold, the trampling in the mob scene; the trauma of it all, I suppose. I kept saying, "Pearl, Mr. Halliday doesn't love me," and Pearl kept saying, "Yes he does, Miss Martin. You'll never find another man like that one."

Richard, when he got my letter, went straight to one of those convertibles and drove all night long. He went every place he could think of—to Arrowhead, almost to Fresno—then he remembered the ranch and guessed I might be there.

At dawn I heard his voice calling, "Mary, Mary," outside. My throat was so closed I couldn't answer. Pearl let him in and I lay in bed thinking, "He's found me. That means he loves me."

He sat down on the bed and asked if I was all right. I whispered I thought so. Then he said, "Stop worrying about the house. We'll sell it. We'll get rid of everything." I wanted to get up and go straight home with him but he said no. He said I needed a rest, I needed to think things over. He told me he loved me but that we both had had a big shock and I should think it over. He arranged for a doctor to come, worked out a way to talk to Pearl every day at a public telephone in town. Then he went away. Life with Richard was never simple, but it certainly was never dull.

Another man might have insisted that I come home right

that minute. Or he might have told me never to come back again, ever. But this man was Richard.

I went back in a week. When I walked into our home there were flowers in every room, fires burning in fireplaces, all the furniture settled, candles lighted. It was utterly beautiful, peaceful, settled. This was to be the pattern of our lives from then on. Always arranged by Richard.

The moment I could do it without his knowing, I telephoned his mother. She was off on a riverboat on the Mississippi. But with the help of Western Union I tracked her down to say, "Mammy, if you love your son you must help me. I love him with all my heart, but I don't know how to run this house, make his home. I love him, but believe me if you don't fly out here, right this minute, it will be over in a week."

Bless Mammy, she did it. She got off the riverboat, flew out, and thought up a good excuse to explain to Richard why she had come without warning. Then she began to teach me. She took me everywhere to show me things; taught me how to organize the staff, let me bask in her judgment and her taste. But most important of all, we became the closest of friends for the rest of her life.

Finally I had to confess to Richard that I had asked her to come. Both he and Mammy went to work building up my confidence. Richard always said afterward that I had innate good taste, good color sense, but I simply had never developed them.

Developed them? I had never even thought about them. For up to that time my mother, who also had impeccable taste, had made all homelife decisions.

I had never met a man like this. His sense of commitment, of discipline, of *hard work* absolutely amazed me. More than that, he seemed to see beneath all the faces of the Paramount Mary Martin. He saw something there—I never knew what, but I did know that the search for my identity was over. All I wanted to be was Mrs. Richard Halliday. That darling Paramount editor had his life work cut out for him—he was to spend the rest of it *editing me*.

IX
Some of the Special Women in My Life

Even when I preferred playing with boys, back in Weatherford, I always had close girl friends: Bessie Mae, Lenora White, Helen Fritz, Myra Akard. Over the years many other women have been important to me: Jinx Falkenburg McCrary, Nancy "Slim" Hawks Hayward—who later became Lady Keith but who will always be "Nancy" to me—Dorothy Hammerstein, Dorothy Rodgers, Kit Cornell, Maj, my Larry's many-talented wife, Richard's sister, Didi Whitcomb, my "sister-in-love," and my one and only Sister.

My closest most special friend is Janet Gaynor. We met in the early Hollywood days and I have loved her always. For herself, for her intellect, her good common sense, the way she has lived her life, and the many things she has taught me.

Then there is Heller, the daughter Richard and I wanted so much. Nobody longed for a child more than we did, and we both wanted a daughter. I was working so hard I was too tired to get pregnant, at first. But after the runaway week at the ranch, Heller was on her way. People have always asked me about her name. Everybody calls every unborn baby something—Sam, or Joe, or Doodleedoo. Our baby kicked like mad, whammo, from what seemed the first moment, and she never stopped. Back in Texas, *heller* means a lively person who raises Cain, so we started calling our baby Heller.

I almost lost her every month, because of my blood type, Rh-negative. We didn't know much about it then. At the end I had to stay in bed with my feet up, for three months. The most dangerous moment was earlier, when Bing Crosby and I were doing *Birth of the Blues*. We were racing to finish because of my pregnancy, and there was a scene in which we were on a beer truck going down the street, dubbing a song. I always loathed dubbing because I could never sing the same song the same way twice.

We were bouncing along, singing like crazy, when all of a sudden I fell off the truck. Bang, right into the street. Bing looked horrified but he never missed a beat. Instead of singing "That's the birth of the blues" he sang "That's the birth of Heller."

I laughed so hard at him that I didn't even feel the bump much. It didn't hurt me, and it didn't dislodge Heller.

Finally she arrived, safely. I had spent weeks preparing a room for her, all dolls, dolls, dolls, as tiebacks for the curtains— I had finally learned how to do these things. When people asked what the child's name was, we both said, "Heller." Heller Halliday. *Well*, it came out in all the papers in the entire United States and the next thing we knew people, ladies' aid societies, were saying, "How dare Mary Martin name a child Heller?" This made us mad. Why couldn't we name our baby anything we wanted?

We did get a little nervous about the minister of the Episcopal church where she was baptized, so we christened her Mary Heller Halliday. Jean Arthur and Judith Anderson were her godmothers. After a while people calmed down about her name. She has always loved it, and she has always lived up to it. We never knew from one day to the next what she would spring on us.

She began when she was very little. Once, when she was only four, Noël Coward was being perfectly lovely to her at his home at the White Cliffs of Dover. He held her in his lap and read a long bedtime story—in French, which she didn't understand. Heller sat there with her innocent big brown eyes fixed on his face, fascinated but uncomprehending. When he finished the story she announced, very solemnly, "You have a rat face."

Noël did have sharp features and kind of Chinese eyes, but it took him some time to forgive her for the remark. Through the years he always asked, "And how is that dreadful 'gull'?"

By the time Heller was five she was onstage with me in

Annie Get Your Gun, earning her own money. She refused to spend any of it. If Richard or I wanted to buy her something, that was fine, but her own money was *hers.* We began calling her Hetty Green.

But that is a little ahead of my story. When she was just a little baby, back in Hollywood, Heller was one more reason for Richard and me to decide to leave. We had been there three years and we both were miserable. We had no time to spend with our baby, no time to see each other.

At this point in our lives Janet Gaynor and her husband, Adrian, the designer who did so many of the fabulous costumes of the great days of Hollywood, were the only people we knew who insisted that we should "go East, young couple."

"Take the chance," they both said. "Do it. Leave Hollywood and go back to Broadway."

We maneuvered a leave of absence from Paramount.

Back on Broadway along came another of those special women in my life, Cheryl Crawford. Cheryl is a brilliant, creative veteran of Broadway and of theater. In 1943 she had a show called *One Touch of Venus,* which had been written originally for Marlene Dietrich. It was to be her theater debut in America. Kurt Weill had written the music, Ogden Nash and S. J. Perelman the words. For some reason Marlene suddenly decided not to do it, and Cheryl Crawford came to me. I couldn't believe it. Me in a part for Dietrich? And Venus? She must be mad. Cheryl insisted, bless her.

Richard and I went off to hear the music, on a very hot night in August, in Kurt Weill's apartment in New York. All my life I will remember that man singing Venus' lovely number, "That's Him," with a kind of quavery, German sound . . . "Ummmmmmmmnnnnnhhh, that's him . . ." I longed to sing that song, but I still could not see myself as Venus.

Richard dealt with my problem in a most imaginative way. He asked if I had ever been to the Metropolitan Museum. Of course, I hadn't. So he took me to that huge place, led me to where the statues are, and said, "Look, this is a Venus." We must have seen fifty varieties: tall ones, short ones, even one who was noticeably broad of beam. All were marked "Venus."

"You see?" Richard asked. "Each sculptor has his own idea of Venus. They aren't all Venus de Milo." After this had sunk in, he said, "You can play Venus. You're going to play her wearing the most beautiful clothes in the world."

That's how Katharine Cornell, Guthrie McClintic, and Mainbocher came into my life. Richard had known Kit and Guthrie for years, but I hadn't. He invited them to our Fifth Avenue apartment for dinner and that night they said I must meet Mainbocher, the famous couturier. He had been tremendously successful in Paris but then the war came and he went to New York, where he had to start all over again. Kit and Guthrie arranged for us to meet.

When I first saw Mainbocher I couldn't believe it. I had always thought designers would be tall, effete, very grand. Mainbocher looked like a businessman. He was stocky, sturdy, with the most clear, honest brown eyes. I trusted him on sight. He listened to our plans for Venus and then he said no. Just "No." He never had designed clothes for a theatrical production, and he didn't want to.

Finally Richard asked if he would at least hear me sing. He promised that we could arrange an audition wherever, whenever, Mainbocher wanted. Main agreed and met us at

Mainbocher, the magician designer, and my Richard discussing how to make me a Venus onstage.

Kurt Weill's apartment. As Kurt played the introduction to "That's Him," I picked up a little chair and carried it over right in front of Main. I sat on it sideways and sang "That's Him" right smack into those kind brown eyes.

When I finished, Mainbocher said, "I will do your clothes for the show if you will promise me one thing. Promise me you'll always sing this song that way. Take a chair down to the footlights, sing across the orchestra to the audience as if it were just one person." And that's how "That's Him" was sung for the next two years.

Then he made for me the most fabulous clothes. Every time I walked on stage as Venus there was applause—for Main's clothes. Gjon Mili took a jillion pictures of me wearing them and everybody printed them, pages and pages in *Vogue*, in *Harper's Bazaar*, my second cover on *Life*.

Main created the color "Venus pink," pale and glowing as the inside of a seashell. My first costume was chiffon in this shade, and the others evolved from it, everything from mauve to shocking pink. Every single costume had a pink silk lining. He said it would make me feel like Venus on the half shell, that when I felt that softness next to me I would feel like a goddess. It worked. He also was the first person who advised me to wear tights under my costumes. We went to Capezio and had tights especially made for me, very light, sheer, flesh-colored. When no inner seam shows the outer line looks longer, thinner. At least the tights made me feel that way.

That blessed Cheryl Crawford, who had stuck her neck out even to think of me as Venus, put up with things in the production which would have driven a lesser woman wild. First there were all those clothes—she must have paid $25,000 for mine alone, more than anyone had ever paid for costumes in a musical at that time. Then she paid another fortune for scenery. When we took the show to Boston for tryouts we saw the scenery for the first time and it was all wrong—great hanging loops, swirls, busy busy; it dominated the stage so much that no one could even see Main's dresses or the great ballets. So Cheryl waved her wand—and her checkbook—and had most of it redone before we went to Broadway.

Then there was the matter of the tenor. Kenny Baker opened in the show and he was marvelous. But when his contract was finished he went back to Hollywood. And believe me, tenors

One of Mainbocher's greatest creations in *One Touch of Venus*.

were hard to find in 1943–44. As fast as Cheryl could find a replacement, he would be drafted. Kenny's first replacement went to war. The second one got so upset when he received his "Greetings . . ." from Uncle Sam that he walked off the stage in the middle of an act one matinee day, walked straight out of the theater, vanished.

Well, panic. We rang down the curtain and stood there looking at each other. A blond, curly-haired chorus boy stepped forward and said, "I can do it. I know the songs, the dialogue, everything." He did, too. He had been quietly watching and memorizing away in the background. His name was Jimmy Sheridan, and he was amazing in the part. He sang the hit number of the show, "Speak Low," like an angel, in a beautiful Irish tenor. He finished the second act without a hitch, and we all gave a huge sigh of relief as the curtain came down. We had a new "barber" to carry on.

That night I went on without a qualm, but to my horror Jimmy couldn't seem to open his mouth. He sang all right, he sounded great, but he kept his mouth closed, his lips together. He looked like a ventriloquist. I thought, "Oh well, it's Saturday night and he's nervous. He'll rest on Sunday, and Monday night everything will be fine."

So on Monday night he couldn't seem to keep his mouth closed. He sang, and spoke, with it wide open and all these big white teeth showing. After the performance I asked what on earth was going on. He had been having his teeth capped. Monday night he had them, all shiny and new and too big. He couldn't possibly close his mouth. After that for a week he sang with the uppers out and the lowers in, or vice versa, while the dentist put things right. I got quite accustomed to seeing him singing away with either his upper lip well down, or his lower lip well up.

Finding Jimmy was a stroke of incredible luck, but good luck was with me all through *Venus*. Agnes de Mille choreographed it, Elia Kazan directed it. Gadge, as people called Kazan, was very young then. This was the first musical he ever directed. He took me to lunch at the Oak Room in the Plaza Hotel. I was absolutely terrified. We talked about everything except the show. Finally he looked at me with those piercing eyes and asked, "How are you going to play Venus?"

I said, "I was afraid you were going to ask me that. I haven't the vaguest idea how I'm going to play Venus."

Then he asked me how I "approached a part." Well, I had only approached one, since I'd only been in one show on Broadway, but I had to say something. I told him I thought in terms of movement, of how I should walk. It was true. I have always thought in terms of movement, of timing. If I can work out the right walk, the tempo, everything else comes naturally.

Kazan said he found this idea exciting. Then he made a brilliant suggestion. At the beginning of the play, Venus appears as a statue in a niche, the property of a wealthy art collector. (John Boles played the collector.) He is so rich that he has a barber come in to cut his hair. In the first act the barber arrives, carrying a ring which he has bought for his girl friend. He keeps trying it on his own hand but it doesn't fit, of course, so when he sees the statue in the niche he impulsively slips the ring on her finger. With that, Venus comes to life.

Kazan said that Venus would certainly find the modern world far different from the one she remembered: now people were in a rush, dashing wildly up and down the streets. Venus would no doubt consider herself the only sane person in the whole world. The others were mad, had no fun, no joy.

"So your tempo, your movement, should be legato, slow and graceful," he said.

Agnes de Mille apparently had the same concept. She used it to create one of the most delightful, funny ballets I have ever seen. I, as Venus, moved legato, slowly and gracefully. The other dancers leaped around staccato, frantically. It was an early version of many of the precision-quick, funny ballets which have been performed in Broadway shows and the ballet theater itself.

For the end of the show, Agnes created a lyric ballet of great beauty. In the plot line Venus and the barber have fallen in love, but goddesses can't truly live on earth. So at the end Venus is taken back by the gods, lifted up, up, up, in a swooping series of lifts by the ballet boys. She vanishes, and the barber is desperate . . . until she comes back, at stage left, as a young girl who wants to be an art student. The barber, it has been well established, is just a simple soul from Ozone Heights. When the young student comes on, dressed in a simple little Mainbocher dress and hat, he looks hard at her. Her face is that of Venus. He looks at the ring, he looks up to the heavens, he looks back at her. Then he asks, "Where are you from?"

When she answers, "Ozone Heights," the happy ending is implicit.

Oscar Hammerstein saw *One Touch of Venus*. He said that the moment he saw me enter as "the Venus of Ozone Heights" he wanted to write a part for the innocent, eager little girl in the white-piqué blouse, pink polka-dot skirt, and matching rolled-brim hat. He wrote it, too—Nellie Forbush in *South Pacific* was a descendant of Venus.

Everyone in every profession, I am sure, has little secrets, tricks of the trade. I began to learn mine in *Venus*. One was the walk. Another was rehearsal in costume. I had fifteen costume changes in *Venus* and I always rehearsed in muslin copies of each costume. I changed for every number, in every rehearsal. When it was time for the real dress rehearsal, I never had to think, "What am I doing now? What am I wearing?" From that moment on I have rehearsed in costume for every show, no matter how much trouble it seems at the time.

I also learned that one can change one's size. The person who taught me how to do it was a young ballerina, Sono Osato, the *première danseuse* of the ballet corps of *Venus,* a tiny, beautiful girl of Japanese descent. She could see that I was nervous about not looking like Venus. I am only 5 feet, 4½ inches, and I longed to be 6 feet tall, statuesque. Sono came to me in rehearsal one day to say, "You know, you can make yourself an inch taller by the way you stand, the way you think."

"Tell me, tell me," I begged.

She did. "Rehearse always in the highest heels you're going to wear in the show. Think tall. Keep your head up; think tall from your solar plexus up. Never relax. Stand straight, think tall. In the audience they'll think you're the tallest person they ever saw."

It worked, it really did. I felt at least an inch taller. I also wore stiletto heels, piled my hair up as high as it would go, and exposed that long neck which had been such a curse in Hollywood. When people came backstage and saw me out of costume, in my flat comfortable shoes, they couldn't believe their eyes.

The high heels which helped make me look tall disturbed my precious motion, however. They clicked. The noise took away from the movement. Besides, I was sure that goddesses shouldn't click. I had tiny rubber caps put on the heels, and from that day onward I have always had rubber-capped heels in the theater. I can move freely without a disturbing, distracting noise.

There was one more secret which I learned in *Venus*, thanks to Richard and to Janet Gaynor. "That's Him" was my big song, but my opening number, "I'm a Stranger Here Myself," was wonderful, too. Mainbocher had made me a huge jersey scarf which went on for about a block. Unknowingly, while I was singing I threw it around in grand, sweeping gestures. One night Richard came backstage to say, "You know, what you do with that scarf is wonderful. In all my life I've never seen anyone do what you do, when you throw it."

I was pleased, of course, but I didn't know what moment he was talking about, what gesture. He said, "When you're walking, you throw it like this." Well, the very next performance, *death*. I couldn't make the scarf move. I didn't know when I had done it, or what I had done. Richard was devastated. He swore that he would never again tell me when I did something specific that he liked.

He didn't understand what had gone wrong and I certainly didn't until Janet gave me The Book. Janet must have read all the books in the world, all kinds, but she has one special inspirational one which she reads every day. It is called *Around the Year* by Emmet Fox. It has a message for every day. One of them is a little poem:

> Do not dissect things too much.
> By the time you have dissected a
>   living thing, you have killed it.
> And you no longer have the thing you
>   began with. . . .

Janet said, "Mary, remember this, whatever you do. When you start analyzing something, then you aren't *you* anymore."

This is the God's truth. I have never forgotten it.

One Touch of Venus opened on Broadway on October 7, 1943, and played 567 performances. Then we took it on the road.

Being a goddess was very hard work. In the summer of 1944 I played at the non-air-conditioned Imperial Theatre in 102 degree heat. Everybody, including the audiences, was uncomfortable but onstage with the heat from lights it was suffocating. I exited backward one smothering afternoon and fell over flat on my back, with heat prostration and a fever of 104. Although I didn't know it, at almost that same moment my mother was having emergency gall-bladder surgery in California. I knew that she had not been well. She had sent Larry east to us. But I had no idea that she was as ill as she was, or that she would have to have surgery. She put it off so long that it was fatal. Sister was with her, and both tried to shield me from the truth. When she left us, when they had the funeral, I was flat on my back in the hospital. Once again, I had not been where I would have wanted to be at the crucial moment.

Once again the theater, and my family's loving dedication to my career in it, had kept me away.

Venus was my first real starring role on Broadway. I had been a "star"—kinda—in pictures, and I had had my name in lights in *Leave It to Me*, but *One Touch of Venus* was different. Everybody wanted me to do everything—photographs, interviews, flower shows here and there, personal appearances. I loved every minute of it and I tried to do all of it. Until one day Richard said, "What do you want most? Do you want to be on the stage and be a star, or do you want to fritter away your time doing all these other things?"

I said, "Both." I have always wanted both, never ceased trying to have both. It doesn't work. All I really know about being a star is the constant responsibility. If all those people would pay all that money to see me prancing around a stage doing what comes naturally, then I owed it to them to be *up,* in voice and full of energy, at every performance. There were years in which I never even talked with friends, because I had to save my voice. Years in which I seldom went out, even for meals, seldom went to parties.

Apart from that, I have never really felt like a star. And I certainly never dared to act like one. Richard would have taken me down a peg or two if I ever tried a thing like that. He surrounded me with the pampered, protected life that a star is supposed to have, but he expected me to behave like Mary Martin from Weatherford, Texas. Which is the only way I ever have felt, or ever will.

X
Staying and Playing Together

At the Drake Hotel in Chicago, during the tour of *One Touch of Venus,* Richard and I made the final decision about our future.

When we left Hollywood all we knew was that we wanted to be together, and be in the theater. We looked no further ahead, asked ourselves no questions. Would Richard produce our shows? Would I play in other people's shows, sometimes on the road while he was in New York? Would he go on the road with his shows while maybe I was playing New York?

I felt such guilt about this brilliant man giving up his successful career. All through rehearsals of *Venus* and one year of performance he had devoted all his time and attention to me. Now we had an extensive tour ahead of us. I was afraid that some day he would deeply regret the move from Hollywood to Broadway, the move which interrupted his career.

We had long, soul-searching talks in Chicago. Our conclusion was that we could live together forever, happily, one way: we would stay in the theater but he would be the boss, the manager, the decision-maker. We also decided that after this, our first road tour, Heller would always go with us. To turn a phrase, "A family that stays together plays together."

That's exactly what we did, for the next thirty years. Heller for years went everywhere with us, made her theatrical debut at age five. For the rest of his life, Richard's goal was to provide the best for us. He managed every phase of our life. He decorated all our various apartments and homes—I think we had twenty of them, altogether—and he decorated my dressing rooms in all the theaters. Each different, each sheer beauty, in his exquisite taste. He also had an extraordinary capacity for detail in business, in contracts, but he was an executive who could not delegate work to others. He had to do it all himself.

Most of all, he did *me*. He was determined to make his Texas tomboy the most feminine, delicate person in the world. Mainbocher and his associate, Douglas Pollard, were his allies. Some of the happiest hours I've ever known were with those men whose one goal in life was to make me look attractive. They succeeded to the point of turning me into Venus—onstage.

Off stage, Richard wouldn't even let me carry a purse. Partly because I always lost them, but mainly because if I carry one thing I end up with a pyramid of things. It's ghastly. He got rid of the pyramid by saying, "No purses, no handbags."

Richard's sister, Didi, once told me that when they were young Richard wanted to make her "the greatest star in the world." As a little boy he wrote plays, put them on, designed costumes and sets all for her. He did this with other people, too. When he was story editor for Paramount he was always discovering writers. He found that more fun, more rewarding, than writing himself. Didi said that Richard's whole life, his desire, his dream, was to make somebody perfect. He had some difficult raw material in me but he tried, he really tried.

He also tried with Larry. Mother and I had shared Larry, with the larger share going to Mother. When she died, Larry came to us. It wasn't easy for anyone. On top of the traumatic shock of the death itself—Larry and I had both lost a mother—was our life style. It was totally in contrast to anything Larry knew. His life with Mother had been complete concentration on him. Now he was with a family in which all the focus was on the mother—a mother in name only, a family whose goal each day was "Get to the theater on time." For a healthy, rapidly growing twelve-year-old boy the atmosphere in a theatrical home was difficult to take: quiet until noon "because Mother's sleeping"; very little talking and playing because "Mother's energy and voice must be saved for the show."

Richard adored Larry but found it difficult to reach him. He wanted to adopt him, but Larry rightly wanted to be Larry Hagman, the son of a father he barely knew. Richard loved

me and wanted to help. I wanted to make up to Larry for twelve
lost years, but there was no time. Heller, thankfully, was still too
little to feel anything but joy in having a big brother.

While we were on the road in *Venus,* Larry and Heller
both lived in our Fifth Avenue apartment with Richard's mother,
Mammy. When we came back we moved to a new home in Norwalk, Connecticut. We thought country living might help but it
didn't, much. We tried to solve our problem by sending Larry to
the best schools as a day student, thinking that meeting new friends
would help. He was miserable.

For the next few years Larry, Richard, and I had a check-
ered career. There were moments of great joy and utter sorrow,
tensions, times when we didn't speak, misunderstandings, anger,
reconciliation, tears, everything. The love and comprehension
Larry and I now have belong to another moment, another
chapter. . . .

During the first crucial years Richard had to juggle many
emotions. I wonder how he did it, because he had just begun "our
career," and he had to make it successful.

Our first show after the big Chicago decisions was *Lute
Song,* a lyrical, lovely thing based on an ancient Chinese legend. It
was the story of a young wife, Tchao-Ou-Niang, who is left at home
to care for her aged in-laws while her young husband goes off to
seek their fortunes. On the way he is either captured by, or falls in
love with, a Chinese princess. I forget which. In any case the wife
goes looking for him, sells her beautiful hair to get money for the
search, and sings the loveliest song of the show, "Mountain High,
Valley Low."

Raymond Scott and Bernie Hanighen wrote the score.
John Houseman directed the show, Robert Edmond Jones did the
scenery, and the famous Russian designer Valentina did my costumes. Because of that show Valentina and her husband, George
Schlee, became friends of ours. Circles again—we ended up living
in the same apartment building in New York, years later.

Again I had a marvelous choreographer, Yeichi Nimura.
He taught me long, liquid movements suited to the Oriental
robes. This time there were no stiletto heels; I wore the flattest
possible ballet slippers. Nimura taught me how to hold my hands
and arms, how to make the graceful hand movements. We worked
together for three months before the show opened and I used to

As a Chinese bride in *Lute Song,* in
Valentina's lyrical costume.

practice the finger movements as I walked down the street, watching to see if I was doing the deft, intricate movements correctly.

One day on the block just before Nimura's studio in Carnegie Hall, I was walking along doing my hand exercises when a man came up and started making what looked like the same movements back. He scared me half to death. When he saw me start talking—spluttering, I suppose—it was his turn to be startled. He was deaf, and of course when he saw me carrying on like that on the street he thought I was, too.

My husband in *Lute Song* was Yul Brynner, whom, I am proud to say, Richard and I really discovered. Somebody told us about him and we invited him out to the Connecticut house. He came with a guitar and sat on the floor, playing. We had seldom seen such an exciting man. He created a special magic around himself, and we knew we wanted him for *Lute Song.* When he moved onstage in that show he was grace itself, pure poetry. He seemed to float in and out of the beautiful panels designed by Bobby Jones. I can't remember whether he was bald then or not. I know he wore a black toupee to look more Oriental.

At the beginning I wore wigs for that show. After I decided

to use my own hair and dye it black—with a special fall which I could "cut off" during the dramatic haircutting scene, I still kept the wigs. Thank fortune I did, because one night I was late to the theater. But not for the overture. I had no time for makeup or a fancy ancient Chinese hairdo, so I just plopped one of the old wigs on my head and rushed out, looking Chinese from the neck down and the wig up.

I hate being late, being rushed. Usually for rehearsals I was so early that we had to ride around the block for a while so I wouldn't be Miss Jerk and get there before the janitor did. The night I was late for *Lute Song* was all the fault of a blizzard. It was an hour's drive from Norwalk to New York, but we always had made it until that night. The snow was so thick, the weather so awful that when we reached New York the car stalled. We had to abandon it and run for the subway. I'll never forget the scene of that packed subway car, people standing up holding onto the rings, many of them trying to get to the theater. All of a sudden they saw me. "What are you doing here?" they asked. "We're on our way to see you."

When the train finally made it, most of the passengers bolted toward the front of the theater and I to the back, headed for the stage door and my wig.

Richard always drove me to the theater in those days, and did the office work in our Hampshire House apartment while I performed. Then he drove me home again, except on Tuesdays and Fridays, the nights before matinees, when we stayed in town. It was fun, we made all our important decisions on the Merritt Parkway. I never have been one to rehearse my lines, brood about the part, before I get to the theater. If I start saying my lines in the car, when I get to them in the performance I get a block— I think I've already said them. I don't begin to get into the part really until I start to make up. That moment, putting the face on, and the costume, is the moment I begin to be whatever role I'm playing. Richard always said I carried the part home with me, that all through *Lute Song* I tried to walk thirty feet behind him. I don't quite believe it.

Michael Meyerberg's production was utterly lovely, and the score was different and haunting. Perhaps it was ahead of its time. It was a critical success but not really a commercial one. We opened at the Plymouth Theater on February 6, 1946, and played only 142 performances.

That time I did not go on the road with the show. Yul Brynner did, playing with the beautiful German actress Dolly Haas. I hate to admit it but she was superior to me in the part; she was a much more experienced actress. Dolly is the wife of Al Hirschfeld, who does those marvelous caricatures of Broadway shows for *The New York Times*. He did one for every show I was ever in, and Richard always bought the original drawings from him, as an opening-night present for me. I have them all proudly framed today, in my home.

There is a sequel to *Lute Song*. Years later, when Dick Rodgers and Oscar Hammerstein were doing *The King and I*, they had trouble finding the perfect king. Richard and I both said, "There's only one man—Yul Brynner." Yul got the part, and Richard and I went up to New Haven for opening night. We loved this spectacular musical. Even in tryout out of town we could see it was going to be one of the great shows of all time.

But Gertrude Lawrence, a star with a capital *S*, a magic woman of whom I was deeply in awe, didn't have an opening song to establish her character as Anna, the teacher the king had brought out to Siam.

Everybody concerned—Dick, Oscar, Leland Hayward— knew it. After the dress rehearsal in New Haven we got together at Casey's, a famous restaurant across the street from the Shubert Theater. Because of our long, happy association together we started to talk about the show.

"Any suggestions?" they asked.

I had one. I knew the perfect melody Gertie should have. But I didn't want to tell them.

"I'm cutting my throat right now," I said to Dick and Oscar. "Do you remember that song we had in *South Pacific,* the soft-shoe number we used about a thousand times in rehearsal?" It didn't have any lyrics then, and in the end we had so many marvelous songs that Dick and Oscar decided to save the melody for another show.

"You have always promised me that melody someday, but it is exactly the one Gertie needs for the first act," I said. Then I hummed it, the first two bars.

They all said, "You're right!"

When Oscar wrote the perfect words to Dick's lovely music, "my" melody became "Getting to Know You."

To My Mistreated Body

XI
Hair, Nose, and Teeth

Everybody has hair, teeth, and a nose, at least part of his life, but people who are not in the theater cannot possibly imagine how much trouble they are.

I don't remember having seen the real color of my hair since I was fourteen. I do recall that when I was little I had short, reddish-brown hair with bangs. When I was fourteen I started putting camomile tea on it. We all did in Weatherford; we'd boil up the flowers, put the tea on our hair to make it blond. This went on until one day Daddy said, "Baby, you shouldn't be out in the sun so much, your hair is bleaching." So I eased up on the camomile for a while.

In Hollywood my hair was long, for me, and it photographed very dark. For *Venus* it was pink, for *Lute Song*, black. We began that show with wigs—elaborate, beautiful things—but every time I moved I could feel them stick, or pull, or unglue, or something. Also, they were big. The more hair I had the thinner my face looked. I wasn't happy, so after *Lute Song* opened in New Haven I asked Richard why we didn't throw away the wigs and dye my hair black. We bought the materials and stayed up all night long in our hotel bathroom doing it. When Heller saw me like that for the first time she was terrified, she thought I was a witch. She always referred to it as Mother's Mourning Period. I looked dreadful in the daytime, but onstage it was striking. I also shaved my eyebrows off to paint in an Oriental look. I must say when they came back in they were rather sparse.

When *Lute Song* closed I had to get rid of the black and make my hair red for *Pacific 1860* in London. No beauty shop would do it; they said my hair would fall right out. Once again

Richard and I did it ourselves. We put some kind of acid on it, very strong. It didn't fall out. It still hasn't, though we turned it bright red for England, dark red for *Annie Get Your Gun,* short blond for *South Pacific,* long and pale yellow for *Sound of Music,* orange for *Hello, Dolly.* Once I made some ghastly mistake and it turned green, chartreuse green. It was too late to do anything about it and I played the entire show with green hair. Nobody noticed. When we were doing *Pacific 1860* I loved to walk through Covent Garden. All the costermongers, the porters there, knew me, called me Mary. One morning as I strolled through I distinctly heard one of them say to another, about my red hair, "It's hartificial!"

Only once did Richard and I try to achieve what had been my natural auburn. We were on a train from New York to Hollywood, where I was to do "My Heart Belongs to Daddy" in a film about Cole Porter's life. I had abandoned Hollywood, but I wanted to go back—briefly—for this tribute to the man who gave me my first big song.

I had to look, of course, the way I did when I first met Cole. Richard and I had packed all the bleaches and dyes and equipment, but doing my hair job on a lurching train is rather more difficult than in a hotel bathroom. We performed a cockeyed ballet between the washbasin and the seats in our compartment. At one point the train gave such a jolt that the hand basin went up and my head went down, this time into the john. But I was the right color for the film when we got to California.

Only once in my life did I go to a famous hairdresser. The whole experience was a fiasco. Part of the lyric for "That's Him" in *One Touch of Venus* went, "You know the way you feel when there is autumn in the air . . . the way you feel when Antoine has finished with your hair." Antoine, the great hair stylist from Paris, had come to open a new salon at Saks Fifth Avenue. When he saw me onstage and heard the lyrics he was pleased. He offered to give me a personal Antoine hairdo. I said to Richard, "Here's my chance. I must go." Richard gave me money for taxi and tips, and I wore a very grand hat, high, covered with daisies. I had practically never been out alone, without Richard by my side and carrying the money, since we moved back to New York. I was so excited about Antoine that I didn't pay attention to what I was doing. I handed the taxi driver all my money, waited for change, and he drove off with it. There I was, without a cent.

Antoine gave me a fantastic hairdo, piled high, way up. I didn't dare even try to put my grand hat on top of such splendor. I arranged with the manager to have Richard take care of the tips later, but I still had the problem of getting home with no money. I called Richard. With great glee he said, "It's a beautiful day, why don't you walk? Just go out to Fifth Avenue, turn right, stroll along until you find our building."

I didn't think he was taking my predicament seriously enough. We had an account at Saks, so I decided to buy a blouse, plus anything else that appealed to me. I'd just buy and buy and charge everything and that would fix *him*. While the clerks were making out the ticket I sat down in a chair, feeling madly elegant in my magnificent pink hairdo, with my daisy hat in my hands. Suddenly I felt something: there was a lady fingering the fabric of my dress. Very intent, she was. I moved, and with that she started to scream. Obviously, she had thought I was a dummy. I've never heard such screaming in my life, just one yell after another until finally she terrified me. I ran off in one direction, as fast as I could; she ran in the opposite direction. By this time there was pandemonium, half the clerks chasing the lady and the other half hurrying after me.

I finally got out of the store and kept right on running up Fifth Avenue, the daisies falling off my hat, my new Antoine hairdo falling down my red neck. It turned out to be a long way. When I finally got home, dozens of blocks later, I went in and yelled, "Richard." He started to laugh as hard as the lady had screamed and he couldn't stop, either. I was so furious, so mortified, that I didn't go back to another beauty shop for years. Richard didn't give me money again, either, except for an allowance, which I usually lost or gave away. He wanted me to have anything I wanted, but it was simpler if he handled the money.

There was also the saga of my teeth. They weren't my worst feature—my nose was—but they caused the first problem. After the two front baby teeth James Porter McFarland had knocked out in the glider, new ones came in big, bright, shiny, and permanent. Beside the big ones were a lot of little-bitty ones which were very much out of proportion. When I opened my mouth to sing, or smile, it looked like all I got for Christmas was my two front teeth.

Dear Lawrence Schwab, when he hired me for Broadway,

said he would pay to have my teeth capped and I could repay him later. His offer left me literally with my mouth open. It was to stay that way for some time. We found a dentist, Dr. Gordon Pace, who was one of the most endearing men who ever helped put me on a marquee. At this point I was singing every night until 2 A.M. at the Trocadero in Hollywood, and I had to be in Dr. Pace's office at eight every morning. He had to grind down all but the two front ones on the top row, put on cement and plastic, put in temporary substitutes while he made the permanent porcelain jackets. I lost fourteen pounds while all this was going on. Poor Dr. Pace lost twelve.

Between sessions I went home to put ice packs all over my face to get in shape for the next performance. One afternoon about four o'clock the doorbell rang. Mildred answered it, then came to say, "Robert Taylor would like to see you."

"Oh, sure," I said, "ho, ho, ho, just show him right in."

Ye gods, it *was* Robert Taylor. He had seen me at the Trocadero, found out where I lived, and brought me red roses. He took one look at me with the fat mouth, the swollen jaws, the ice packs, smiled a sickly smile, dropped the roses on the floor, and walked out. I didn't see him again until we did a radio program together called *Good News*. By then I think he had forgotten the whole episode; perhaps he didn't even realize I was the same girl.

Just a few days before the permanent caps were to be put on, Oscar Hammerstein called. He had been trying hard to get me into the St. Louis Light Opera Company. This time he thought there was an ingenue part I could do, with some dancing. He asked if I would go to Fanchon and Marco's for an audition. When I got there, the heads of everything were sitting on benches, with Oscar in the middle.

This was one of the times I decided perhaps my dancing was more impressive than my singing, so I threw myself into the whole Eleanor Powell-Ruby Keeler-Ginger Rogers act, dancing away, rat-a-tat-tat, doing fast turns, faster, faster. All of a sudden my temporary plastic caps flew out across the floor, landing at Oscar's feet.

Poor Oscar, every time he tried to help me, something happened. He didn't want to laugh but he just doubled over. I made a dive for the caps, our eyes met, and he said, "Did you drop something?" I stuffed the caps back in my mouth (they were all in one piece), said "Excuse me" and "Thank you very much," and left the room. I didn't get that job with the St. Louis Opera Company.

Dr. Pace's caps lasted until 1953, when I had to have most of them redone in New York. By this time I owned a house, a lot, a yacht—all in my mouth. I still have the two big shiny front ones, my very own, and one nice porcelain one left over from Dr. Pace's efforts.

By the time I did *Sound of Music* in 1959, I had talked my New York dentist, Peter Yoshitomi, into giving me some cement powder so I could take care of any emergency in the theater when dentists are off duty. Reluctantly, he also instructed me carefully about its use. He kept saying, "Mary, people don't do this, you might ruin everything." But I felt safer with my little repair kit nearby in my dressing room.

Weeks went by before I got to use it, but one matinee day Muriel O'Malley, who played Sister Margaretta in the convent, the one who always defended Maria—me—came tearing up to my dressing room. She was in her robes, her makeup, and a panic. "Mary, have you got anything? My two front caps just fell off; they've called 'five minutes'; I can't sing without them. What can we do?"

My big moment had come.

"Muriel, you just sit right down there," I said.

I pushed my sleeves up, settled Muriel with her head tilted back at the right angle, mixed the ingredients very quickly because "five minutes" *means* five minutes in the theater, took careful aim —and put her caps in.

I made sure they were firmly set; she ran her tongue over them a couple of times, then I said in my best professional dentist's voice, "Now smile." Merciful heavens, they were in backward! We couldn't get them off to turn them around. It was quite difficult for the members of our abbey, that Wednesday afternoon, to keep straight faces when Muriel sang "How Do You Solve a Problem Like Maria?" when Maria had just ruined her.

My own dentist had to knock off my handiwork between shows. Fortunately, both he and Muriel still speak to me.

Knocking off was what a lot of people thought should have happened to my nose. Personally, I never thought it was that bad. Not as bad as it was made out to be when I went to Hollywood. My face was thin, what was called "heart-shaped," with high cheekbones and pointed chin. In the middle was a roundish pug nose; I guess it did sort of stick out there. If I didn't have enough money to have my teeth capped until Lawrence Schwab gave it to me, I certainly didn't have enough to have my nose fixed. Anyway, I didn't want to.

My most vivid recollection of what I have come to think of as my "nose audition" was with Harry Cohn, head of Columbia Studios. It took place in his office, which had a desk about twenty feet long, half covered with telephones. Harry Cohn was a stocky, burly man whose ears seemed permanently attached to telephones. I began to sing, I think it was "Il Bacio." Before I could even get to the swinging part, he interrupted to answer a telephone. Then he said, "Sing another one." I started, he interrupted. "Sing another one"—and another phone rang. Finally I was singing "Johnny One Note" and holding the note, loud, as long as I could. I was determined to hold that note as long as he could talk. Just as I was about to turn blue he put down both phones, looked straight at me, and shouted, "Will you stop that noise?"

"Will you stop talking on all those telephones and listen to me?" I shouted right back. I didn't care anymore that he was president of his tacky old company.

"Okay, okay," he said, "you sing fine, just fine. But you have to go and have your nose fixed."

"What's the matter with it?" I asked.

"Too round," he said. "Something like a W. C. Fields nose."

Since the moment he said it I have been unable to get the image out of my mind. But I did get even with Harry Cohn. One night during *Leave It to Me,* I heard that he was in the audience, in the front row, watching every move I made. I peered out and saw him. He was there all right.

That night I tried to sing "Daddy" better than I ever had before. Just before my exit in the lynx coat, the little fur hat, I always sang, "He treats it and treats it and then he repeats it . . . my Daddy he treats it so well. . . ."

That night I put my hand up to my nose and made a complete circle around it with my thumb and forefinger. I aimed that pug nose straight at old Harry, smiling my dazzling porcelain-tooth smile just for him. I had made Broadway *sans* teeth, but with nose.

It was a very satisfactory moment.

XII
Some Royal Occasions and a King-size Fight

I guess I've been in love with England and the English ever since I saw Noël Coward in the Palace Theater in Weatherford. He played a terrible man, a villain, in *The Scoundrel,* but from that moment on I dreamed of meeting him, just seeing him. Then it was Noël who first took me to London. It was he who presented me to the royal family; it was with him that I had the worst and silliest fight of my whole career.

We first met, briefly, backstage while I was doing *Venus.* Later, during *Lute Song,* a cablegram arrived between acts asking if I would come to London to star in a musical comedy which he was writing for me. I read the cable about three times, with my jaw dropping farther and farther. Finally, I said to my maid, "Give me a cigarette."

"You don't smoke," she said.

"I know I don't, but this is from Noël Coward. I have to start."

I was so excited all through the next act that I had trouble keeping a British accent from creeping into my Chinese wife's mouth. When Richard was backstage I asked him to cable Noël instantly to say we were interested. Richard wasn't exactly mad about the project at this point, because he thought we should hear the music first, and see the script. I told him I didn't care if it was written in Sanskrit or in Braille. I had to see England and I had to work with this man.

From then on, for months, there were telephone calls, cablegrams, letters—Noël wrote fantastic, marvelous letters. We never saw the music before we left, because he explained he was still writing it. He did send along the story idea. Richard read it first and made no comment. I read it and thought, "Welllll, I don't know . . ." My part was written not only for a high soprano but also for an opera singer—an opera singer who had traveled all over the world, spoke seven languages, was called Mme. Eleanor Salvador. That alone should have stopped me, but it didn't. I *had* been to California, and New York and Nassau and Tijuana, Mexico, after all, and I couldn't wait to work with my hero.

Richard and Heller, who was four, and I sailed on the *Queen Mary* in the summer of 1946. Larry, who was fourteen, flatly refused to go when he heard he couldn't wear his cowboy boots at the Savoy Hotel, where we were going to live until the show opened. He stayed in the United States with Richard's mother.

We had a rough crossing, with fifty-foot waves. The *Queen Mary* had been a troopship during the war and she still was hardly a luxury liner at that moment in her glorious history. This upset Richard because he wanted my first trip to be perfect, but I adored every minute of it. Noël met us, whipped us through customs, drove us from Southampton in an enormous Rolls-Royce equipped with a nanny for Heller, and into a Savoy suite right on the Thames with two huge bedrooms and a living room, all filled with flowers. I couldn't decide what to do first—pinch myself, feel the fabric of those beautiful draperies, sniff the flowers, or hug Noël, Richard, or Heller.

Noël Coward is—was—for me, the greatest host in the world. He took us to his Mews house in London, a small place with a huge living room and an enormous fireplace and, up on platforms, two grand pianos. Two, for heaven's sakes, what luxury! Then he took us to his country place at the White Cliffs of Dover. We could still see where the bombs had hit, again and again, but he had flowers and fires in every room, hot-water bottles in every bed, and those fat down comforters which always either fall off during the night or else cook you in the middle of the bed.

Richard and I were eager to get to work, but Noël explained that there was nothing we could do because they had to rebuild the Drury Lane Theatre Royal, which had been bombed, before we could open the show. And they didn't even have a building permit yet. He confessed that he hadn't wanted to tell us before, because he was afraid we wouldn't come to England.

Every time I complain that I never had a vacation—I complain about that sometimes—it is because I have temporarily forgotten those next three absolutely glorious months. Almost all of it was holiday, sheer joy. It was also very expensive, but Richard was so thrilled watching me be Miss Wide-eyed of 1946 that I don't think he minded very much.

Noël showed us London, then whisked us off for ten days in Paris, to be wined and dined by his friends. There I ate my first *escargots*, with champagne, and had too much of both. Edward Molyneux, who was a great friend of Noël's, had a party which included everybody in the fashion world—Lanvin, Patou, Schiaparelli, Dior, Balenciaga. I wore a beautiful, simple, understated dress Mainbocher had made for the opening night of the London show. There I was in the reception line with Molyneux on one side of me, Richard and Noël on the other. I didn't speak French so I just said *enchantée* to everyone I met and *oui* to everything anybody said. *Enchantée, enchantée, enchantée, oui, oui, oui,* all night long.

Finally some man said to Edward Molyneux, "I hope her husband isn't jealous."

Molyneux said, "Well, I don't know him very well, but what do you mean?"

The man said, "We've just made a date, she's meeting me at such and such a place after the party." He followed me around for the rest of the night and I kept saying *oui* until somebody finally had to explain to him that I was not going to meet him after the party.

Then Richard gave a dinner at Maxim's for all of Noël's friends who had been so kind to us. King Peter of Yugoslavia and his Queen were the honored guests. There I was, with kings and queens and *enchantées*, living it up.

Meanwhile Heller and her nanny, back in London, were having their own social life. When Heller asked if she could have a birthday party—she was five on November 4, 1946—we said, "Of course, but whom shall we ask?"

"I know a lot more people in London than you do," she answered, "and I've already invited them." "Them" were the page boys of the Savoy, darling youngsters who looked about ten or twelve but probably were sixteen. They came impeccably dressed in their uniforms, with white gloves and each with a little bouquet, in lace, for Heller. Nobody in the whole Savoy got page service that day.

Noël had invited John Mills and his wife, Mary, with their two little girls, Hayley and Juliet. Also, the actress Adrianne Allen Whitney with her two children, Daniel and Anne, whose father was Raymond Massey. We let Heller wear a little black-velvet dress which had been made for opening night of the show. Noël, who had forgiven her for saying he had a rat face, knocked himself out with presents. We had a double-barreled party with cake and ice cream and presents in one room, martinis and hors d'oeuvres for adults in another. The pages, of course, went back and forth between the two rooms. Before the party ended there were twelve handsome boys swinging one little girl—our Heller—in the air. What a birthday!

Then reality struck us all. Prince Littler, producer of the show, received a permit for rebuilding the Drury Lane Theatre. We had to begin work. I had received a letter in the States from this man, a letter which came with a fancy kind of seal on it. I thought he really was a prince, only to learn later that it was his first name. It's a good thing I hadn't yet met my friend the New York producer Saint-Subber, or I probably would have thought he was a saint, even though there aren't many of them around writing letters.

We first heard Noël's music for *Pacific 1860* in his Mews house. There I met my leading man, Graham Payn from South Africa. He had done terribly well with a song called "Matelot" which Noël had written, and *Pacific 1860* was supposed to make him a star. He was a beautiful dancer and sang well enough—let's say as well as I did, though I was supposed to be an opera singer, ho, ho, ho.

Noël played some of the songs. I thought every song he wrote was the most divine thing in the world, but I kept wondering who was going to sing them. They certainly didn't sound like me. Noël said they were for the trio, or for the chorus, or for

Graham, or somebody. The plot of the show was that Mme. Salvador's husband had died, she went off on a tour of the world, stopped at a little place on an old plantation in some island somewhere, and the governor invited her to stay with his family. He had a lot of daughters and one son, played by Graham, and, of course, the boy fell in love with the older woman. It was all veddy British.

The main song Noël had written for me was "Alice Is at It Again." Probably this was because he had heard me sing "Daddy," which was naughty. A few years older and wiser when I read the lyrics to "Alice," I nearly dropped dead. Alice was really *at* it, with the birds and bees and the beasts of the field. I thought it wasn't right for a gal from Texas to make her London debut with this scandalous song. I also didn't think it was right for Mme. Salvador, for her character. I knew it was funny, terribly funny, and now I know that I should have sung it. It would have stopped the show every night. But I refused. Noël was very sweet and said he would write me another. He later sang "Alice" himself, in nightclubs and revues, and made it a tremendous number.

What he wrote for me as a replacement was a song that went, "There is nothing so beguiling as a One, Two, Three, A One, Two, Three and a hop!" All very quick, clipped, British. Noël could play it very well, in his own keys, and he did. Well, in the middle I was to sing all this in seven languages—French, Italian, Spanish, German, and whatnot. It was hysterical. He kept asking, "Do you like it?" and I kept saying, "Yes, yes," forgetting that I not only couldn't sing the words in all those other languages. I couldn't sing them in English eye-ther. But I was so enamored of this man that if he'd said "Sing the alphabet," I would have done it.

Finally came the day when we went to a beautiful hall for the first reading. In London they don't make you rehearse in some dusty half-lighted empty theater, but in a whole hall. Noël assembled the company. He was so loyal, he always had the same people for all his shows, the same stage people, same managers, same costume designers, everybody. I loved them all, and the hall, but I thought if I had to read one word in front of all of them I would drop dead, I would go straight through the floor and never come up again. I was the only one who spoke Texas—solid, solid Texas—which I don't really do onstage, but I certainly couldn't speak beautiful English English.

Noël saved me. He said, "I will now read the entire thing," which he did. He also ran through the songs and we all just sat back and enjoyed it. Never was *Pacific 1860* performed so well, because he could perform everybody's parts better than most people in the cast. Then he stood up and said, "It's been marvelous to be with you. I will see you again in two weeks. You will be letter-perfect. I do not wish to see one script in one person's hand."

Talk of tricks of the trade. This was the first time in my life I had to be letter-perfect on first rehearsal. Noël didn't care how you said the lines in the beginning. He was interested in directing the movement, from the first day of rehearsal, with no wasted time. You can't do that with a script in your hand. For the rest of my career I took care to be letter-perfect before I went to rehearsal. This approach has been debated. I suppose it wouldn't work for a lot of people, such as those in the Actors' Studio, who improvise. Certainly one changes moves, lines, business all during rehearsal and even after opening night, but for me it was a big step to know the entire part before we began. It might drive the improvisers up the wall, but for me it was perfection.

I still had to learn how to sing in English English, so I asked Noël if he would work with Graham and me at night. He said he'd love it. That blessed man spent hours teaching me the clipped, quick voice that the London audience understands. My first line, I'll never forget, was "She wouldn't laugh, nor would she be angry. She would be touched and veddy grateful." Over and over again I said it, faster and faster and faster, clipped, clipped, clipped until I sounded like a record running at the wrong speed. I learned the cadence by practice, but I am such a mimic that I sounded exactly like Noël Coward. Which wasn't very good for me, or for the show.

I can never exaggerate how much stagecraft I learned from Noël. It was he who taught me two of the most important techniques of acting: first, how to really let go onstage; second, how to express emotion without feeling it so much that it absolutely destroys you.

His lessons almost destroyed me in the learning. There

was one scene in *Pacific 1860* in which I, being a temperamental operatic diva, was supposed to get furious with my impresario and hit him in the face—really sock him. I couldn't do it, just couldn't hit that man. We went over it and over it, with Noël saying, "Hit him." I tried, but I couldn't. Finally Noël became so desperate that he began to gig me as one would gig a horse in the bullring. He said everything ugly he could think of—to me.

"How could you be so dumb?" he asked, or "Haven't you ever learned anything?" I was crushed, killed. How could this man I worshiped turn on me like that? After all, he knew all about me. He had asked me to come to London. He had written this bloody (a word I had learned from him, by the way) part which I couldn't play.

He kept it up and kept it up until I got so mad one day, just before lunch break, that I hauled off and socked that poor man as hard as I could. Hit him, *bang*, almost knocked his head off. His ears may still be ringing, but I was the one who was destroyed. I couldn't believe what I had done; I wanted to cry. But Noël suddenly was on his feet, laughing, clapping his hands.

"Thank God I got you to do it," he shouted. "I never thought I could. Haven't you ever hit anybody before?"

"Of course I have," I said. "But only my best friend, James Porter McFarland, and only with boxing gloves."

I tried to apologize to the darling man I had socked, but Noël did it for me. "She had to do it," he said. "She got so mad she had to hit somebody. She couldn't hit me, even though she wanted to."

He explained that once I had had the emotion, and had let it out onstage, I would be able to hit but pull my punch on cue, without damaging either of us too much.

Then he taught me how to cry on cue, with a variation of the same technique.

"You must really have the emotion, once or twice or three times, then train yourself to summon the tears without suffering the emotion," he said. I couldn't agree with him, at first. He told me that once, during the war, he had been performing for British soldiers and he became so emotional that he broke down and cried during the performance. The men didn't believe him. They roared with laughter, had hysterics, because they thought he was putting them on. By expressing his own emotion, Noël explained, he had become incredible. Worse, he had robbed the audience of its right—the audience has the privilege of *feeling* the emotion; the performer must only express it.

I still thought it would be impossible to do anything unless I felt it, deeply. To convince me he said, "I will now cry for you." He turned around a moment, turned back, and he cried. I could hardly believe my eyes.

He was absolutely right. Always before, if I had had to cry onstage I would think of something sad . . . my father's death, my mother's, something that had hurt me. That made me cry all right, but I had to sing over real tears. Believe me, that isn't easy. But once I had had the real emotion, really cried, I found that I could use Noël's technique. I could give myself a word—I don't even remember the word now—and make myself cry on cue without tearing me to pieces inside.

This is stagecraft, learned from the master.

Pacific 1860 ran for nine months. Despite all Noël did and I did, I never really felt comfortable as Mme. Salvador. Both the audiences and the press were kind to me, and I adored London. I also got to meet some people I had admired from afar for years and years, the royal family. The first time I met them was at a charity performance on January 23, 1947. King George, Queen Elizabeth, Lord and Lady Mountbatten, Princess Margaret—all came. The present queen, who was young Princess Elizabeth then, was home with a cold.

We were asked to come to the royal box between acts to be presented. Noël was to take us up. The royal family had a little sitting room behind the royal box. Noël asked me if I knew how to curtsy and I replied, "Naturally." Not that it mattered; I was in my first-act costume, a big red crinoline. Nobody could see under that wide skirt to see if I curtsied right or not. Anyway, I did.

They couldn't have been more darling. We talked and talked; they asked if I'd ever been in London before and I said I'd never been *anywhere* before, and they asked if I liked it. Time was passing and I began to worry about being *on* too long, and the second act, with all those people sitting out in the theater. So I said that I had had a lovely time but I thought I should go. All the time there had been in the royal box a royal footman with a white wig and knee breeches, and as I backed away, I suddenly felt something stopping me. Something like the un-royal foot of the royal footman.

Later I discovered that you just don't dismiss royalty; they are supposed to dismiss you.

That dear sweet queen understood what had happened. Quickly she said something about how she was sure I wanted to get back, the show must go on. The footman removed his foot, and I removed myself from the royal box.

I was presented once more about five years later when we played *South Pacific* in London, again at the Drury Lane. The king had been so ill he hadn't been anywhere for months, but he wanted to see the show. He came with the queen and Princess Margaret. Princess Elizabeth was on a tour with her husband, the Duke of Edinburgh. They were going to Australia, but at the moment they were in Africa. This time Richard and I were invited to the royal box and there was the same footman with the same white wig and knee breeches. This time I wasn't so scared. What I remember best was the great applause, the love and devotion of the crowd to Their Majesties that night when they saw the king out in public again. He asked me if it wasn't very difficult to do the same lines, sing the same songs, every night for three years. I said, "Well, it must be a lot more difficult to do what you do, meeting thousands of people, making hundreds of appearances, always having to be in form and know what to say." His Majesty showed me his hand, all doubled up; he said sometimes it got that way from shaking so many hands. I felt such affection for this man. I asked if he had a favorite song from the show that I could sing for him. He said he loved them all but he could only listen to them when he managed to get the record away from Princess Margaret.

At the end of the show, when the orchestra played "God Save the King," the audience rose, faced the royal box, and sang from their hearts. There wasn't a dry eye in the Theatre Royal that night.

A week later, on a Wednesday Richard came in to tell me there would be no matinee. Nor would there be a performance that evening. The king was dead.

Right then, and forever after, I have wished that I had had the courage to say to the king, or the queen, "I just think you're the greatest family . . . the example you have set in your marriage . . . what you have taught your children . . . the image you have given your people . . ." I don't know another family I admire so much.

I never met Queen Mary, but I have her music stand in my home. Richard went to an antique fair where he found a beautiful wooden stand with brass hinges and fittings which had been Queen Mary's. I have it always, standing beside my mother's violin.

I didn't ever really know Sir Winston Churchill, either, but Richard and I had lovely hours with Sir Anthony Eden and his wife and son. He occasionally came to have dinner with us at the Savoy because from there he could see the lights of Parliament and he would know if he had to go back. Once he took us to Parliament to listen to a tremendous debate about India and independence. He put us into a small gallery looking straight down into that beautiful room. The debate went on and on, and it began to get close to curtain time. When we tried to get out we found the door was locked. Richard finally wrote a note and gave it to a guard. The guard took it to Anthony Eden, and he arranged to have the door opened a crack so we could slip out. I thought we were going to be there all night, and I kind of wish it had happened.

The irony of all this is that we met these wonderful people because of Noël, and by the time he presented us to the royal family for the first time, we were no longer speaking. It was the silliest, most awful, painful fight of my whole life and it was all over a hat and a bow.

Before we went to England there had been long correspondence about costumes. Of course, I had to wear period dresses—the show was 1860, after all—but Richard had explained that there were certain things I couldn't or shouldn't wear. I was so skinny, and my face so small, that I couldn't wear large hats because my face just vanished. I also couldn't wear big bows. Little ones were all right—Mainbocher always made little tiny ones—and so were simple lines. Noël had a marvelous friend named Gladys Calthrop who designed costumes for all his shows. We sent over my measurements and the warning about hats and bows. Noël wrote back, "No problem."

Then came costume fittings in England. My first dress, the opening-scene dress, I thought was a little busy, a little big for

me—the sleeves and all were too big—but I didn't say anything.
Neither did Richard. Then came the dress parade, when all my
costumes were laid out. There was the first costume with a huge
organdy bow, right on the bosom, and out of the blue a big picture hat with long ties for under my chin. Everybody was there,
Noël out on the stage, Richard out in the darkened theater. I
came out with the dress and bow on, but the hat in my hand.
Noël said, "I asked Gladys to do that, because it's a long walk on
your first entrance and I don't want the audience to recognize
you right away. I want the hat so they can't see your face until
you're down front."

I didn't want to make a scene, so I said, "May we discuss
it later?" It got very tense, however, as I went through the other
costumes. There was another big hat for one of them. Afterward,
in the dressing room, Richard told Noël that I couldn't wear the
opening-scene dress the way it was, or the hat. Everything was
too big, and didn't Noël remember all the letters back and forth
about costumes? Noël said, "Yes, but Gladys knows a lot more

Noël and his designer, Gladys
Calthrop, looking over my
first-act-finale costume for *Pacific 1860*, moments after our
previous *big* millinery crisis.

about the clothes of the eighteen-sixties than you do." It turned into a fight.

I said I would not wear the hat and the bow the next night at the opening preview. Noël said if I didn't wear them I would not step foot on the stage. Further, he would tell all the papers the reason the show didn't open was that Mary Martin was stubborn and impossible. This went on and on until finally we compromised: I said I would wear the hat but I wouldn't wear the huge organdy bow. We were almost hitting each other, and we were both in tears, and I can't even remember for sure what I wore at the opening preview but I had the bows removed and we never spoke again. Never . . . for years. We had one final scene backstage, screaming at each other at the top of our lungs. Then he left. Just walked out.

We were all invited everywhere in London, but never together. If we were invited to his friends' homes, Noël wouldn't be there. If he was invited, we weren't there. I wasn't even speaking to Graham anymore, though we had to kiss on the stage. Actually we adored each other but he, poor young man, was caught between Noël and me. Well, it was like death. I cried and cried, but I wouldn't give in. Neither would Noël.

One summer later on Richard and I went to Westport, Connecticut, to see Tallulah Bankhead in *Private Lives*. Noël was in the audience, in the back, but I didn't even turn around, never got out of my seat. Then I went home and cried some more. Richard woke me up and said, "You're crying again."

It was Noël who made up. One night during *South Pacific* a box about the size of a casket was delivered to my dressing room. In it were white lilacs—dozens and dozens of white lilacs—out of season, with a card saying, "Mary, darling, I'll be in the audience tonight, may I come back afterwards?" Could he! I couldn't wait to get on that stage and perforrrrrm, for Noël.

Richard said, "I'm not going to be with you backstage," but I said, "Yes, you are, you're in this, too."

When Noël came Richard just opened the door, showed him in, and vanished. Noël took my hands and said, "Forgive me," and I said, "Weren't we idiots?" Then Richard came in and we all cried and kissed and laughed and we took Noël straight home with us to Connecticut that night, without his pajamas or a toothbrush or anything.

There was one more scene. While we were all in England, before the fight, he had painted a picture for me of the White Cliffs of Dover. I had put it away somewhere, I truly didn't know where, and the night he came home with us he found it over the john in the guest bedroom. Of course, he came charging out to say, in his clipped voice, that he didn't mind so much being hung in the bathroom, but he did wish I had put his painting where the ladies could see it—on the other wall.

After we made up I had the privilege of doing two shows with Noël, just the two of us performing together. The first was a Sunday-night benefit at the Café de Paris in London, in 1952.

We rehearsed in our spare time for three months for a single two-and-one-half-hour performance. I remember asking Noël if we couldn't get Maurice Chevalier to join us. It would be so exciting, I told him, to have Paris, Texas, and London all in one show. He absolutely refused, however. There went my chance to work with Chevalier, my third hero.

Then in 1955 Noël and I did a ninety-minute television

Together again, at last, with Noël in the TV show
Together with Music.

special in America. Noël wrote a song for it called "Ninety Minutes is a Long, Long Time," and I remember being terrified that reviewers might use those words as a headline. Noël seduced me into accepting by saying we could rehearse in the swimming pool of his house in Jamaica. We did, too, hours and hours of floating around on inflated mattresses, under gorgeous skies and shadows of palm trees, singing like crazy. Rehearsal was bliss and the show was a success.

Another of Noël's gifts to me was an introduction to the funniest lady I ever met—Beatrice Lillie. I can't remember the occasion when I met her, but I'll never forget the first time I saw her. It was in New York. I was singing "Daddy" eight times a week but I managed to go to a Sunday-night benefit starring Bea Lillie. She walked onstage without a word, then went into her famous Garden Club Lady act, crawling around the stage tacking down a grass rug, doing a pantomime with her feet in those funny laced shoes. It was every gardening lady I had ever seen in Weatherford, being done in total silent pantomime by an English lady in New York. I laughed so hard I cried.

Then on one of the coldest days in the world, in London, she came to see *Pacific 1860* and sat in the front box, which is practically onstage. People had stayed away in droves, it was so cold, but there was Bea in a fur coat, fur hat, fur earmuffs, fur gloves, fur boots, and over it all a fur rug—with a hot-water bottle underneath. She smiled that wide wonderful smile, applauded like mad—perhaps to keep warm—and made my day.

The next time I saw her she was done up in fur, too. It was in New York, just before Easter. I was going into Saks to buy gloves when up the street came an apparition, absolutely swathed in furs which dragged on the sidewalk, topped with the inimitable Bea Lillie pillbox hat. I rushed to greet her and she didn't even act surprised. She never does. We hadn't seen each other for two years but we went quite casually into the store. It was packed with last-minute shoppers; nobody would wait on us. They wouldn't even look at us. So Bea hustled right around behind the counter and started pulling out boxes of gloves. Talking the whole time: "What did Madame have in mind? Would Madame prefer them wrist length, or near the elbow?"

It went on and on, I trying on gloves, Bea getting out boxes, nobody paying any attention. She was completely straight-faced and businesslike, but how could anybody have missed the pillbox hat, the fur coat, the *voice?* That English voice in the middle of Saks? I picked out what I wanted, she came out from behind the counter, I paid Bea. She handed the money, plus the sales slip she had made out, to the nearest uninterested clerk and we left the store.

Another time, during a brief vacation from *Sound of Music,* in about 1960, Richard and I went to visit Edward Molyneux in France. Elsa Maxwell was there and she gave another of her parties—not on a bus this time, but in Monaco on the terrace of the famous Grand Hotel de Monte Carlo. Bea was there. I accused her of either not having come to see my show or else of having hated it so much she wouldn't come backstage to see me. She insisted that she had seen it, standing up at the back of the theater because she had to catch a plane for London. She is far too much of a lady to get up and walk out of a performance, even to catch a plane.

I said, "That's a likely story," and she said, "I'll prove it to you. I'll play your part, Maria the postulant in the abbey." Whereupon she did. She picked up two pieces of Melba toast, put them beside her face like a nun's wimple, got down on her knees, and played my scene which began, "Oh, Mother Abbess . . ."

The whole terrace at Monte Carlo was in hysterics. Then Bea got carried away and made up a whole story about how she had fallen in love with a priest. She was going to confession, saying "Father, Father . . ." and ended up with her own punch line: "But don't get into the habit."

She wrecked the dinner. None of us could eat because we were laughing so hard. She wrecked the dinner, but she made the party.

Later in the evening we left the terrace, looking for the ladies' room, and somehow we blundered into the men's room. There wasn't much traffic, just the two of us, so we went about our business and then Bea, still feeling giddy, gave that famous pearl-slinging gesture of hers, the one in which she throws a long rope of pearls so they go around and around her neck like a Hula-Hoop. This time the pearls were real, they were her own, and they broke.

About half of them landed in the urinal, the rest on the floor. We finished the evening on our hands and knees in the men's room, picking them up and chanting "One for you, one for me . . ."

Darling Bea as I write this is very ill, in a nursing home in the United States. I have been to see her, but I don't think she knows me. Yet I shall have her always, in my memories and in a painting she made for me. I have many paintings done by friends, and even a few I did myself, but Bea's is special. It is a much larger-than-life painting of a bouquet. It isn't quite finished but it is signed, with a great flourish, "Bea Lillie—" in nail polish.

It is so like her, like her comedy, that painting—the great sweeping gesture, always a little askew, not quite finished, always making you want more, more, more.

To Annie

XIII
Texas Will Out

Both *Lute Song* and *Pacific 1860* were written for me, but neither was the real me. The show I had dreamed of was written for somebody else. The moment I saw it, I knew that one day I would play it. It was Irving Berlin's *Annie Get Your Gun,* starring Ethel Merman.

Richard saw it first, while I was still playing *Lute Song* in 1946. He came after opening night, handed me a knife, and said, "Cut your throat, Mommy. This is the part you have always wanted to play."

I might as well admit, right here, that when we started to have our first baby we promised we would never call each other Mommy and Daddy. We thought it was awful. Corny. Then we called each other that for the rest of our lives. Richard never, after Heller was born, called me Mary unless he was a little cross with me. He would ask, "Is Mommy home?" When he was serious he would say, "Now listen, Mary . . ." It was like Mother, who always called me Mary Virginia when she was annoyed.

If Republic Pictures had never thought of casting me in a western, why should anyone else? Certainly not Irving Berlin, or Dorothy and Herbert Fields, who wrote the book of *Annie Get Your Gun.* By this time, thanks to Richard's vision of me, I had become known for delicate, ethereal parts. Who would have cast Venus, or a Chinese bride, as a gun-shooting, fast-riding song belter? Nobody. But Richard knew the real me as well as I did.

When I finally got to see a performance of *Annie,* he asked, "Well, what are you going to do?"

"I am going to play it," I said.

I gave my first performance—impromptu—at Edna Ferber's farm in Connecticut and almost scared her to death. She and Richard had been friends for years, from the day he, at about the age of seventeen, had interviewed her for an article for *Liberty* magazine. He was longing for me to meet her and finally I did, at dinner. After dinner as we chatted, I announced that I wanted to play Annie.

"You couldn't," said Miss Ferber. She was a very definite woman. "You're too feminine. Anyway, you can't sing that way."

There was an umbrella around somewhere, in a stand, I suppose. I snatched it up, held it like a rifle, and said—no, shouted —"You cain't get a man with a gu-nnnn." Miss Ferber nearly collapsed. Nobody had heard me sing like that before.

I was so pleased by surprising my hostess that I had to go and ruin it all by saying, "You see? I told you I could make myself heard from here even to Kalamazoo."

She hit right back. "What do you mean, *even* Kalamazoo?" That was her hometown and she was always a bit touchy about it. What a dynamic woman! I adored her caustic wit.

After my startling success at Edna's house, I tried it once more at Lawrence and Armina Langner's house in Connecticut. Dick Rodgers and Oscar Hammerstein and their Dorothys were there, Terry Helburn, Ina Claire. After lunch everybody had to get up and do something. Ina Claire is the greatest mimic of all time; I had to think of something spectacular to show her. So again I let go with "You cain't get a man with a gun."

Dick and Oscar, who were the producers of *Annie,* couldn't get over it. At least they didn't forget it. While I was still doing *Pacific 1860,* in 1946, they cabled to ask if I would stay on in London to star in *Annie* there. Much as I had yearned for the part, much as I loved London, I couldn't do it. Richard and I were so heartsick because of the fight with Noël that I simply couldn't stay there any longer.

Richard said, "How would you like to play it on the road, all over America?" There have been a lot of different versions of how this came about, but the truth is that it was our idea to take it on tour. I wouldn't have played it in New York; that was my friend Ethel's territory. But anywhere else—I'd love it.

This was one of the first times a musical star had gone on the road in a role somebody else had made famous. Most of my family—young Larry, Didi and her husband—and most of my friends thought I was crazy. But I have never been afraid to try anybody's role, any other person's part, if I thought I could do it. The challenge of my life, of everybody's life in the theater, I think, is "If you think you can do it, then do it."

I had no intention of imitating Ethel, of "competing." I wanted to create my own characterization. That is what the theater is all about.

I did ask if Joshua Logan, who had directed the stunningly successful Broadway version, could direct our national company. I had never met him, but I knew I needed him. While Richard was still trying to get New York on the telephone from London, I had another idea. "Ask Dick and Oscar if I can open the road tour in my home state, in Dallas."

The *real* me, finally, in *Annie*.

That's what we did. We went home. I could stop being that lovely opera singer speaking seven languages in a very high so-rano. I could stomp in boots, shoot guns, shout at the top of my lungs, have a ball.

Opening night in Dallas was fantastic. Busloads of people came from Weatherford, Fort Worth, Houston; all of my old friends, my kin, kissin' and otherwise. I was made a Texas Ranger, and I was given a solid-silver six-shooter, pearl-handled, with a steer's head and ruby eyes, a belt and a silver buckle, silver bullets. The gun was inscribed, "From Mary's Texas friends." The mayor of Weatherford himself handed it to me onstage—in a brown paper bag.

On opening night Stanley Marcus, who with his family ran the famous Neiman-Marcus store in Dallas, gave a fantastic, beautiful party. He took over the entire theater lobby and filled it, covered it, with flowers. All out of season; he had them flown in. He served such lavish champagne that half of the first-night audience came in loop-legged.

I have known Stanley Marcus since I was a teen-ager. When I had my first success in New York, singing "Daddy," he sent me a beautiful dress. It came in a fancy Neiman-Marcus box, and I could hardly believe it. It was a *gown,* a grand evening dress which I wore to sing in the Rainbow Room. When I did *Venus* I was a guest of honor at one of Stanley's spectacular parties at the Hotel Pierre in New York, an evening to introduce a jewelry show. He had the whole collection displayed in a series of shadow boxes, with ice sculptures covered with jewelry. The decor was all Venus pink, and a beautiful diamond necklace was called *One Touch of Venus.* Through all the years, every time I played Dallas, Stanley and his wife, Billy, gave parties for us.

Beginning with *Annie,* Richard bought presents for every-body in the company—from Neiman-Marcus. For Christmas, or for opening night. Every dresser, every electrician, everybody in the production got a present. Richard worked it out with Stanley, and with a wonderful woman who ran the Neiman-Marcus pack-aging department, so the boxes were beautiful. The first year everyone got an Annie doll, made of handkerchiefs. They were handmade, with the hat, the gun, painted faces. People never used the handkerchiefs, because they didn't want to take the dolls apart. They became collector's items. Forever after, Stanley al-

ways helped us find an appropriate and enchanting gift for each
show.

Our national company of *Annie Get Your Gun* was very like
the Broadway one, except for the different styles of Ethel and me.
She has a pure, honest, God-given voice. Like a trumpet! She's right
on every note, like a great tenor, like Rodolfo singing "Mimi." My
voice isn't as big as hers; the timbre is different. It used to be more
soprano. I stripped all the gears in my throat belting the big songs.
Some were a little different in our version. "Moonshine Lullaby"
became more of a lullaby in our show, for example. After all, I was
singing it to our own little Heller, who at age five played with me
for the first time onstage as Annie's little sister. It was Heller who
really tried to be Ethel Merman; she sang so loud the stage manager had to ask her to hold it down a little.

One of the proudest moments for all of us came when Ethel
and the Broadway company watched an afternoon run-through of
our national company in New York before we went to Dallas.
There was a special moment for me, at the end of the first act.
That good old sharpshooter Annie Oakley—I—had just been initi-
ated into the Sioux Indian tribe, hoisted to the top of a huge Indian
pyramid, and then dropped into what was supposed to be a semi-
split on the floor. Annie was supposed to cry, because she'd just
had a letter from the man she loved, Frank Butler, saying he was
leaving her forever. That day I dropped off that pyramid and went
right back into my Fanchon and Marco position—a touch beyond
a split. As I read Frank Butler's letter I poured buckets of tears.
From pain. I wasn't sure I could ever get up again. The only thing
that gave me heart was the sight of two long white gloves, in
the second row, applauding like mad. They belonged to Ethel
Merman.

I did somehow get up again, but there was no time for
doctors. The second act was almost upon us. I swallowed Empirin
pills and everything else I could find, went back on, and finished
the show. By the time we hit the road I didn't hurt so much anymore.

We toured for eleven months, from the end of 1947 into
1948, and ended in my beloved San Francisco. I never wanted to
stop, but everything has to end, even tours. San Francisco I always
thought was one of my lucky towns; so lucky that ten years after

that first *Annie* closed it opened again, right back in San Francisco, in August, 1957. That time it was a limited run, ten weeks, for Edwin Lester's Civic Light Opera Association. We played it in both Los Angeles and San Francisco, in a limited repertory season, back to back with *South Pacific.*

In this second *Annie* John Raitt sang the role of Frank Butler. Earl Covert had sung it with me the first time. John Raitt and I never had played together before; he was wonderful.

The album of that show, done with him, is one of the best I have recorded. I'm not a fan of mine; I'm much too critical of records, but I do like that album because we were fresh, not worn out. Ordinarily what happens is that you work yourself to a frazzle getting the show ready. Then you open, do two shows on matinee days, and the very next Sunday, the first free day, you make the cast recording of the entire production. It can have vitality, because the cast can create that, but no one is in best voice. They can't be, they're too tired. Unfortunately everyone who buys and plays a show album risks hearing just about everybody at his lowest ebb.

It was Richard's idea to make this album before we opened. I had been in Brazil, resting; I felt wonderful. The part was easy to relearn after months on the road, even though it had been ten years. John was fresh and *up.* Our voices weren't pushed. We were full of enthusiasm. You can hear it in the record.

As always, we wanted to make this production more spectacular than it had ever been before. The biggest inspiration—and innovation—came from Richard. All through our marriage he kept telling me how exciting, how magic, theater had been when he was a little boy. He remembered the Hippodrome, where he said they had galloping horses on treadmills, chariots, all kinds of goings-on. Just telling me about it got him excited—and that's how we arrived at the horse and treadmill.

In the original *Annie,* both Ethel's and mine, we had a motorcycle scene. The cycle stood absolutely still but there were flashing lights going around and we stood up on it to shoot at a bull's-eye target onstage. Richard decided we should have a horse instead of the motorcycle.

"You'll love it," he assured me. "It will be fun to ride on a treadmill. Just think of shooting your silver six-shooter from a real horse."

When we told Ed Lester our inspiration he turned about ten shades of green. He asked Richard, "Do you love your wife?"

"Of course I love my wife, and I can't wait to watch her ride a horse onstage."

Finding a treadmill was the problem, but Ed never stopped once he put his mind to something. Finally they dug one up in New York, had it shipped to California at vast expense. Then it had to be set up; somebody had to audition horses; audition men to handle the horses; audition the treadmill itself.

At last came my turn to try out. The first thing I did was fall madly in love with the horse. He was big, brown, lovable, and smart. He had been trained as a trick horse; he could do anything. I loved him so much that when the show closed Ed Lester tried to buy him for me, but he cost something like fifty thousand dollars. The Civic Light Opera Association couldn't afford that price and still do other shows.

I've never known for sure how a treadmill works, but it is

The horse, the treadmill, and "me" in *Annie Get Your Gun*.

all fastened down securely; the horse has a guy wire around his middle to hold him on it. He can walk, gallop, canter, depending on how fast it moves, up to thirty miles an hour. I watched the horse and the man do it; it looked like the most fun in the world. One day they adjusted the stirrups for me; I was up, up, and awaaaaaay. Oh, joy, I was in my natural habitat. I'll never forget Richard's face as long as I live. His dream had come true; he was a little boy again at the Hippodrome.

Just before we opened there was a press preview so the reporters and photographers could see the treadmill and take pictures of me riding my horse. John had his own, a white one, which we both rode for the finale of the show. Just when we thought it was over, somebody asked for one last shot "of Mary and John on the white horse on the treadmill." It had never been on the treadmill.

The trainer objected, but the press can be pretty insistent. We agreed to try it, very slowly. I clutched John around the waist, we put on our best smiles, they started the treadmill. Slowly. But the horse started fast. With this little difference in signals he went straight up in the air. I fell off. John managed to jump clear before the horse fell on him. Nobody was hurt, merciful heavens, but after all those beautiful pictures they had taken, what did they print? Me flat on my backside and the horse straight up in the air, of course.

When we got into performance the prop manager, Dick Rodda, made it his personal business to hold my horse steady, get him set on the treadmill, supervise my mounting. The horse was always securely fastened and he quickly became an expert. But he was too smart for his own good, and for mine. He was also a bigger ham. He just couldn't wait to get *on*—first. My dressing room was where he could see it from the corner of his eye. The moment I came out he would look around, see me, and start running. They tried putting blinders on him. That didn't help; he could sense my coming.

It ended that the horse had not only his guy wire but also somebody behind him holding his tail, four men holding his feet, Dick Rodda at the ready to help me up so I could at least get into the saddle before the horse took off. Then off we'd go, lights, music, action.

Then that darned horse learned to count. Our act was

timed so I could shoot all six "bullets" with the horse at full gallop. Then the curtain descended. At the first performances I shot once, twice, sitting down. Then I'd stand up in the stirrups and shoot the others. Within days that horse figured out that he should stop at six. He began to slow down on the fourth shot. By the time I had fired six he knew his act was over and he would stop. Just stop, dead, before the curtain could fall, never considering that it was *my* act, too.

I tried everything to outwit him, changing the rhythm of the shots. In desperation I asked for a second gun, so I could do six shots with one, then start over. It worked briefly, but that smart horse could count to twelve as easily as he could to six. All the drama was gone from our elaborate act. The trainer suggested we try the understudy horse. He wasn't as bright; maybe he couldn't count. He couldn't, and he galloped very well, but he wasn't half as exciting as my horse. I don't know if the audience noticed the difference, but I thought he was dull.

The incredible thing was that my horse understood even this. The trainers held him in the wings, to watch the other horse on the treadmill. He couldn't bear it, couldn't stand to have another horse out there in the lights getting the applause. After about two experiences as a spectator, he shaped up. He never tried any of his tricks again. He got out there and galloped, and he didn't stop until the curtain came down. By that time I liked the idea of two guns so much that I always used them.

There were crazy experiences with guns, too. Like Annie's entrance, which is one of the greatest entrances of all time in musicals. From the wings, Annie shoots a bird she sees out there on the stage. She doesn't realize the bird is a decoration on a lady's hat. Several times in San Francisco I would shoot, but the bird didn't fly off the hat. Boom, I shot again, and it didn't go. Shot again . . . nothing. So I'd think, "Oh, nuts," and make my entrance. *Then* all of a sudden, plop, the bird would go off the lady's hat. It was fixed to the hat with a spring gadget which didn't always function on time. The lady with the hat, played by Reta Shaw, and I would look at each other. We'd both think, "How do you like that bird?" but we never broke up. I can't stand actors who break up. The thing is to go ahead, stare at that crazy bird for a moment maybe, but keep a straight face and let the audience do the laughing.

The orchestra in the pit seldom breaks up either. But they did once, in California. Somebody neglected to take care of my horse's daily business and just at the end of the first act, while he was galloping like everything, nature called. The treadmill caught the whole load and threw it—all over the orchestra, all over the instruments, all over the first three rows. It didn't exactly stop the show, but it took quite a while to clean up for the second act.

Part of our plan for the second *Annie* in 1957 was to go straight from the theater run to a live performance on NBC television. Irving Berlin had never given permission for a television performance, and he had been very ill. Ed Lester asked me to telephone him to request permission. It was a poignant, unforgettable conversation. Irving sounded so weak, but so gracious. "Yes," he said, "of course. I would like to see you do Annie on television."

I thanked him, and he added, "Of course, I won't be here to see it."

"Why, where are you going?"

"I'll be on the other side," he said. I thought he meant he was going to Europe. He said no, he meant he wouldn't be alive. Thank heaven he *is* alive, painting and writing new songs. More important, thank heaven for Irving Berlin.

There was one more accident waiting for me to happen to it—maybe my nickname should have been Accident Annie—and one more *faux pas* before it was over. By this time Joan Crawford, a friend from Hollywood days, was married to Albert Steele, chairman of the board of Pepsi-Cola. Pepsi was the sponsor for the telecast and had arranged to shoot it live at the Warner Brothers studio.

In an area the size of Warner Brothers everything could be bigger and fancier, so the circus set we used onstage for the "I'm an Indian Too" number could be a real ring. That was wonderful, but the sheer distance between one set and another was enormous. There were so many costume changes, set changes, it was impossible to get from one place to another fast enough. A marvelous young man named Red was appointed to help me. He was about 6 feet 7 and strong as Samson; the plan was that I should make my changes and jump on Red's back, and he would run to the next set to deliver me on time for my next number.

All this was fine except nobody pointed out to me that the new set had a wooden barrier, a low fence like a regular circus ring, all around it. On the dress rehearsal Red ran up to the ring, I jumped off his back, straightened my Indian costume, ran full speed into the ring—and right on my head because I tripped over the fence. I got up, entered on cue, went into my dance. Suddenly I looked down and saw blood. I was covered with blood. Up in the TV monitor booth people were horrified. Blood is pretty impressive in full color. I looked down and there was a hole in my right leg, just below the knee. I hadn't felt a thing when it happened, but it was a gusher.

Everything stopped while people ran for ice. Mr. Steele himself came running. Someone inquired, "Can we bring you something?"

Still dazed, I said, "Oh, please, I'd love a Coca-Cola."

Richard, who was propping up my bloody leg, said quickly, "She would like a *Pepsi*-Cola, please."

It was too late, but Joan and Al forgave me. They even gave a spectacular party for us at Chasen's. Half of Hollywood was there, to see the show on television sets positioned all over the restaurant.

There is one final circle to Annie. When Richard and I were first married I had about a dozen protégées in Hollywood, young girls whom I had been teaching dancing, singing, how to select the right clothes for auditions. After my marriage I simply couldn't be a bride, make movies, sing on radio with Bing, and also have all those protégées. I had to give them up. All but one, a darling fifteen-year-old who was 5 by 5. Young as she was, she had a most exciting, mature voice. When she sang "How deep is the ocean," it was the deepest ocean in the world, and "how high is the sky" was the highest sky. I coaxed her to lose weight, bleached her dark hair blond, gave her a permanent.

Later we took her to New York for auditions. Oscar Hammerstein heard her and never forgot. When I had to turn down *Annie* in London they hired her. My chubby little girl had grown up to be the slim, elegant Dolores Gray. She made a tremendous hit in London.

A fine libretto, wonderful music, a role full of vitality can make milestones in the careers of entirely different personalities in the theater. Annie was one of those roles. It was one of Ethel

Merman's unforgettable ones; it gave Dolores her first big break; it afforded me many of my happiest hours onstage.

And that brings up one more thing I have learned: beware of any role which somebody says is "written especially for you." If the role isn't written so well, so strongly, that any professional can play it, *don't* get involved. That, too, is what theater is all about.

XIV
There's Hope for Everyone

South Pacific was one of the most fabulous things that ever happened to me. It was one of those magic shows that comes along once in a decade—maybe once in a lifetime—and stand for their era forever after.

When I think that I almost turned it down, I nearly die. Richard first mentioned it to me in the car one night as we were driving from Los Angeles to San Francisco to open in *Annie,* in early 1948. Dick and Oscar, Josh Logan and Leland Hayward had an idea for a musical, he said. There was a star part for me, as a nurse.

"A what?"

"A nurse."

Me, a nurse? Richard wouldn't allow me in the room if he had a cold, because I'd sail in with a lusty hand pat and a big "How are ya?" If anybody around me was ill he wanted me out of the house as fast as possible. If I even walked into the room it made his head hurt.

"An army nurse," Richard added.

"An *army* nurse?" I repeated. "You mean I'd have to wear a uniform all the time, one of those tacky khaki things?"

Richard discreetly dropped the subject, for the time being. It didn't come up again until after *Annie* closed. The night before we left California to drive home to Connecticut, Dick and Oscar telephoned, all excited.

As Nellie Forbush in *South Pacific*.

"It's set," they said. "We're going to do *South Pacific*. We have Josh Logan to direct, we have Ezio Pinza to sing the French planter, Emile de Becque. We would like Mary to play the nurse stationed on his island; she's to be Nellie Forbush from Little Rock, Arkansas."

The very thought of appearing on the same stage with an opera singer terrified me. Besides, my voice had sunk what seemed like several octaves from belting out the *Annie* songs so long. I remember saying to Dick Rodgers on the phone that night, "What on earth do you want, two basses?"

There are different versions of whose idea it was to adapt James Michener's book *Tales of the South Pacific* as a musical. So far as I know, Josh Logan and Leland Hayward may have suggested it to each other. They had just had a huge success with *Mister Roberts,* a straight play about the Navy in the Pacific. Then Michener's book came along. It was a series of lyrical tales about life in the islands during the war. There was a native woman who chewed betel nut and sold souvenirs to the sailors; there was her lovely daughter, Liat, who fell in love with a lieutenant; there was a French planter, a widower with beautiful half-caste children; there were Seabees; and there was Nellie Forbush. Each of Michener's stories was different, but a single thread ran through: the slow growing of tolerance, of understanding, of love as two completely different cultures collided in wartime.

Josh and Leland took the book to Dick and Oscar, asking them not only to do music and lyrics but also to produce it. Oscar and Josh were to do the libretto. At first they thought they would build the show around Liat and her lieutenant, Cable. Then they were caught by the idea of the French planter and the nurse. In the end they decided to have two plots, a central one with Emile and Nellie, a subplot with Liat and Cable. The character of the betel-chewing woman was, of course, the unforgettable Bloody Mary.

If I was frightened at the thought of singing with Ezio Pinza, I was absolutely paralyzed with fear after the first time I heard him. Richard and I went to Brooklyn to one of his concerts and sat way up in the gallery because there never were seats available for a Pinza performance. Oh, that glorious voice! I rushed home from the concert and telephoned Dick Rodgers to say he couldn't, he wouldn't, dare to put us together on the same stage. Dick promised he would never have us sing "in competition," and he never did.

Our only song together was a soliloquy in the first act, a kind of counterpoint called "Wonder How It Feels." Ezio sang his thoughts from his side of the stage; I sang mine from my side. Each of us in our own style; never a duet, never in competition.

I'll never forget the first time I heard our soliloquy. Dick Rodgers, who was our neighbor in Connecticut, called and urged us to come over to hear some of the numbers. We still weren't convinced that I should do the show, but we went over. He played and Oscar sang "Wonder How It Feels." There were other songs, I've forgotten in what order, and then there was "Some Enchanted Evening." Oh, the impact of that song! They said they had no idea how long it would take to finish the score but they wanted me. They said we should go away and think it over for two or three days.

That night in bed Richard and I talked about the glorious "Some Enchanted Evening." We both were sure that no matter whether the show was a success or not, that would be one of the memorable songs of the musical stage. It wasn't "mine," it was Ezio's, but that didn't matter. It was three o'clock in the morning, but we picked up the phone and asked, "Do we have to wait three days? Can't we say yes right now?"

The marvelous songs kept rolling out . . . "Bloody Mary," "There Is Nothing Like a Dame," "Happy Talk," "I'm Just a Cockeyed Optimist," "Bali Ha'i," and "Younger Than Springtime."

One night Dick called to ask us to go to Josh and Nedda Logan's apartment in New York. He said he and Oscar had a present for me. Richard and I arrived late, driving in from Connecticut, and Dick sat down at the piano to play "I'm in Love with a Wonderful Guy" while Oscar said-sang the words.

"This is your song, Mary," they said.

It went straight to my head, my heart. I had to sing it, right that moment. I sat down on the piano bench next to Dick and began "I'm in love, I'm in love, I'm in love," getting more and more excited, singing full speed ahead, waving my arms around. Finally I got to "with a WONDERFUL GUYYYYYY" and finished it—and *clunk,* fell right off the piano bench onto the floor.

Dick Rodgers turned his head, looked down at me rather solemnly, and said, "Never sing it any other way." My darling Dick Rodgers.

I couldn't stop singing it that night. Before long telephones started ringing like crazy. People in the apartments above, below, on both sides, were complaining, "Stop that terrible noise. We can't sleep."

Josh was so exhilarated that he told them all, "You'll be sorry. Someday it's going to cost you I don't know how much to hear all this."

We often thought of that night later, when scalpers were

My wonderful guy Oscar writing "I'm in Love with a Wonderful Guy" for me.

selling *South Pacific* seats for one hundred dollars each. After "Wonderful Guy" came "I'm Gonna Wash That Man Right Out-a My Hair." I have never written a song in my whole life, but I can take some credit for that one. It all started with a crazy idea of mine. It came to me in my shower one day. Richard was working at his desk and I came tearing out of the shower, dripping wet, without a stitch on, to say, "Richard, always in movies and the theater people say, 'I've just washed my hair and I can't do a thing with it.' But they looked utterly perfect. Now, wouldn't it be great if sometime I washed my hair, right on stage, maybe even singing a song, and then came out all dripping? Wouldn't that be a great scene?"

Richard looked a little bit patient and more than a little bit worried.

"Don't you dare tell that to anyone," he said. "Not a soul. If you do, they'll go for it, and then you'll have to do it onstage eight times a week."

The very first person who telephoned after that conversa-

"I'm Gonna Wash That Man Right Out-a My Hair,"
and I did, and loved it, for three years.

tion was Josh. I heard my equally crazy husband saying to him,
quite clearly, "Josh, Mary has a great idea . . ."

"Don't you dare tell Dick and Oscar," said Josh. "You know
what will happen."

So, naturally, we all told them both, the very next time we
talked. They said I was balmy, but if I was willing to do it they
loved the idea. Then they wrote "I'm Gonna Wash That Man."
The song really helped the plot along. It established Nellie's re-
luctance to fall in love with Emile, and it helped set up her collapse, her surrender, in "I'm in Love with a Wonderful Guy."

From the very beginning, *South Pacific* was pure joy. Dick
and Oscar, Josh and Leland, Richard and I were all close friends
who loved working together, but it was more than that. Josh and
Leland had auditioned forever to cast it, so everybody in the show
was somebody special. Everyone had a beautiful voice, great talent.
We couldn't *wait* to get to rehearsals. No matter how many hours
we worked we never wanted to stop. We couldn't wait to get back.
It was like the excitement of an operating room, when somebody's

life is being saved by the team, or like a delivery room when a new life is coming.

The show kept growing from the first day, getting better, because we were having a ball and everybody was contributing. The idea for the show-within-a-show, when the Seabees and the nurses put on an evening's amateur entertainment for the troops, began with Myron McCormick. Myron was a marvelous actor who had gone to Princeton with Josh. Somewhere, somehow, he had learned to do a belly dance. He was just dying to do it onstage. Josh liked the idea. I announced that I could do a soft-shoe number with some of Sister's waltz clog steps included, of course.

At just about that time an old girl friend sent me a picture somebody had taken of me at Camp Mystic in Kerrville, Texas, about 1925. Like most children, I absolutely adored summer camp; I went as often as I could and stayed as long as I could. In the Camp Mystic picture I was standing in semishade, grinning with delight, wearing a pair of men's shorts with wide stripes, a long shirt, a sailor hat, and a man's necktie. The predominant features of the picture were two rather large round water pitchers which I held in my hands, two round knees, one round nose, and one long neck.

I thought the photo was so funny that I gave it to Oscar Hammerstein. He took one look at that gangly girl and then put the picture by his mirror where he shaved every morning. Under it he wrote, "This proves there is hope for everyone."

When Josh Logan saw the picture, he said, "You've come a long way, honey, but you're still a baggy-pants comedian at heart." Then he dreamed up my costume for the show-within-a-show: I was to wear a sailor hat, baggy pants, and a long black tie. I was to be the baggy-pants comic sailor and Myron, who played the Seabee Luther Billis in the show, was to be my girl friend, done up in a grass skirt and coconut-shell "bazooms."

Then Dick and Oscar wrote our number, "Honey Bun" . . . "A hundred and one pounds of fun, that's my little Honey Bun . . . Get a load of Honey Bun tonight. . . ." I will never forget the half-embarrassed, very pleased look on Oscar's face when he first sang me the lyrics. Never in his life had he written such corny words, but I shrieked with joy. It was my kind of song, my kind of singing. I learned it in nothing flat and we set the routine in one afternoon. This was right down Josh's, Myron's, and my alley.

"This proves there's hope for everyone"—Oscar Hammerstein.

Then Josh went to work improving it all. Of course the sailor suit had to be a bit large for me because I was supposed to have borrowed it from one of the Seabees. Josh kept making it larger. He kept saying, "Make the pants bigger," "Make the tie longer." The pants got longer and longer in the crotch, the sleeves grew so long that they covered my hands. Then he thought of elastic suspenders being attached to the pants under the oversized blouse. The elastic made the pants bounce up and down as I moved.

His final piece of business came before one matinee in Boston. Josh came into my dressing room and said, "This afternoon, when you've gotten all the laughs on your dancing, bouncing pants, at the last minute put your leg through the tie. Right up to the crotch, so the tie finally holds up the pants."

I thought this was going too far. We argued for quite a while—we often did, with wild affection. Then we compromised. I wouldn't try it at the matinee, with all those ladies out there, but I would do it at the night show. Josh was right, as usual. That

"Honey Bun" was one of the most joyous moments in *South Pacific*.

little business brought the house down, and from that moment on
you couldn't have taken it away from me on a ten-foot pole. Of all
the fun moments Josh staged for me in theater, dancing and singing "Honey Bun" was the most.

He had the same skill with everybody else in the cast. He
was forever asking, "What can you do?" and somebody would
jump out and show him. One of the girls could do acrobatic dancing. Somebody else could do a barrel roll. Juanita Hall, who played
Bloody Mary, could do everything. She sat down on the floor one
day with Josh and with beautiful Betta St. John, who played Liat.
The three of them worked out all the hand movements for "Happy
Talk." I can still see the concentration and hear the stillness as the
three of them perfected that beautiful song.

Even now I can hardly believe, though I saw it, the way
Josh choreographed the Seabees in the "There Is Nothing Like a
Dame" number. All these gorgeous guys, playing Seabees, were up
there on the stage and Josh jumped up with them. The music
started and he began to pace around, saying "Follow me." He directed some of them forward, others backward. He was singing all
the time—Josh always knew the words—tramping, gesturing, shouting "Follow me," or "Reverse." Big, massive Josh with all those
guys. He knew the whole lingo of the servicemen, their spirit. He
was magic that day. The entire ballet of pacing men, directed by
Josh, was done on the first day of rehearsal. When it was finished
everybody who was watching stood up and screamed, just screamed.
"That's it, Josh. Never touch it."

There kept being screaming moments in *South Pacific*. One
day just before we went to New Haven for tryouts the cast was
asked if we would mind having an audience for one of the rehearsals. Fortunately, we didn't know that they intended to fill the
theater with professionals—actors, dancers, singers, composers, directors. We were working with rehearsal props, old benches, and
junk. We didn't even have proper lights. When we finished, it was
so quiet it was like church. We didn't know what to think, because we couldn't see the audience. Then all of a sudden there was
an unbelievable roar. I've never heard anything like it in my life.
Our peers approved. Some people say that this rehearsal was the
best performance they ever saw in the theater. I have seldom heard
such yelling, whistling, applause.

From that exciting day we went to New Haven. In spite of

the wealth of music, the richness of every melody and every lyric, there were still a few problems. One was a song worthy of Ezio Pinza's voice for the second act. He had "Some Enchanted Evening" for the first act, but he needed something for the second. Dick and Oscar kept saying, "We'll get one; we'll do it," but Ezio was getting very nervous and upset. They had one called "Will You Marry Me?" which was lovely, but it didn't have the dramatic intensity for the scene. Just the week before we went back to New York they came up with "This Nearly Was Mine." Ezio by this time was so worried that he didn't even think it was good. Then he settled down to learn it, and I was delighted to discover that this great basso didn't read music much better than I did. He had to learn it note by note, with his accompanist. The song, of course, was fantastic. All my life I shall hear that great organ of a voice as Ezio sang it.

There was also the problem of Lieutenant Cable. He was played by William Tabbert, a darling boy with a wonderful voice, but he was about to be fired in New Haven because he didn't look right. He had soft, fine, brown baby hair that had to be plastered down. He just didn't look sexy enough. Nobody wanted to let him go, but they thought they had to. By this time Richard and I were pretty expert on hair and metamorphoses. So we asked Josh if we could borrow Bill for one afternoon. We bought some bleach, a home permanent and some razor blades and went to work. We cut his hair, bleached it, curled it. Poor boy, he was a captive in our bathroom for about five hours, and he kept asking, "What am I going to tell my wife?"

When we finished he had soft blond curls that made his brown eyes stand out like anything. He looked taller, handsomer, a perfect foil for dark-skinned Liat. Then Josh came along, with the wardrobe mistress, and redesigned his costume. Josh kept saying, "Tighter, tighter," and the wardrobe lady made him some of the sexiest pants anyone ever had. He could hardly sit down, though he was supposed to do most of his numbers sitting down. When Josh, Richard, and I unveiled our new Bill in New Haven, the night before we opened, half the people in the cast thought he was a replacement. But nobody could have replaced his voice. It was a new Bill Tabbert with the same wonderful voice. Later he told us that his wife found him pretty sexy, too, with that short, curly blond hair.

This was the one and only Ezio Pinza!

Bill was my first triumph as a hairdresser in *South Pacific*. For the rest of the show, the Polynesian children, the stage manager, the Seabees lined up outside my dressing room on certain selected matinee days, and I cut their hair before evening performances. That's when the production staff bought me the barber pole, and put a fake New York City barber's license smack on my dressing room door.

Our tryout performances in New Haven were as wild as that final big rehearsal in New York. People stood in line outside the theater, in the corridors, outside the dressing rooms. On opening night I found Mike Todd and Joan Blondell, who were married then, facing me. They were the last in the line. They had been standing there, waiting quietly, while everybody else shouted, "This is the greatest," and yelled, and kissed each other.

Joan and Mike said, very solemnly, "Don't take it to New York." It was like Mike Todd's great balloon going around the world in eighty days and suddenly he deflates it.

"Why, Mike? Why, Joan?"

"Because," they said, "it's too good for them. It's too goddamn good for New York."

It is absolutely terrifying to have such a hit out of town. It could be overrated. It could be a fluke. In Boston it was even more of a hit than in New Haven. Almost every number in the show demanded an encore, and we began running forty-five minutes late because of the applause. We had to cut something, somewhere. After all, we couldn't run on until 1 A.M. like an Italian opera.

Josh and Nedda Logan brought their friend and ours, Emlyn Williams, the actor and playwright, from London to act as a surgeon. He stayed with our company from New Haven to Boston to New York, and on Broadway's opening night they gave him little golden scissors because he had snipped away, so delicately and so carefully, forty-five minutes from the show. He did it with consummate sensitivity. I was particularly pleased because, although he had cut a duet I had with Lieutenant Cable, the cut made Cable's lovely "Younger Than Springtime" even more poignant. I adored it; that was the song I always hummed, or whistled, throughout *South Pacific* when I was making up, waiting for my cues, or just sitting around.

We opened at the Majestic Theatre in New York on April 7, 1949. We came in with a $500,000 advance sale, a record at the time and a tribute to the welcome we had had in the tryouts. It was quite an opening night. I never can hear a thing on nights like that, just the roar of blood pounding in my ears as we really go *on*, during the "this is it" night. My friend Jinx Falkenburg McCrary was in the audience that night, and she remembers it all. Richard had arranged four front-row seats for Jinx and her husband, Tex, and Jock and Betsy Whitney.

Jinx says she has never heard such sound: song after song stopped the show. Josh permitted no encores, no second choruses, except the crossover in "Wonderful Guy." A second chorus then actually progressed the action. The movement, of book and music, was magic. When the final curtain came down the audience not only refused to leave the theater, they all stood up and crowded toward the front, shouting and clapping and calling for more, more, more.

Afterward there was a gala at the St. Regis Roof, an enormous supper dance with flowers, candles, very, very elegant. The electricity that had been inside the theater was transferred to the party—the air just crackled with it. I remember very clearly that Main had made me a gorgeous royal-blue satin dress with tiny black stripes, an enormous ankle-length bouffant skirt, no sleeves but a little strap that went across from one shoulder to the other. And a *turban*, a Persian turban that covered my entire head and had a black egret feather going straight up, and a diamond pin. Shades of Sister's Persian Princess costume. But I didn't really look so much like a princess as like a little prince, with that turban on. Main had designed it to hide my hair, which had been a story point all evening, and to make an elegant contrast to the Nellie Forbush of the South Pacific.

Ezio and his Doris came in, the orchestra played "Some Enchanted Evening," I arrived with Richard, and everybody kissed everybody all night long. I wish I could remember what night it was, but it couldn't have been a Tuesday because I got to stay clear to the end of the party, and Richard would never have let me stay to the end if it had been Tuesday, with Wednesday matinee and evening performances facing me the next day.

Around midnight word passed around that the reviews were going to be raves. Somebody had telephoned the newspapers to ask. Then the first papers came in, about one-thirty in the morning. There were little knots of people around the St. Regis Roof, all huddled with their heads together reading, and shouts of "Listen to this." The critics used the words "utterly captivating" and "truly great." Brooks Atkinson of *The New York Times* began with "Nobody will be surprised this morning to read that Richard Rodgers, Oscar Hammerstein 2nd and Joshua Logan have written a magnificent musical drama." He ended up, "*South Pacific* is as lively, warm, fresh, and beautiful as we had all hoped that it would be."

Time magazine wrote, "Hammerstein and Logan have contrived a shrewd mixture of tear-jerking and rib-tickling, of sugar and spice and everything twice." *Life* printed a cover of me in my sailor suit, taken by Philippe Halsman, and wrote, ". . . she and Pinza create what the theater attempts much more often than it achieves; a rare and touching love story of two gallant people . . . a show to go down in theater history."

What a night, what a show, what a man! Only one *South Pacific,* only one Ezio Pinza come in one's lifetime. How blessed I was to be part of it! I played Nellie Forbush for three and one-half years, in New York and in London, to five different Emile de Becques. But the French planter who had this Nellie's heart forever was Ezio Pinza. Oh, golly, besides everything else, he had that glorious voice. He was the most earthy, peasant, darling man, with such an easygoing, warm personality. And the chemistry, I cannot tell you. Our first scene together, in the first-act soliloquy, we sang on opposite sides of the stage. The music swelled and Ezio walked toward me, carrying a brandy glass. It was a long walk. Every time he started my way, with that face of his, that magnetism, that music, a spark came across like nothing that ever happened to me before and never will happen again. Every curl on my little knucklehead began to stand up. Straight on end, all the way, every night and twice on matinee days.

Never in the whole time we played together did we have a fight. But we did have a feud. A genuine, long-lasting feud—about steam heat. Ezio wanted his dressing room in the Majestic Theatre like a Turkish bath. I wanted mine cold. The trouble was that our rooms were right next to each other and we shared the steam pipes. I turned my radiator off, wrapped asbestos around the pipes. If I felt a little chilly I put on a warm robe and woolly socks. Heat literally made me sick; I could not go from a hot room to a cold stage and sing. Ezio said he couldn't go from a cold room to a cold stage and sing.

Out in the hall, a tiny corridor between our dressing rooms, was a huge radiator. Ezio wanted it on full blast. I couldn't even walk past it without choking. By the time I got onstage I was hoarse. I took the temperature in that corridor and sometimes it reached 100. Ghastly. Every time I passed the radiator I turned it off. Ezio turned it back on. Everyone else pretended not to know who was fiddling with the knobs.

One night I made a scene. The corridor temperature was

over 100. I called for our understanding stage manager, Charlie Atkinson, and said, "I cannot go on like this. No matter what I do about that blasted hall radiator, the heat, and the horrible smell— I can still smell it now when I think about it—creep into my dressing room. My throat is completely dry by the time I get onstage. Please, please, do something."

Charlie said, "Mr. Pinza turns it on. You turn it off. I am between the devil and the deep blue sea." I hoped that I was the deep blue sea.

For a while we tried to compromise and turn the radiator down a little, but radiators do not respond well to a compromise course. Ezio kept catching cold and being out of the show. Every time he was out I turned the radiator off. Every time he came back he turned it on. Once I removed the control knob and took it home. Next day he brought in a monkey wrench so he could manage the controls without the knob.

Then he was out of the show again and I called Charlie and said, "Take that thing out of the theater. Remove it. Seal the pipes."

The deed was done but I thought, "Ye gods, what will Ezio do? He'll be furious. This is the end of a beautiful friendship." But he came into my dressing room with that devastating smile, those naughty, twinkling eyes, that sexy voice of his, and said, "Tex-aaahs, you win!"

From opening night on, there was never an empty seat in the house. There were lines, queues outside, advance sales—and standing room. One day our family doctor came into my dressing room and asked, "What is Larry doing out there in the line? I just saw him." Larry was then in boarding school in Vermont. He had seen the show but his roommate Roger hadn't, and the two of them stood outside that theater for hours, waiting to buy standing-room tickets, then stood through the entire performance. Larry was too proud to ask Richard and me for help getting tickets.

Oddly enough, the one scene in *South Pacific* which we had to keep working on was my hair washing. It was easier said than done, onstage. It wasn't difficult to set up the shower stall, or even to get the water supply delivered, though it wasn't always completely reliable. The real difficulty was that the audience didn't believe it. They simply did not believe I was really washing my hair up there, because they never had seen it done.

At first I went into the shower stall and pulled the chain on a makeshift shower which the Seabees of the show had constructed with a huge barrel on top of a rickety frame. Each performance that barrel had to be filled with hot water. Then I would wet my hair, dump on a handful of liquid soap to make instant lather, and proceed to wash. It was too instant. The audiences were so skeptical that Josh restaged the number.

In the later version my nurse friend, Roz, handed me a huge bar of Ivory soap. In full sight of the audience I then stepped into the shower and with my downstage left hand rubbed my hair with the bar of soap. In my upstage right hand I used liquid Prell because it made instant lather. Then, just to make the whole point perfectly clear, I emerged from the stall to dance around the stage, flicking soapsuds all over the place.

Even after that, during one matinee I heard two little old ladies in the front row saying, very loudly, "It's a wig, you know."

It was not a wig. It was me. Of course, my hair had to be very short for this, so that it would dry in time for my next number. Richard and I cut it short, with razor blades, and it was straight as a post. It needed to be fluffed up so it wouldn't just hang flat on my forehead. This was in the early days of home permanents, so we began to experiment. We tried several, settled on one, and Richard, who knew absolutely nothing about hair, had to help give me a permanent every three weeks. I put in the front and sides, and he did the back. We always did it in Connecticut so I wouldn't have to go to beauty shops. My hair was always too curly the first week, better the second, smashing the third. Then we had to cut it off and start all over again.

I never could get all the soap out onstage, so after every performance I washed my hair again in my dressing room. Then I washed it again every day at home, before a performance, so it would bounce back and not be flat. We tried to count up, once, and it came out to something like twenty-six or twenty-eight hair washings a week. For more than three years. It's a wonder my hair didn't just give up and fall out, or that I never caught pneumonia.

Elizabeth Montgomery did the costumes for *South Pacific* and her efforts for me were something of a miracle. My pants had to look exactly like dungarees but shed water so I could dance and act without being soaked to the skin. Elizabeth also did a precious little jacket for me, with a cowl neckline. We had a terrible time with the bra that went under it. I had to have the jacket off, the bra on, for the hair-washing scene. No bra we tried was ever quite right until the last week in Boston, when a surprise arrived from Mainbocher. He had been working on the bra problem and finally he came up with a red-and-white candy-striped number which was perfect. That's what I wore on top forever after, for "Wash That Man." Mainbocher's bra was personally delivered to our suite at the Ritz-Carlton in Boston by—ahem—Sir Cedric Hardwicke.

The whole New York run of the show was a dream time. The new Bill Tabbert, the steam-heated Pinza, the baggy-panted Martin, the rarest of all companies, the four wise men of Broadway—Dick, Oscar, Josh, and Leland—all had a long, long ride on the crest of the wave. Richard used to tell me, half in fun, that it was too bad I couldn't have lived in the days of Lillian Russell, when stars were stars, feted and courted; when they rode around in carriages and lived on oysters, caviar, champagne, draped with fabulous jewels.

This always made me laugh, but then came my last night in *South Pacific* in New York, after two years. Ours was the last Broadway curtain to come down, at about eleven-thirty in the evening, and as the last act progressed the back of the theater began to fill with even more standees—actors from other shows, photographers, critics, stagehands, even taxi drivers, policemen, ushers from nearby theaters. The crowd grew so thick it pressed downward into the aisles leading to the stage.

Emile de Becque—now played by Ray Middleton—and I touched hands in the final scene, the curtain came down, bedlam began. The whole theater seemed to be wall-to-wall, aisle-to-aisle people, shouting. Suddenly, as the company was taking its last bows, out of the wings stalked four Seabees in fatigue uniforms, carrying on their shoulders a long pipe with some crazy prop hanging from it, part of an airplane engine or something. These four were definitely not part of the routine. Yet here they came, their backs to the audience. When they turned around there was more bedlam than bedlam, if that is possible. They were Dick Rodgers, Oscar Hammerstein, Josh Logan, and Leland Hayward.

Each made a little speech of one line about my leaving our

South Pacific. We all loved it that Josh, who was always at us if we did anything wrong, completely forgot his line and had to be prompted by Leland. Then they said they had a present for me, in a black velvet box, hidden somewhere in the prop. I had to find it.

I searched and searched; the audience crowded closer and closer to the stage. Finally I found the box, opened it, and when the lights hit the contents it was like an exploding rainbow. Inside was a diamond-and-pearl bracelet, set in gold; fantastic and in such exquisite taste. I learned later that Nancy Hayward had helped choose the design, from Schlumberger's.

That night as Richard and I drove home to Connecticut, very late, after a cast party, I told him, "Lillian Russell never had it so good."

When we got home, Heller, who was nine, woke up to greet us. We showed her the bracelet and she got so excited that we had to leave it with her to get her to go back to sleep. Next morning she greeted us with "Mommy, Daddy, do you know how many

Richard Rodgers, Oscar Hammerstein, Josh Logan, and Leland Hayward surprise me on my closing night in *South Pacific*. Diamonds and pearls! Even Lillian Russell never had it so good.

pearls and diamonds there are in this bracelet?" I no longer recall the total but she had spent the night, apparently, wearing the bracelet and counting the jewels. She was still in her Hetty Green period.

Later, Richard designed and had made for me earrings to match the bracelet. Those beautiful things became the heart of a collection to which Ed Lester, Richard, Dick and Oscar, Leland, and others have added through the years. I never thought I would care about jewelry as a possession, and I never have bought any for myself. But these beautiful pieces are presents from persons I love, so I treasure them. I wear them constantly, *love* to look at them, and remember . . . and feel like Lillian Russell.

Then came another glorious year with that glorious show, in London.

We opened in late autumn of 1951, back at the Drury Lane Theatre Royal, where I had played *Pacific 1860*. It is a very beautiful but very drafty theater. The winter of 1951–52 in London was one of the coldest of the century. Half the pipes in London burst from the frigid temperature, and just about every night my wet dungarees froze. I would come out of the shower, do my love scene with Wilbur Evans, who was then playing Emile the planter, sit down on a little canvas-covered box to sing "I'm in Love with a Wonderful Guy"—and my pants would freeze. When I finished, I had real ice on my dungarees and my dressing-room maid had to crack it off to get me out of them.

Josh had to restage the entire opening of the show, and several other scenes, to fit the raked stage of the Drury Lane Theatre. The night before we opened, he kept all of us at work in rehearsal until well after midnight. When we finally walked out into a London downpour, we found one of the most heartwarming sights in the world—the London "first-night gallery," people willing to wait for eighteen hours on the sidewalk to buy unreserved gallery seats for opening-night performances. They are a special, hardy, theater-loving people, armed with little folding stools, blankets, umbrellas, Thermoses of coffee—and the will to wait.

Some of them remembered me from fifteen years before in Noël Coward's play. Most of them had heard recordings of the American production of *South Pacific*. When we emerged from the theater they started calling out, "Mary, Mary, sing us a song before you go home." I asked if they intended to stay there all night, though I knew the answer. Then I said I would sing if they would sing along with me.

Josh, Richard, and I stood there in the rain on the steps of the Drury Lane Theatre and I sang "I'm in Love with a Wonderful Guy" and "Wash That Man." My heart was so full of being back in London, being with these people who really love theater, of having my son, Larry, in a show with me for the first time, that my face was wet the whole time. And it wasn't all just London fog or rain.

Larry had, truly, begun his circles. After the rebellious years, the total dislike for anything connected with theater or a career, he had decided to play a small part in the London production of *South Pacific*. His conversion had come gradually. During his adolescence he decided he wanted to go back and live with his father in Texas. He thought he would become a veterinarian, maybe, or work in a circus. He and his father and Juanita got on well, and Larry went to Weatherford High School, where I had gone. There he drifted into school plays. He was a natural—like mother, like son, a ham. He got the lead in one high school play and wrote his name—above mine—in the wings of the old auditorium, on peeling posters of "Mary Martin in *Smiling Through*" or some such. When he was about seventeen he took a job baling hay in the summer to earn enough money for a bus ticket to Connecticut. He turned up at our home one day, looking tall, strong, tanned, wonderful. He walked in and said, "Mom, I think I made a mistake. I like the theater."

This was the boy who refused to go to London because he couldn't wear his cowboy boots at the Savoy Hotel! Now he was so tall, so thin, so dearly vulnerable. We had one small scene together—he played a Seabee—and neither of us knew that it was the beginning of an exciting career for him in movies and television. Never once in his career did he ever trade on my name, or on Richard's. Larry Hagman made it all on his own, his own way. I am so deeply proud of him.

London opening night, except for Larry's presence, is the usual blank for me. Once again Jinx Falkenburg McCrary remembers it for me, because she had flown over to do a television interview with me the night of the opening. We did it live from London at twelve-thirty in the morning. That was six-thirty in the evening,

New York time, and Jinx's husband, Tex McCrary, used it on his *New York Close-up* show, on NBC, from his studio at the Hudson Theater. The entire New York cast of *South Pacific* was in the Hudson Theater that night to see it.

Jinx says that on opening night in London there was the same applause, the electricity, we had felt in New York. That night, on that huge stage, the cast had to sing each song over again on the curtain calls—for more than forty-five minutes. When I left the theater to get into the limousine and go back to the Savoy Hotel for the broadcast and the opening-night party, the audience—and what looked like half of London—was out in the street, shouting for "More!" and blocking the way to the limousine. Richard and I couldn't fight our way to it, until the police made a path. When we got in, that crowd lifted us up, car and all. They just reached under and picked up the whole thing. Talk about Lillian Russell in her carriage! I kept calling out the windows, "Please, put us down. Just put the whole thing down. We all love each other and that's wonderful, but I don't want you to get hurt."

Finally the police, rather gently, made order and off we went. I remember Jinx saying to me, sitting in our bedroom at the Savoy, "Wouldn't it be funny if the London critics didn't like it?"

This is hard to believe, but they didn't. Not one critic liked it much except Kenneth Tynan, who didn't work for a daily but for a weekly. He liked it. All the other reviewers found it sort of racist: "What is this message of tolerance, what is your problem?" "Doesn't everybody know this?" "Why sing to us 'You've got to be taught to hate'?"

It was a revelation to me. London *did* have a problem, the same as the United States, but they didn't seem to admit it. One of our great dancing Seabees, Archie Savage, had trouble finding a London hotel room. So did Muriel Smith, who played Bloody Mary in London. I couldn't believe it.

In spite of the critics' reservations, London audiences loved *South Pacific*. It was sold out for the year that I played it there, and it sold out for all the other Nellies who played it through the years. One night the little princess who had grown up to be the beautiful Princess Margaret came to see the show, and came backstage. I longed to have something special to welcome her. Here was a young lady who had launched ships, opened hospitals, walked on royal-red carpets. I thought up a very private, special treat for her. For three and one-half years I had been working on something which became known as the Family Rug, my first attempt at needlepoint and petit point. It was a monster, that rug, two panels, 9 feet by 12 feet, containing stitch by stitch all of the symbols of Richard, Heller, Larry, and the theater's life with me. I had dragged it all over the world, working away, and finally it was finished. I decided to put it down on the dressing-room floor. Forever after I would be able to say, proudly, "Princess Margaret once walked on this."

Noël Coward, who was to bring Princess Margaret backstage, had seen the Family Rug about a thousand times, at his house or on country weekends, but he didn't know I had finished it. I set up champagne and glasses in the dressing room, put the rug at the door. When Noël brought the princess back he flung open the door and focused on the needlepoint.

He blurted out in that Noël Coward voice, "Oh, no, not that bloody rug again!"

Once, in London, we sort of touched history. General Dwight D. Eisenhower was in Paris as head of SHAPE, which became NATO, the North Atlantic Treaty Organization. Everybody was trying to get him to run for President, but he wasn't sure he wanted to. One day Tex McCrary called Richard from New York to say there was going to be a huge public rally at Madison Square Garden to demonstrate popular support for Ike. Tex said, "I know Mary likes Ike. Would she sing to him personally, on a closed-circuit line, to his home in Paris?"

I couldn't wait. Tex set up the most extraordinary hookup. He said I should go to a studio in London, where technicians would have a microphone and earphones ready. They would connect me to a studio in New York where Dick Rodgers, with the same setup, would hear and accompany me. There would be a direct line from both of us straight to the General.

I went to the studio, put on the earphones, heard Tex's voice in New York saying "We're ready," heard Dick say, "Hi, I'm here." Then Dick played the introduction and I sang to Ike, a guy I adored, "Wonderful Guy." At the end I heard him say, "Thank you, Mary," from Paris.

Tex also taped my song, and they played it the next night at a huge public rally in Madison Square Garden. I couldn't be there, of course, but they flashed pictures of me on a big screen while they played the tape. Tex made a kinescope of the entire rally and the next day he and Jacqueline Cochran, the famous aviatrix, flew with it to Paris to show it to Ike. They went on a commercial airliner; Jacqueline didn't fly the plane. They showed Ike the entire two-hour show and they said he had a tear in his eye. That huge popular rally was one of the main reasons he finally decided to run for President.

When I left *South Pacific* in London after a year, nobody in our whole family wanted to go home. Heller was studying in the Sadler's Wells ballet school. I had begun studying opera—get me!— with Dino Borgioli. Richard, as always, wanted me to go on learning so he was willing to stay. Larry liked London so much he enlisted in the U. S. Air Force there so he could hope to do his service in England.

In the end Heller finished her course but never became a ballerina. I learned Puccini's *La Bohème* but never sang it in public. Larry found the Air Force something other than his life's ambition, but he met his future wife, lovely Swedish-born Maj Axelsson, and courted her while he was in uniform.

All our lives had changed. The magic of *South Pacific* had touched us all, brought us together, widened our horizons. As strongly as if we had lived on the frangipani-scented islands of James Michener's tales.

Years later, Jim came to visit us for one night in Brazil. We welcomed him with our own exotic blossoms of coral, pink, yellow perfumed frangipani which grew in wild profusion on our own "special island." I like to think that as he went to sleep that night the palm trees waved a benediction over his head.

XV
The Other Side
of the Coin

My mother loved to gamble, but only on horses and only two-dollar bets. I have never liked gambling in any form, except with life. There I am always willing to take a chance. Richard and I took the big chance of marriage without knowing each other very well, because we had to—we loved each other. In the theater we didn't always have *South Pacific*s. We both turned down some winners, gambled rashly on some losers.

On the flip of a coin—a quarter, I remember distinctly—we missed one of the most memorable, most lucrative shows of half a century. While we were still in Hollywood, late in 1942, Vinton Freedley, who had produced *Leave It to Me,* offered me a starring role in a new show called *Dancing in the Streets,* with music by Vernon Duke. At the same time, Oscar Hammerstein and Dick Rodgers had been commissioned by the Theatre Guild to compose a musical based on the play *Green Grow the Lilacs*. It was the first time these two giants of musical theater had worked together. They, too, offered me a starring role, but in a part that wasn't yet written.

I was deeply torn between Vinton, the man responsible for my then single Broadway success, and Oscar, who had believed in me for so long. I didn't know Dick Rodgers well at that time.

Richard and I honestly didn't know which to choose. So we flipped the coin. It came up *Dancing in the Streets*. We telephoned both Oscar and Vinton to tell them our decision.

Both shows tried out in Boston, practically within shouting distance of each other. One show closed there—ours. Dick and Oscar's show, which was provisionally called *Away We Go,* was in difficulty. First they had had trouble raising the money for it in New York. When they played New Haven, one critic panned it hard: "No girls, no gags, no chance."

At first our show, full of girls and gags, seemed to have a chance. We packed them in in Boston, largely on the strength of my movie "name." By coincidence, one of the last pictures I made, *Happy Go Lucky* with Dick Powell and Rudy Vallee, was showing at a cinema right across the street from the theater where we were doing *Dancing in the Streets.* Maybe one audience fed the other, I don't know. In any case we didn't deserve it. *Dancing* just wasn't a good show. We closed it in Boston, never went to New York.

While we were deciding to close, Dick and Oscar wrote a song, in Boston, which changed their luck, changed the title of their show, changed show business. *Oklahoma!* opened in New York on March 31, 1943, and it is still playing somewhere in the world more than forty years later. The "No girls, no gags, no chance" critic was totally, utterly mistaken. *Oklahoma!* was an innovation in musical comedy, created by two of the finest talents in theater, working together for the first time. Agnes de Mille, who had never done musical comedy before, added immeasurably to the joy by creating the show's charming, carefree ballets, as fresh and as sprightly as spring.

For months afterward I got roses from Dick and Oscar because I had turned down their show. Had I accepted it, they said, they would have written a star part for me and probably ruined the musical. When I turned it down they wrote it for four people with almost equal parts. Their roses were the nicest thing that happened to me after *Dancing in the Streets* folded. Richard and I had left Hollywood forever but we had no home to go to. We didn't have a show; we didn't have a house; Richard got pneumonia.

His sister, Didi, and her husband, Newell Whitcomb, came to our rescue. We went for a weekend to their home in New Canaan, Connecticut, and stayed for two months. This was the beginning of our love affair with that beautiful state and mine with my sister-in-love. We eventually bought a house and lived in Connecticut for the longest consecutive period of our lives.

In the months we spent with Didi and Whit—talk about the man who came to dinner—there were weeks and weeks of worry before our personal fortunes turned. Cheryl Crawford gave us the break by offering *One Touch of Venus*.

I have always regretted that I never got to play *Oklahoma!* though the part I coveted was not the ingenue. It was funny Ado Annie. Once I dreamed of doing it in repertory, perhaps for Ed Lester in California, alternating it with *South Pacific* and *Annie*, but the cost of doing three or four musicals on alternating nights, in repertory, was too fantastic for anyone to consider.

My batting average of losses is spectacular, to say the least. Just as I was finishing the first *Annie* on the West Coast in 1948, Cole Porter called to say he had written a new score he wanted us to hear. The book was by Bella and Sam Spewack, who had done *Leave It to Me*. I hadn't worked with any of these wonderful people since they started my career with "Daddy." Richard and I rushed to Cole's house and utterly adored the music. There was one song, "Always True to You in My Fashion," which enchanted me. I said, "Cole, it's marvelous. It's another 'Daddy.' "

"But I don't want you to play that part," he said. "You must do the lyric soprano, the star."

Back when he first met me I was a soprano, but I wasn't anymore. After yelling the *Annie* songs for months I simply could not have sung Cole's songs at that moment. Richard and I had to say no. Years later we read a long, beautiful story about his life and found out for the first time that we had hurt him, deeply, by turning down the part. I thought he had understood that we refused only because I literally could not sing the role. The show was the wonderful *Kiss Me Kate*. We also, just to make sure we kept that batting average up, turned down *My Fair Lady*, and *Mame*.

We accepted some disasters. One was *Kind Sir*, in 1952. After *South Pacific*, I would have done anything with Josh Logan. He had two ideas. One was a musical to be called *Fanny*, with Ezio Pinza and Tyrone Power. This would take a year to prepare. In the meantime he had a play by Norman Krasna which could

Dear Josh Logan and I.

go into rehearsal immediately, costarring Charles Boyer. It was a very amusing light comedy about a suave diplomat who meets an actress. Both are unmarried, but the diplomat finds it convenient to pretend that he is, so he can devastate the ladies without having to consider marriage. The actress discovers his deception, decides to get even, and, of course, they wind up getting married to each other.

It was a challenge to me—my first straight play with no singing and no dancing, plus the chance to work and learn from one of the most deft, exciting actors in theater and motion pictures. I couldn't wait to do *Kind Sir*.

We should all have waited: Charles, Dorothy Stickney, Margalo Gillmore, Robert Ross, Frank Conroy, all exceptional actors and intimate friends, all of us loving Josh. From the first rehearsals, the show was ill-fated. Darling Josh, without knowing it, was in the throes of a breakdown. He was under psychiatric treatment. Although I certainly believe in the profession, we were to learn later that this man's treatment was not correct for our Josh. He insisted that Josh keep on working, and he cautioned all of us to cooperate in anything Josh asked, never to cross him. This led to some rather wild moments.

Josh decided, among other things, that we should open in New Orleans and go there for the final weeks of rehearsal. Why New Orleans I don't know, perhaps because of Charles Boyer's wonderful French accent. Off we went, to be installed in the Hotel Pontchartrain. There is still a suite there named for me, with a star on the door, put there by the hotel's owner, Mr. Aschaffenburg.

As if that weren't enough, Josh decreed that each member of the cast was to have his or her personal limousine, to whisk us grandly from the hotel to a tiny gem of a theater which he had commissioned to be renovated and reopened just for *Kind Sir*.

The circus atmosphere attracted quite a lot of attention. Every photographer from the New Orleans free-lancers to New York's Milton Greene was there. Also *Life, Look, Peek, Squeak,* you name it. We posed on plantations, on Basin Street, riding on the river. We were photographed upside down, inside out, so much that we hardly had time to rehearse.

As a result, the dress rehearsal ran for an intolerable three and a half hours. The next day we sat down in Josh's hotel suite for script cuts. He sat there cutting, cutting, cutting, until it got so late I felt I had to leave, bathe, do my hair, get ready for opening night. I asked Richard to take my cuts for me. The next thing I knew, Josh appeared at my bathroom door, shouting, "Get out of that bathtub and come right back! Richard cannot take your cuts for you."

More or less dripping wet, I went back. Opening night was pretty bad. Dorothy Stickney, that fabulous pro, who played my sister, had to carry her script onstage with her because it had been so mutilated, and the rest of us bumped along uncertainly.

The sets, the production, were beautiful. Josh in his state of euphoria wanted us to have everything beautiful. He bought several thousand dollars' worth of red velvet curtain, with gold tassels. He hired about a hundred pretty girls to throw fresh flowers from the audience while we took our bows. The audience, overwhelmed, screamed *bravo*. Photographers were shooting off strobe lights, we were all being pelted with flowers, bang, crash, plop. We had a fine time picking up the flowers and throwing them back. Oh, there was a hot time in the old town that night.

The flower throwing actually was the best scene in the whole show. It was so successful that in the next city we played—St. Louis, I think—Josh had us throw flowers on all our bows. And we had a lot of bows. Somewhere in the plot, Charles, as my lover, gave me yellow roses, always real ones, onstage. Then an ex-lover sent me red roses. Or maybe I sent them to myself to make Charles jealous; I really can't remember the plot because it was changed so often. Anyway, for a couple of weeks Charles and I threw one red rose and one yellow rose at the audience on our very last bow.

This proved to be such a popular, personal touch that Josh thought up an even bigger surprise for our next city, Detroit. I had a prop bracelet in the show, loaded with emeralds and diamonds, which Charles gave to me in one scene. Charles also had a pocket handkerchief which he used to very good effect throughout the play. Josh decided that at the end of each performance, after we had thrown our roses, I should take off my bracelet, wrap it in Charles's handkerchief, and throw it into the audience—with a note inside which said something like "Please bring this backstage afterward and I will give you an autographed picture."

I thought it was a dreadful idea. So did Charles. We couldn't imagine anyone wanting my picture when they could have the bracelet and the handkerchief. But there was always that psychiatrist lurking in the background, saying, "Don't argue. Don't cross Josh in any way."

So, reluctantly, I put the bracelet in the handkerchief and slung it as far as I could into the audience. Then we all went backstage to wait.

Josh said I should leave my costume and makeup on, so the lucky recipients of that little package could see me as I had looked onstage. Josh, Richard, Charles, and I sat, and we sat, and we sat. Charles finally went home. I said nobody would come. Josh said, "You all [he's southern too] don't have enough faith in people."

Finally the stage-door man knocked. "There's a couple here to see Miss Martin."

Josh jumped up and said, "Didn't I tell you?"

In walked the saddest, sweetest, white-haired couple. When I threw that bracelet into the dark theater it caught the lady right in her glasses and crashed them into a million pieces. Her husband groped around on the floor to find the flying object—and the rims of his wife's glasses—then led her out of the theater and took her home. They lived quite a way out of town, and not until they got home and turned the lights on could they see what had hit her. Then they found the note, which also said, "Please

bring this back, it's a prop and we need it." Bless their kind
hearts, they got back into their car and drove all the way back
to the theater.

I was so mortified I could have died. Even Josh was aware
of the fact that two nice people had had an awful lot of strain and
trouble. He said to them, "I just wanted you to have the pleasure
of meeting the greatest actress in the world." That dear man
really thought I *was*. But he did agree that I wouldn't ever have
to throw my bracelet into the audience again.

Kind Sir eventually moved to New York. Josh moved into
a hospital for care. When we opened on Broadway about the only
thing the critics could find to praise were my Mainbocher clothes.
When they review the clothes, you know something is wrong with
the show. We played out the limited run in New York, from
November 4, 1953, through March 27, 1954, and closed after 166
performances. It hadn't been a total loss: I got to work with
Charles Boyer, and I became so bored with having no music that

I still cannot believe I played opposite that fabulous actor Charles
Boyer.

I started taking piano lessons at the Juilliard School between performances. I still can't read music terribly well, but I know a lot of crazy chords.

I also learned, as if I hadn't before, the importance of a director who is in total control of a production. We were like a rudderless, unhappy ship, all trying to play light comedy in the tragic atmosphere of the suffering of a man we loved. All through that dreadful period my mind kept going back to the classic theatrical masks of Comedy and Tragedy—the wide smiling mouth of Comedy, the down-turned one of Tragedy. It is the same mouth, if you look closely, the same mouth in different phases. There are comic twists in the midst of tragedy; much tragedy in true comedy.

The conduct of everyone involved in our tragic light comedy made me proud of our profession. Margalo's husband, Bob Ross, who also played her husband onstage, died during the run. It made me grow up a little to watch her carry on through that bitter period, overriding her grief with hard work. Watching Nedda Logan, Josh's wife, help him and help all of us was a lesson, sad but valuable. I have seldom seen such strength of character as Nedda and Margalo displayed. Josh came out of the experience a well man, thank heavens, with new doctors and a new drug called lithium, about which he now lectures in order to help other people.

What makes it a happy ending is that Josh and Nedda and I are closer friends now than ever before. And Norman Krasna's *Kind Sir* later became the marvelous motion picture *Indiscreet,* with Ingrid Bergman and Cary Grant. It deserved to be great.

In 1955 a show came along which had both ups and downs, Thornton Wilder's wonderful *The Skin of Our Teeth.* It is a knockabout comedy on the surface; a rueful, ironic, very warm tribute to the human race underneath. The main characters are George Antrobus, his wife, their two children, and their maid, Lily Sabina. It is difficult to explain the plot because it is complex, but all of them are grappling with all the problems and destinies of the human race. Mr. Antrobus invents the alphabet, the wheel, and mathematics; they survive the Ice Age, a plague, floods, war, and they never lose courage. I remember my script summed it up: "They have survived a thousand calamities by the skin of their teeth. Here is a tribute to their indestructibility."

Tallulah Bankhead starred as the maid, Sabina, in the original production in 1942, with Fredric March as Antrobus and his wife, Florence Eldridge, as Maggie. A young unknown by the name of Montgomery Clift played their son, Henry.

Our 1955 production was put together for the State Department, to open in Paris at the Sarah Bernhardt Theatre. Helen Hayes played Mrs. Antrobus, George Abbott was Mr. Antrobus, and I was Sabina. Heller was in the cast, too, as the Antrobuses' daughter, Gladys. Don Murray played the son, Henry. Larry came over from London to create an unforgettable drunk in one scene. He brought his wife, Maj, to meet us for the first time. Maj likes to say that she had the shortest theatrical career in history— she had a walk-on in *The Skin of Our Teeth*—but she spent hours helping with costumes backstage. She was well equipped; she had been a designer for Harrod's. It was altogether rather a family affair: Richard was there, and Helen's husband, Charles MacArthur. Their son, James MacArthur, who is now a big television star, came along to handle the lights.

We played it in English in Paris, and the audience had simultaneous-translation earphones, the kind they use at the United Nations. I'm not sure they really understood it even then, it was all so different from anything that they had ever seen. I, as Sabina, had to step out of my stage role very often and address remarks as "the actress" straight at the audience. One remark, during a long soliloquy in the first act, was "I don't understand one word of this play." That got a roar from the French audiences, because they didn't either.

Opening night was disastrous as far as I was concerned.

All the sets were designed to break down, fall over, fly up, all over the place, on purpose. The idea was to symbolize destruction—another war, a flood, some catastrophe. Sabina, the maid, has to run around and put them all together again. Mrs. Antrobus is the determined, practical one who always says we must Do Something, but it is Sabina who has to do it. Well, on opening night I went to work putting the sets back up, and all the French stagehands, who were supposed to be invisible backstage hauling on ropes to help me, came rushing out on the stage. I hissed at them, "Go away, get out, go back!"

And they hissed right back at me, not understanding English, *"Madame, s'il vous plaît, vous avez besoin de secours."* They wanted to help.

We explained and explained but they never did get it right. Every single night for the two-week run one or two of them would plunge out there gallantly to help me.

I guess the French liked it well enough, but I was miserably unhappy long before we left to take the show to Washington. I knew I wasn't good in it, and I thought I knew why. The role of Sabina had been written for Tallulah Bankhead. The marvelous asides to the audience, the tough wisdom of Sabina, *were* Tallulah, and should be played more or less that way. But our director insisted that when it was time to be "the actress" I should be me, Mary Martin. But Tallulah and I were very different types. A Tallulah line coming from a Mary Martin-type character doesn't work. I argued and argued but the director was unmovable. That was the way I had to play it.

Helen Hayes was absolutely marvelous about it. She knew something was wrong, that I was unhappy, and she tried to help. Richard knew, everybody knew.

Then came a man to my rescue, a man with whom I worked later in many shows and loved perhaps more than any other: Vincent J. Donehue. "Vinnie" was the kindest, wisest, gentlest man. He appeared to rescue me from my dilemma because part of the whole program for *The Skin of Our Teeth* was that after Paris we should do a limited Washington engagement, play in New York, and then do it live on television as an NBC special. Vinnie had been chosen to direct the television version.

He came to see the show in Washington, then went to Richard and said, "Mary is not any good in it. She's terrible. But I can fix it."

I didn't want to meet him, talk to him, even think about it anymore. I was so miserable I just wanted to finish the run and get it over with. Richard finally persuaded me at least to talk to Vinnie. I did, and he said I was the most hostile human being he had ever seen at the beginning of our talk.

He said, "I think I can help you."

Whereupon I burst into tears and wailed, "Nobody can help me." He could, and he did. We got a script and locked ourselves into a hotel suite and went over it.

"Play any actress you want to," he said. "Play Tallulah, or play Vivien Leigh [she had starred in it in London], or anybody else you want, but do *not* play Mary Martin." My savior. I knew what was wrong, but no one would listen to me.

We worked for two hours, with him reading the cues and me responding. We didn't change one single line, we just changed the mental approach, which changed the delivery. Then we had to go tell Helen that my performance would be different that night. We didn't want to throw her off. Nothing throws off that marvelous actress, but that evening's performance threw me off for a while. My ten-minute soliloquy, which had fallen so flat before, went on for about fifteen minutes because it got such great applause, such spreading laughter, for each great Thornton Wilder line. Helen, bless her, watched in the wings with tears in her eyes. At last it was going to be right.

Ironically enough, it was the sensitive, brilliant Vinnie Donehue who directed the next show on which I gambled and

Playing Sabina, in
The Skin of Our Teeth.

That kind, wise, and sensitive director, Vinnie Donehue.

lost—*Jennie,* in 1963. Fortune in the theater is a very strange thing. It is hard to understand how veteran actors, producers, directors, writers, backers can guess wrong in spite of all their experience. It's like a book, or a painting, a sculpture, or even a baby. You begin with high hopes and the best will in the world. But it takes a long time for it to come out, to see what you have. In the end only God and nature can make a tree—and sometimes even that can be twisted.

Jennie was based on the extraordinary life of Laurette Taylor, one of the greatest actresses of American theater, whose career spanned the years between her biggest hits, *Peg o' My Heart* in 1913 to—a world away—Tennessee Williams' *The Glass Menagerie* in 1945. Between the two she had a very difficult life in many ways, including years of touring the country in her husband's repertory company, playing "mellerdrammers." Laurette was forever being tied to railroad tracks, dangled over waterfalls, being pursued by an assortment of exotic villains.

Jennie was a difficult format because it was to be a play

within a play—Jennie's own life with her husband and two children set in the framework of their touring company and its productions. This technique was successful in *Kiss Me Kate* and *Gypsy* but it never quite came off in *Jennie*. Richard and I believed in it passionately, at first. We plunged in with real joy.

Howard Dietz and Arthur Schwartz had done a magnificent song, "Before I Kiss the World Good-bye," for another production called *Mrs. 'Arris Goes to Paris,* which had not been produced. They played it for me and I loved it from the moment I heard it. I couldn't wait to sing it. I was also looking forward to wearing the beautiful period costumes designed by Irene Sharaff. But from the day we started *Jennie* we had problems —getting the right leading man, the right book writer, everything.

In tryouts the show absolutely refused to jell. The second act desperately needed comedy. It needed a comic song. That's how I got my favorite exercise machine written into the plot. It was a great whirling gadget which fascinated reviewers—*Time* magazine called it "a giant Roto-Broil of a torture wheel."

It wasn't torture to me. As much as Mother loved gambling, I love gadgets, especially exercise gadgets. Besides, I had always secretly wanted to sing a song standing on my head, or, more exciting, swinging from a trapeze upside down.

I first saw the Wheel, the Thing, just inside the door at Hammacher Schlemmer's one day. It was tall as a room, 12, 15 feet high, made of iron, with a long canvas stretcher thing suspended in the middle on big circular supports. I couldn't imagine what it was, so I went in and asked a clerk. He said it was a Japanese invention. You got onto the stretcher and were fastened in something like a parachute harness, with your feet held in position, your body and legs and shoulders secure, your arms free. Then by changing your balance, moving your arms, you could go around and around. Or you could balance with your head down and your feet up, any angle or degree you wanted. It was marvelous for the circulation, he said.

Naturally, I *had* to try it. I had on a dress with quite a full skirt but the man assured me it wouldn't fly over my head once I was fastened in the stretcher.

I took a quick look around. The store was almost empty. I explained that I couldn't ask my husband for such an expensive gadget if I didn't try it out. Please, could I? The man was delighted. He helped me get into position, fastened all the straps and belts, and told me to be careful.

I started slowly, waving my arms, testing the balance, moving just a little, like rocking in a cradle. It was such fun that I went back a little bit farther. The stretcher swung up. The man said, "Move your arms"—and the next thing I knew the thing was going round and round.

This looked a bit odd to people walking up the street, and they stopped to watch. Somebody shouted, "Good God, there's Peter Pan in Hammacher Schlemmer's going round and round on a *thing*." More people collected; some started running up the street, pouring through the door. The clerk looked appalled; I couldn't figure how to stop. It became a small riot. When the man finally got me down I took off as fast as I could, back home.

Richard thought I was crazy when I told him about the Wheel. He said, "Don't you think you should try it before I buy it?" I had to confess that I had, uh, well, sort of tried it a little bit.

We installed it in the bedroom and I spent many happy hours upside down. It felt divine; fatigue just evaporated after a few minutes on the wheel. Greta Garbo lived in our building, and on one of her rare visits she watched while I was spinning around. Those beautiful, expressive eyes popped, and the sight brought instant speech to the silent lady. That *voice* intoned, "You arrrrh a crazy voman."

She left, but she came back a few days later and wanted to try it. I resisted. Richard would never forgive me if somehow she hurt herself on my gadget. She longed so to test it that finally one day, with the help of George Schlee—her great and good friend—we put her into it. After one tip backward she had had enough. I was very happy when that beautiful, fun woman was back on terra firma.

No thought of demonstrating the Thing outside the privacy of the bedroom had occurred to me when Richard let me buy it. Then when we got into trouble over the second act of *Jennie*, I thought this might be just the touch we needed. We already had some *Perils of Pauline* scenes in other parts—I was chased by bears, hung by my heels over a waterfall that cost about fifty thousand dollars to create onstage. So I suggested the Wheel. Everyone thought it a grand idea. Howard and Arthur wrote a

song called "Shalimar" and dreamed up a number in which I was
being chased by a sultan, played by Kirby Smith, my Nena's husband, from Peister near Poolville, another circle. He kept saying, "I want you," while I ran around in a harem veil crying,
"Never, never." Finally his men caught me and locked me up
in the Wheel. It was painted gold for the occasion. As the
sultan's men poked at me I started to go around and around,
singing at the top of my lungs. I whirled about eighty times,
full speed, enjoying every minute. We got letters from doctors

Me on the torture wheel, having a ball, with Kirby Smith as the Sultan,
in *Jennie*.

saying I was going to have a stroke or something right on stage, but it didn't hurt me a bit.

Oh, the best-laid plans! No matter what we thought up, how hard we worked, how long we rehearsed, the show just wouldn't come together. It was too complicated, in plot and script. Constant changes in cast, songs, dialogue didn't help. It became more and more a patchwork quilt. Even that marvelous song, "Before I Kiss the World Good-bye," was not right for the character I played—the character was too young for it; she had not seen the world. Richard, as producer, and both of us as investors, felt we should not take *Jennie* to Broadway. Arthur Schwartz and Howard Dietz, however, were investors as well as composer and lyricist. They wanted it to open. There was an advance sale of $2 million in New York and their lawyers told us if we didn't permit the show to open they would sue us for the whole sum.

It all got very tacky. Richard and I finally agreed, to avoid a lawsuit. I loved Irene Sharaff's costumes; the critics were kind; but it was not a success. It could have been so marvelous, so funny, had it only been right. Things were so strained that no one spoke to anyone else for years. Early in 1974 I was at a New York party given by that famous lawyer and party giver, Arnold Weissberger, which Howard Dietz also attended. I always forget that I'm mad at anybody, so I went rushing over to Howard and said, "How marvelous to see you again." He said he was writing a book and he sounded a little ominous as he mentioned that "In a book you have to say all the bad things as well as the good."

"Oh, Howard, life's too short," I told him. "What does it matter? Why don't you and Lucinda visit us in Brazil?" Within twenty-four hours I got a call from a mutual friend. He said Howard had suddenly recalled the manuscript to "take out all the bad parts about Mary."

That's just a funny theater story, but life *is* too short. Friends are associates, associates are friends. We end up all wound together like the threads for the beautiful tapestry which we all wish to make of our lives. The threads get into tangles and knots when we least want them to. If we yank and break them, in anger, or cut them in haste and frustration, it upsets the whole pattern.

Sometimes snarls turn up almost at the end, hidden underneath the fine pattern we are making. This can be funny. It can also, with luck, improve the pattern. I know, because Leland

Hayward, who was not only the greatest producer but also a close friend, made a marvelous tangle once.

What he did was hatch a plot. To accomplish it he dissembled to me—that's a polite word for lying—and he also dissembled to a lady who is a close friend. He upset my digestion and my aplomb, but at the end he helped create one of the great experiences of my life.

It began in Cuba. Richard and Heller and I had finally left London, in 1952, and hopped on a freighter which was going vaguely in the right direction toward the United States. We made up our minds and got on in such a rush we didn't know for sure where we were going. As we floated blissfully along I worked on some needlepoint and helped Heller with her multiplication tables. She got to ten times ten on that trip because that was as far as I could go. Then Richard took over.

One day in the middle of the ocean—I wasn't even sure which ocean—the radio operator came looking for us with a teletype message in his hands. It had been addressed, literally, to all ships at sea, asking if Mary Martin was on board. As we were the only people on the boat, under the name of Mr. and Mrs. Richard Halliday, he wanted to know if I was me. The message was from Leland Hayward, whose gestures were always grand. He had no idea where we were, or on what boat, so he simply contacted *all* of them. The message said that he had something to discuss with me, that he and his wife, Nancy, wanted to meet us wherever and whenever the boat landed. It turned out to be Cuba.

We had a wonderful weekend, but there was more than fun and games on Leland's mind. He wanted me to do the shortest run of my life—a one-shot television show. I had never done television because I was so afraid it would be like Hollywood: "Stand here, stand there, don't move." Leland knew this; right away he said it would not be like that. He said he had a whole new thing called the TV spectacular, which was live, done only once, marvelous.

I was to be mistress of ceremonies of a two-hour show with special material, skits, written for me. Leland thought he could get Oscar Hammerstein to play a scene from *Our Town* with me. He would get Jerome Robbins to direct, get the best cameramen in the business. Most important of all, I would have approval of everything on the show. Every single thing.

I was still skeptical enough to ask, "Can I *move?*"

"Of course you can move," he said. "It's a special; it's live. We have a sponsor, the Ford Motor Company. We'll even get you a symphony orchestra if you want."

By now I was pretty excited. On the last day of our week-end Leland said, very casually, "I have another idea. If you like it, fine. If you don't, forget it. But wouldn't it be sensational if you would sing a song with Ethel Merman? Something like 'Friendship'?"

That did it. In all the years we had known each other, been friends, Ethel and I had never worked together. I went for the idea instantly. Leland said, "Okay, I'll ask her."

From the beginning rehearsals, Ethel and I got on like gang-busters. Anything she didn't think of, I did. But the genius of Jerry Robbins really made the show possible. It was his idea that we do a number sitting on high stools, side by side, on an empty stage doing songs of our different roles. That got both of us going. I suggested we sing different songs but together, the

Merman and friend whooping it up on the Ford Show in 1953.

old trick I had learned back in the Cinegrille. Just as I had done then, we started with "Tea for Two" and had all the other songs come off that. It was Ethel's idea that we do the "I" songs, songs like "I Cried for You," "I Can't Give You Anything but Love, Baby,"—all the songs beginning with "I." But the stools were Jerry's idea, just rehearsal stools. "Let's not clutter it up," he said. Wow! Did he ever start a trend. No one stands up anymore.

We rehearsed our heads off ten, twelve hours a day. Every day we made millions of changes. Ethel always said, "No worry. I'll type everything out tonight and give you a copy." She did, too; she's a wonderful typist. Billy Rose won a shorthand contest once; Ethel could win a typing contest anywhere.

In addition to the duet the show included Marian Anderson singing "Battle Hymn of the Republic," and me doing Jerry Robbins' absolutely sensational skit called "The Shape" in which I put on one simple tube of jersey, designed by Irene Sharaff, and to the accompaniment of music and a veddy, veddy grand voice doing a fashion commentary, turned the tube and a succession of hats into a style show ranging from 1900 to the 1950s. It was a brilliant skit; I'd like to do it again sometime.

We polished that show until every facet gleamed, working out split-second timing. I had my favorite accompanist, Johnny Lesko. Our orchestra conductor was Jay Blackton, who had always been Ethel's conductor. I had not worked with him before. He is one of the great ones of all time. After weeks of work we never had to look at Johnny or Jay; they hardly had to look at us. We *knew*.

Finally it was time for the dress rehearsal, which we did before an invited audience in the huge Center Theater in Rockefeller Center. It has since been torn down, but at the time it was as famous as the present one where the Rockettes perform.

Just before we were to go on, Leland came to tell us we couldn't have Johnny Lesko and Jay Blackton.

To our wails of "Why, why?" and "Oh, no," he shook his head. He had just found out that they didn't belong to the television union.

Well, gloom and doom. We couldn't do the show without them. No other conductor, no matter how good he was, could step in and execute the timing, the beat, we had rehearsed so long. Leland was as miserable as we. He promised to keep trying.

But the audience was already filing into the theater; we had to start the dress rehearsal; and we had to do it with a television conductor.

It was a disaster. The whole effect, the whole punch, went right out the window. Henry Ford, who had been to earlier rehearsals, was in the audience. He couldn't understand what on earth had gone wrong, what had happened to the beautiful show which his company was paying for.

He came backstage to join the general panic. There was almost no time left: dress rehearsal and performance were on the same day. In three hours we had to go on the air over both NBC and CBS, the first time two networks had carried the same commercial program simultaneously.

Ethel and I retired to our dressing rooms, which were next to each other. I was in an absolute state, couldn't eat, couldn't sit down, couldn't think, could hardly breathe. Ethel, who refuses to let things bother her, sat down and started eating a sandwich.

Richard and I both thought we should cancel the performance, right then. No performance at all would be better than a disastrous one across the country's television screens. Ethel finally spoke from her room.

"Mary, it's too late. We've all worked so hard, let's just go ahead and do it."

"I can't, I just cannot," I told her. "Could you, honestly, go on? Would it be all right with you?"

"Of course it isn't all right," she answered, "and my contract gives me approval. But what difference does it make? It's too late."

Approval? Contract? By this time we were both up, out, staring at each other. I asked, "What do you mean you have approval?"

Now it was her turn to look puzzled. "Why, Leland came to me and said, 'I have this great idea for you, and you have total approval, and . . .'"

I finished the sentence for her. "And then he said, 'Maybe it would be fun to get Mary Martin to sing a number with you . . .'"

Light dawned on both of us at the same moment. Leland had told the same story to each of us. Richard was so mad he could have killed him, but, of course, Leland had been right—

With the incomparable Leland Hayward.

he couldn't have persuaded either of us to do it had he told us anything else. In spite of everything, Ethel and I burst into howls of laughter. We had worked too hard together, loved each other too much, to be mad now at Leland.

Then came the second bolt from the blue. We got our Johnny and Jay back again, in the nick of time. Nobody, not Mr. Ford or Leland or Richard, ever told us how they did it. I suspect that Mr. Ford agreed to pay the full salaries of the entire television crew.

We went on the air the night of June 15, 1953. Everything went perfectly and the showstopper—if you can call it that, because you can't stop a television show—was Ethel's and my duet, sitting on our stools. When we laughed together that night we had a special joke. When we tried to outsing each other, which we did, it was because we'd had such a cliff-hanger and because *each* of us knew that we *each* had "total control" of the show.

I can still hear the applause of the studio audience, see the big laugh in Ethel's eyes. A recent book about the 1950s, called *This Fabulous Century, 1950–1960,* said, "For sheer theatrical excitement, nothing yet seen on television had matched their performance; suddenly it was clear that TV could be great entertainment."

Those are nice words to remember it by. And to remember the one and only Leland Hayward.

XVI
Pits and Falls—and Walls— I Know Intimately

Peter Pan is perhaps the most important thing, to me, that I have ever done in the theater.

I cannot even remember a day when I didn't want to be Peter. When I was a child I was sure I could fly. In my dreams I often did, and it was always the same: I ran, raised my arms like a great bird, soared into the sky, flew.

In the early days in Hollywood one of my closest friends was Jean Arthur. One of our bonds was that we both adored Peter Pan. She and her husband, Frank Ross, and Richard and I often were invited to costume parties; and Jean and I both always wanted to go as Peter Pan. It got so bad we would call each other up to declare our intentions—whoever called first got to go as Peter. We had endless discussions about how Maude Adams had played the role, and Eva Le Gallienne, and we mourned that we never had seen them in it. We vowed that we, too, would play it somewhere, someday.

Jean did it first, on Broadway in 1950. She was absolutely wonderful. I hate to admit it but she *is* Peter Pan. She is youth, joy, freedom, all the things Peter tells Captain Hook when Hook asks, "Pan, who and what are you?"

My chance didn't come until 1954. That year Edwin Lester, director of the Los Angeles and San Francisco Civic Light Opera Company, asked if Richard and I would be interested in an entirely new musical version. Richard was to be producer, I was to be Peter, and we had our choice of composer, director, choreographer.

Ed's telegram looked to me like a ticket straight to heaven. Once again I couldn't wait to take on a role which other actresses had made memorable—several generations of them, in fact. I dared to do it because we could make our production different, create our own theater around a role, a plot, which had been beloved for years.

Our first decision, I remember, was to wire Ed Lester, "Yes, if we can get Jerome Robbins." Jerry Robbins then was a young man making a name as ballet dancer and choreographer, but he had never directed a musical book for the stage. We felt his genius, however, and we talked him into staging the entire production. We were repaid a thousand times for our belief in that young pixie, Jerry, who has become one of the supergreats in our business.

For the villainous Captain Hook, Peter's sworn enemy, we had only one choice—the great Australian actor Cyril Ritchard. I had seen him perform only once, in a Restoration comedy with his wife, Madge Elliott, and with John Gielgud, who also directed, but I had never forgotten his perfect timing, his presence. He would be the ultimate Hook, and he was.

My flying instructor was a young Englishman named Peter Foy whom Ed and Richard brought over from London. One single English family had "flown" all the stage Peters there for fifty years, and Peter Foy had learned his trade from that family. He arrived in California with all his wires, ropes, pulleys, machines, and right away he had his work cut out for him. No Peter Pan had ever flown very far—just through the window of the stage set, over to the mantelpiece, around the room, and back out the window.

I was determined, instead, to fly all over the place. I wanted to fly at least sixty feet across the stage, up to the top of the wings in the back of the theater, in and out the window, everywhere. I also wanted a flying ballet with Peter and the children, Wendy, Michael, and John, all sailing around together.

Peter Foy sort of gulped, but he agreed to try. Jerry Robbins and Richard were almost as excited as I, but Ed Lester was a little leary. He didn't want to lose this Peter in a flying ballet accident. Peter Foy planned the whole thing like a military

The villainous Captain Hook—marvelous Cyril Ritchard.

campaign, making charts of stage positions, calculating what can only be called trajectories of people in midair.

There is no secret about how it was done: it was all piano wires, harnesses, ropes, and expert rope-pullers. I was hooked to a very strong piano wire which was attached to a harness that went around my waist, over my shoulders, through my legs. The main support, around my waist, was an enormous thick belt, the sort of thing motorcyclists wear, about two inches thick and eight inches high at the back. It was padded, as was the shoulder harness and the bit that went between my legs. It wasn't madly comfortable, but once I was in the air I forgot all about it.

Peter Foy and an assistant held control ropes in the wings. When they pulled I was hoisted up by the harness and away I went. They worked so skillfully, in tandem, that I could swing back and forth, zoom up and down. They became so expert that they could drop me, wherever they wanted me onstage, as lightly as a trout fisherman drops a fly at the end of a fishing line, wherever he wants it to land.

I wish I could express in words the joy I felt in flying. I loved it so. The freedom of spirit—the thing Peter always felt—was suddenly there for me. I discovered I was happier in the air than on the ground. I probably always will be.

Balance in the air was no more difficult than on earth, and graceful movements were far easier, as they are in swimming. I found I could use all the ballet movements I once taught back in Weatherford, but now they were effortless. I never knew how all the mechanics of harness, hoist, and pulley worked. I simply trusted them, and Peter Foy.

Our new *Peter Pan* was a tremendous hit in San Francisco and Los Angeles in 1954, on Broadway in late 1954 and early 1955, and on a nationwide television live performance that same year. Everything came together right. Perhaps I transmitted some of the joy to audiences, I don't know. Jerry Robbins' staging was perfection. Cyril and the entire cast were magnificent. We had lovely original music, some of it written by Carolyn Leigh and Mark Charlap, the rest by Jule Styne, Betty Comden, and Adolph Green. There was an odd story in that, too. One night Richard and I were driving home to Connecticut on the Merritt Parkway when we heard on the radio a song called "Young at Heart." We decided whoever had written those lovely lyrics, that haunting melody, should work on *Peter Pan*. Richard did one of his detective acts and tracked down, through ASCAP, Carolyn Leigh. She came to see us, brought along her collaborator, "Moose," and they wrote "I've Gotta Crow" and "I'm Flying" for us. We opened in California with their songs and added some others later.

Just before the final triumphant performance of that *Peter Pan*, the television special of 1955, I had my very last flying dream. I dreamed I was flying through the Holland Tunnel, straight through, between the car tops and the tunnel top. Never touched a thing, not a single car or the tip of a finger. It was the best flying dream I had ever had. Bliss. When I woke up, I couldn't wait to tell Richard.

Then I never dreamed it again. Perhaps it was because I had experienced at last the joy of really flying. On the end of a wire, of course, but audiences could barely see the wire and I often forgot completely that it was there.

Strangely enough, such a simple thing as my costume

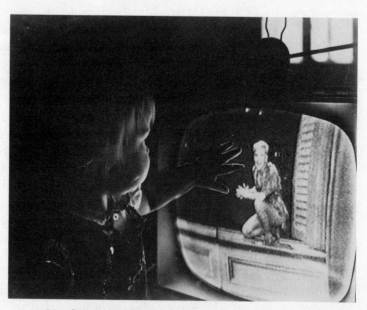

My first grandchild, Heidi Hagman, trying to catch her grandmother, Peter Pan, on the TV screen.

caused more trouble than the complicated business of flying. I had to have something that would cover the harness without making me look like a football player, but which at the same time would fit me well enough when I wasn't wearing the harness. We experimented with five different costumes before we found the right one, starting out with leather and ending up with jersey. The answer came in finding Dorothy Jeakins, a Los Angeles designer who since then has won many Academy Awards. She made me a jersey tunic covered with fabric leaves and gold beads of "fairy dust." We were up all night long, both of us, while she lovingly pinned every single leaf in place on the jersey so the costume could be stitched together for the opening-night performance. Her costume, as had Mainbocher's costumes before, helped me to crystallize my characterization.

Then we had to figure out how to make me look like a boy. I wonder, now, how important that really was. Nobody ever seemed to care—certainly the children didn't—whether Peter was a boy or a girl. Peter Pan is, and should be, any age or any sex.

Still, some people are literal-minded and my name *was* Peter, so I got Richard's barber to come and cut my hair short, and I flattened my already more-or-less flat front. I never was what one would call amply endowed. Not until I reached fifty. Heller, who has inherited some of my characteristics, keeps asking "Mother, do I have to wait until I'm fifty to be sexy?"

I solved my front problem by wearing a short girdle with a nice, soft lining. I cut the legs off and then pulled it on upside down, over my shoulders. The cut-down girdle was also handy for holding the microphone, because all during the "I'm Flying" number I was sailing up so high into the wings that the sound wouldn't come down unaided. I had a mike which slipped into a little green pocket which slipped into the place where the girdle and I met at the top. The batteries for the mike were attached to my harness by a belt at the back, and I used it only during the flying ballet. This innovation is now in common practice. The only two things I ever checked before going on, every single performance, were the microphone and its batteries, the tension and "feel" of the piano wire.

My understudy in that *Peter Pan* was Billie Worth, who had also been with me in other shows, playing opposite me in *Annie Get Your Gun* the first time. She later became a star and played, among other things, *Call Me Madam* in London. She had to work out on the wire, too, and it was funny—every time she had used it I could tell the difference. It had a different feel. No doubt she noticed it, too. That wire was rather special.

It never failed me, though once, during a San Francisco tryout, it slipped a cog on top and dropped me thirty feet, then whiplashed me back up again, hard. I was stunned and dangling; everybody else was scared to death. The audience thought it was all part of the show. The stage manager closed the curtains quickly and made an announcement about "technical difficulties," and there was a slight delay while they got the technical difficulty—me—safely back to earth.

We finished the performance, but the shock had jammed every nerve and muscle in my back so painfully that for months I had to have deadening shots up and down my spine to ease the pain enough for me to get into the harness. Richard, Ed Lester, Jerry Robbins were all beside themselves because I wouldn't stop flying. But there simply was too much involved. All the money spent by the producers, the money spent by the people who paid to see it. I know I'm cracked on the subject, but I think that after all that money, and faith, and anticipation, a few shots and a little pain are far less important than the performance. Mind over matter is more important. Besides, I cannot bear giving up.

As long as I live I will hear the sound of the children's voices at *Peter Pan*. All that energy sitting in the audience— well, not exactly sitting. They always stood on their seats, ran down the aisles, tried to reach Peter. He belonged to them. Always, at every performance, the children whose parents had paid to see the show performed as much as we "children" did onstage.

At first their, shall we say, unfettered reactions upset Jerry Robbins, who was accustomed to the more polite reactions of ballet audiences. He kept saying, "But I can't hear the laughs," or "I'm losing what's going on." The children made so much noise. They would shout, "Look out, Peter!" or "He's right behind you, Peter!" I loved it. They were *in* the show; the noise didn't matter.

Our flying ballet always went without a hitch—except for one time early on when I almost killed poor Wendy, played so perfectly by Kathy Nolan. I never could distinguish left from right. It's like reading music, I guess; either you can or you can't, and there's little to be done about it. Everyone on every stage for every performance has his "spot" marked on the floor. It is always important, but when you're hooked to a piano wire and about to fly into the air it is somewhat more important than normal. Peter Foy always hooked my wire to my harness himself, in the wings. Then he would say, "Go stage left," or "Go stage right," and I would go.

One night I got into Wendy's position, her spot, instead of my own. When they flew us out the window we collided and I crashed down on her back. Again the audience couldn't see what happened, because the set broke and there was a blackout. The children and I simply sailed out into the starry sky and vanished. That's when I hit Kathy, and hurt her. From that time on Peter Foy always said, very carefully, "Miss Martin, come toward me," or "Miss Martin, go away from me." No more of that stage right or stage left business.

Peter's attentiveness saved me once more when I wasn't on the wire but should have been. It was a scene in which I was high up on the pirate ship and had to fly off to have a sword fight with Captain Hook, hand to hand. I was all charged up, ready for action, and I forgot to back up to the spot where I was hooked up. Just before I leaped into thin air I heard Peter hiss, "Miss Martin, don't move. Don't jump. You're not hooked to the wire."

Adrenaline is a strange thing. It made me quite ready to launch into empty space in *Peter Pan*. It sent me crashing into sets and orchestra pits and props. I can chart every single show by some lump, bump, or scar on my body, and yet I never felt a thing at the time when I banged myself. I always was just going too fast, and too concentrated, to feel a thing. Except once. That was during rehearsals for the third and last time I played *Peter Pan*, in 1960, on television.

By 1960 I was performing in *The Sound of Music* eight times a week, so Richard rented the Helen Hayes Theatre, right across the street from *Music*, so I could conveniently rehearse for the new *Peter*. Cyril Ritchard was going to do Hook again, and we still had many of the original pirates and Indians. But the children had all grown up. Cyril and I had been through three generations of Wendys, Michaels, and Johns by now, and even my Heller, whom we asked to play with us again, was grown up enough to be in college. One of our dreams, Heller's and mine, was for her to play Wendy to my Peter. But she reluctantly said, "Mother, I'm in college, and if I'm going to college I must stay there." She really had grown up.

So with an entirely new cast of children we began rehearsing daily. Peter Foy was there to fly us. He never had gone back to England, except for visits, because he had made a marvelous career in California, flying people in circuses, on TV, everything. He did *The Flying Nun* on TV. By the time we were ready for our 1960 show he was available but his assistant had left and he had a new man. On the first day of rehearsal I went up on the wire to show the children how to move and turn. Suddenly I had a strange feeling that something was wrong. I was going faster and faster in the pendulum swing, but it didn't feel as though anything was pulling me back again. I kept getting closer and closer to the brick wall of the theater and I knew some decision had to be made. Quickly, and by me.

I knew how to do fast turns on the wire and a fast turn was needed. I had to turn away and hit that wall with something which wasn't my head. It turned out to be my left elbow.

There was a sound like a rifle shot when I hit the wall, and for once I felt it. It was all dark in the theater, but out there were Richard, Vinnie Donehue, who was directing this production, and Johnny Lesko, my conductor. They were frozen with fear. There was a terrible silence for a moment, then Peter Foy's voice, saying, "Pull her down, pull her down."

Thank fortune I didn't faint or scream or do anything to scare the children. Richard called our family doctor, David Bachrach, who had patched me up through all our shows, and he rushed me to the theater and in my dressing room drained about two cups of fluid from my elbow. It looked like a melon by then. Over Richard's and Vinnie's and Dr. Bachrach's dead bodies, I went right back out and flew again. I had to. The children would have been terrified if I hadn't. They might never have flown again—and maybe neither would I!

Later we found out what had happened. Peter Foy's new assistant had dropped his rope. He was watching me and he "believed." He thought I was really flying, and he forgot what he was supposed to do. That poor man, he looked far sicker than I felt. He said he would never, never, never come back to the theater again, never help fly me. We all told him of course he would—he probably was the only man in New York who would never forget again. It wasn't his fault, really, he just believed, and that is what *Peter Pan* is all about.

The children never knew for sure what happened, and, oddly enough, neither did audiences at *Sound of Music*. I went on that night, four hours after the accident, but in the meantime we had all trooped off to the hospital. I had a broken bone in my arm, not in the elbow, thank heavens, but just below it. It was a nice, clean fracture, with no splinters, so Dr. Bachrach set it, taped it, put a sling around it, and off I went. Poor David Bachrach, he had to be called constantly to put my legs back in, my neck back in, my arms. I think I saw him every Wednesday and Saturday of my entire life while I was playing. He would come to the theater between shows and give me osteopathic adjustments, B_{12}, whatever. He kept me well and fit enough to go on; he probably knows my bones and muscles and my stubborn head as well as anyone in the world.

Peter Pan rehearsals were held up while my arm healed. But I still performed eight shows a week in *Sound of Music*. Fortunately I was playing the role of a postulant and my arms were crossed a lot. Then came the great day when we could go back to work again. The first time I flew up, right back to the too-familiar brick wall, I was convulsed with laughter. Somehow the stagehands had gotten up there and fastened to the precise spot a huge mattress with a sign on it which said, "MARY MARTIN SLAPPED HERE."

Now wouldn't that make you want to stay in the theater forever, and fly, and find a funny like that? I have always adored those magicians, the stagehands and crews. Richard and I had the same electricians, carpenters, sound men, propmen, light crews, for show after show because we loved them so. It sounds corny to say we were "family," but we were.

My only frustration, through our California run, the Broadway run, the two television performances in 1955 and 1956, was that I never was able to fly from the stage across the theater itself to the spotlights up back. Eva Le Gallienne, I had read, used to do that at the end of every performance and oh, how I longed to do the same! I knew, of course, that in her day there were fewer rules and regulations. Now there were fire laws, asbestos curtains, all the rest. Once the asbestos curtain comes down in an American theater nobody is allowed beyond it—not even for flying.

Then came a glorious afternoon in Poughkeepsie, New York, about 1958. I was doing a concert tour of the country with two shows a day, one for adults at night, one for children at matinees. The matinee performances included some things from *Peter Pan*. When we got to Poughkeepsie, we found we were booked into a huge IBM auditorium. Peter Foy came to me and said, "Mary, this isn't a theater. It doesn't have an asbestos curtain. If you want to fly to the spotlight, I can arrange it."

That darling boy. I told him I'd love him forever if he could fix it. There was no time for rehearsal. Peter showed me the spot onstage where I should stand when the performance ended. He assured me that he would be up at the spotlight himself, to manage the ropes.

Did I fly that afternoon! I sailed over the heads of the children, clear across the auditorium, up to the spotlight. I don't know how far it was, but it was *far*. I didn't fly just once, but over and over again, sailing, up, up, and awaaaaay. The children went mad. They clapped and cried, stood on their seats, reached for my legs. "Peter, Peter," they screamed. "Take me with you, Peter."

They didn't want to go home, ever. If the truth were known, neither did I. No amount of crowing, no amount of fairy dust blown into the audience could persuade them to go. It became a full-scale riot. Somebody had to call the police, the fire department, I don't know what all, to clear the theater and to get people away from the entrance and out of the street. Once the children were coaxed outside the auditorium door, they had no intention of going any farther.

We in the cast, and the crew, absolutely had to get out of there because we were on a tour and we had to reach the next town. But for hours I didn't dare show my face outside. We all cowered in the basement until things quieted down enough so we could slip out, like thieves, and get into our cars and trucks to move on.

I have so many priceless memories of Peter Pan and his fans. There was the day Princess Grace of Monaco brought little Caroline backstage to meet me, and Caroline was so bashful she just stood, silent and big-eyed, looking up. The day in San Francisco when a tiny little girl, a darling little girl, got away from her parents in a theater box, which was within crawling distance of the stage, and suddenly appeared onstage. About 3 feet tall, all in white, with a straw hat on, and clutched in her hands a bouquet of flowers wrapped in lace.

Suddenly there she *was*. The audience had seen her, too. I stopped—I must have been onstage alone at that moment—and started toward her. She looked absolutely terrified, so I stopped. Everything stopped. There was such a silence, the quietest moment I've heard in a theater. I got down on my hands and knees then, and crawled across the stage toward her. She backed away, so then I backed off and she came toward me. It became like a ballet, back and forth, back and forth. It was clear that she longed, yearned, to touch Peter, but she didn't dare. Finally she came close enough to hold out the flowers, which were a little limp by then. Her tiny hand came out. I said, "Thank you, little one. May I pick you up?" She shook her head, but she didn't say a word. I did pick her up, and carried her back to her mother and father. They asked if they could come backstage after the show, and I said yes.

We started the show all over again . . . but the story goes on. Backstage that afternoon the little girl walked in, put her arms around my neck, and kissed me. When I asked what her name was, she didn't reply. She was deaf or autistic, and when she climbed out of that box and walked onto the stage it was the first thing she had ever done all by herself, with no direction. Such is the magic of *Peter Pan*. I still hear from her and her family; she has been to special schools and has learned to speak, to live in the world.

For her, for all the thousands of other children, I made a point of never getting out of my costume until they had all left the theater. So many of them came back, and it would have been too awful for them to see plain old Mary Martin standing in the dressing room, instead of Peter Pan.

We used to give them all fairy dust; we must have dispensed tons of it. We started out with tiny gold beads, but came down to little gold stars. We had them put up in plastic bags so the children could take them home. Some people still have them. They collected them, kept them; they waggle them at me at parties sometimes, to prove that they never forgot, never lost their fairy dust.

It never ends. Early in 1974, I was flying from Texas to California to begin my new life. A young soldier sat down beside me, in first class, but I was so tired I didn't even want to talk. The soldier started to read, and a man across the aisle who had been staring hard at me suddenly got up, leaned over us, and said in a loud whisper, "Tell him who you are."

I shook my head, but the man persisted. About three more times he came over to say, "Tell the boy. It would be awful for him not to know."

Finally lunch came and the soldier had to put down his book. I was just so curious about him I couldn't stand it, so I asked where he was stationed. He said somewhere down by the border in Texas. He was maybe nineteen or twenty, and he intended to be a career soldier like his father. He had just been out on some kind of survival course, with backpacks in the mountains, and he told me he had won an award for the man who had spent the longest time out there. He was on his way home for a leave with his family in Arizona, to show them his certificate and his emblem, his award. Then he asked me where I was going, and what I did. I said, "I've been a housewife, and I have a place in Brazil, and I've got children and grandchildren . . ."

"But that man over there keeps saying 'Tell,'" he said. "What do you do?"

I said that I had been in the theater, and on television.

"On television?" he said. He stared hard at me, for a long time, and then he said, "Are you . . . are you Peter Pan?"

Then he started ruffling around in his duffel bag, and he pulled out the emblem he had won and gave it to me.

"But you should take it to your mother," I protested.

"No," he said. "I'll give her the certificate. This, that I won, is for Peter Pan." I don't even know his name, but I cherish the emblem he gave me.

My favorite Peter Pan memory of all is of a darling old lady in the wilds of Brazil. Right after the 1960 television show,

Richard and I went back to the farm we had bought there some years before. Our *fazenda* was pretty far out in the jungle but we knew there were much more remote farms than ours, places where literally the snakes hung from the trees in the Amazon Valley. We had always wanted to see the interior, so when an American who had once been ambassador to Brazil asked us to pay him a visit, we were delighted. He sent the word to us through mutual friends because his farm had no telephone and there was no telegraph service. We were simply to come see him whenever we could.

Richard and I chose what seemed a likely weekend, made a date with the ex-ambassador's friend, George Homer, who had been in Brazil for years, and with Jibran, our best Brazilian friend. George had a Jeep station wagon, which was required for trips into the jungle. We all put on jungle clothes, packed some sandwiches and a chocolate cake I had baked, piled into the Jeep, and off we went. It was quite an expedition in those days. There were no real roads, no place to stop along the way. We started at four-thirty in the morning, to be sure we could get there, and find a refuge at the end of the trip. The jungle is not healthy at night.

We drove and drove, pushing through underbrush. Just before dark we arrived at a clearing and a marvelous house by a huge river. The relief, I cannot tell you. We had arrived. But the house was closed. Doors shut, window shutters shuttered. Richard, George, and Jibran got out and knocked, loud. No answer. Then they tramped around the house, looking for a sign of life. Nothing. Obviously the ex-ambassador was not home.

This was a dilemma because we absolutely could not drive all the way back to our house that night, and we could not camp out in the jungle.

I was sitting in the Jeep, looking at the closed house, when I thought I saw a shutter open, just a little, and behind it a small white figure. White face, white hair, white everything. I shouted, "Look, there's somebody in there!" and at that instant the shutter closed. The three men came back and I said, "I saw something, I know I did." I wasn't at all sure it wasn't a ghost, but the men suggested I go and knock on the door. If it was a ghost, maybe it would be less afraid of a lady than of three men. I climbed out, in my jungle pants and boots and short hair, and went over to knock lightly on the closed shutter of the window where I had seen the figure.

There was a pause, then the shutter opened again, very slowly. Behind it was the face I had seen, a lady's face. The lady looked at me for a moment and then she said, "Peter! You've come to my window."

I wondered if maybe it was all a dream, but I replied, "Yes, I have."

Then she said, "Peter, I didn't think you would ever come. Come in."

I stepped right through the open shutter, the open window, and there we were, face to face. She was very tiny, frail, and old. She said, "I have prayed for this, but I didn't think it would ever happen." Then she looked out at the Jeep and asked, "Have you friends with you?"

Solemnly, I replied, "Yes. I have a few Lost Boys out there."

"You must bring them in," she said. Then she ran for her front door. I climbed back out the window, went to the Jeep, told the three men that from this moment on they were Lost Boys and they were invited into the house—by the front door. My Boys were a little startled by all this, but they were very grave and polite when they walked in.

Our darling little old hostess was in her eighties. She was the sister of the former ambassador. Her brother was away on a trip, so she was alone in the house with only a thirteen-year-old Brazilian girl to help. She bustled around, getting rooms ready and saying to herself, "Peter and the Lost Boys are here. . . ."

It turned out that she had recently been in Washington, and the last thing she had seen on television was *Peter Pan*. Then she had left, gone straight to the jungle house to be with her brother, and the first human being she saw, except for the little Brazilian girl, was what she believed to be Peter Pan, standing outside her window in boy's clothing.

As I was washing up for dinner she came to my room.

"Peter, I have a surprise for you which you won't believe," she said. She led me off to her own quarters, then into her bathroom, and—she was right, I didn't believe—there was a crocodile in her bathtub. It wasn't a very big one, and she apologized because it didn't have an alarm clock in its stomach. But she said, "Peter, there's your friend."

The little Brazilian girl cooked us all a marvelous dinner. After we had eaten I decided it was time to produce my chocolate cake.

"Now I have a surprise for you," I said, and I brought it out. That darling lady burst into tears.

"How did you know?" she asked. "How on earth did you know that it was my birthday?"

The Lost Boys and I were all in shock by this time, so all I could think of to reply was, "In Never Land, you just know. . . ."

Next morning we left, without ever meeting her brother. It was a long trip. None of us knew if we would ever return again to the house by the rushing river in the depths of the jungle. The last time I saw the little old lady she was standing with her hand in the air, waving, and calling out, "You'll come back next spring, Peter?"

I have been back each spring, in spirit and in my heart. I will go back that way forever, each springtime.

XVII
Which Led—Among Other Miracles—to the Lunts

I must have some of the instincts of a gypsy, or of a carnival pitchlady, because I have always adored taking a show on the road. It's a hard life, but rewarding: I love the changing scenery of the vast countryside, discovering cities I never knew before, the challenge of facing new audiences.

My first experience, though it certainly couldn't be called "taking a show on the road," was a publicity tour for my first movie, *The Great Victor Herbert,* in 1939. Allan Jones and I made personal appearances wherever the picture was showing, starting with the Paramount in New York City. We did seven "shows" a day, sometimes starting at 7 A.M. and ending after midnight. Eventually we made our way to Texas, where we must have played every town over pop. 20,000 in the whole state.

On New Year's Eve we were in Fort Worth. It was pretty exciting being a mild celebrity in my home state, but the real thrill was that Alfred Lunt and Lynn Fontanne were there, too, on the road with *The Taming of the Shrew.* They had planned a company party at their hotel, and asked if I would come. Would I! I even had the nerve to ask if I could bring Sister, and my accompanist, Ray Sinatra. They said yes. The Lunts' curtain, because they were legitimate theater, rang down long before I was released from my movie duties. By the time Sister and I got to the party it was in full swing.

I never had seen such a glamorous affair. They had taken

With my idols, Alfred Lunt and Lynn Fontanne,
in Fort Worth, Texas, New Year's Eve, 1939.

over a hotel ballroom, an orchestra was playing, and there were
balloons and streamers hanging from the ceiling. The Lunts—
who were always the most glamorous stars to behold—were
sitting in the middle of a table as long as the room, being
toasted in champagne by their huge company. When they saw
our entrance Miss Fontanne with one regal nod of her white-
turbaned head started the orchestra playing "My Heart Belongs to
Daddy."

Sister and I were bug-eyed and bewitched from that moment until we floated home at dawn. We danced with the entire
company—Sydney Greenstreet, Dicky Whorf, midgets, blacks
. . . Cinderella never had a better ball.

Everybody in the cast did an impromptu act or stunt, and
all of a sudden Miss Fontanne rose and said, "Now I'm going to
ask Miss Martin to sing my favorite song, 'Battle Hymn of the
Republic.' "

"Sing the what?" I asked. "The what? What?" When she
repeated, I had to confess that though I would dearly love to

sing it for her, I didn't know the words. She looked disappointed, and I added quickly, "But I would like to sing you a song from your country, if you don't mind." I had already planned to sing it for her because it's one of my favorites. I had rehearsed it with Ray, who was a marvelous conductor and accompanist; we made many albums together. It was a swinging version of the "Tit-willow" song from *The Mikado*. Ray began the accompaniment and I started in my high soprano, singing the song as Gilbert and Sullivan wrote it. In the middle I swung it, as I had done with "Il Bacio." It brought the house down.

It was Lynn and Alfred who first explained to me the importance of the road. "If you intend to make the theater your life, you must tour," they said. "You build your career, get the experience, create your own audiences, on the road." They were the perfect example of the proof of this, and I decided then and there that if the royal family of the American theater could stand the rigors of the road, so could I. They later became dear, close friends. Alfred had grown up in Genesee Depot, Wisconsin, and both he and Lynn loved the old family farm there. They retreated to it as often as they could, and whenever I played Minneapolis they would drive for hours, sometimes through sleet or snow or whatever, twenty degrees below zero sometimes, to pick up Richard and me and take us home to the farm with them for a weekend. I always thought—hoped, I guess—that in their minds Richard and I had the same kind of lovely relationship that they had together.

My first real tour was in 1945, when John Boles, Jimmy Sheridan, the whole company, and I took *One Touch of Venus* off Broadway and across the country. Richard and I left Heller and Larry in the New York apartment with Mammy, and set forth to "see America first." I still have the diary I kept on that first tour, and pretty naïve it is, too. I labeled it rather grandly "Venus Uncovers America (Our First Road Tour)," signed it, and dated it Sunday, March 11, 1945. Actually it was February 11; I always seem to be a month ahead of myself. The first entry reads, "Left Penn. station—had a compartment—it was fun, a little sad—and exciting."

Next day was opening night in Philadelphia, and in my diary I complained about butterflies in my stomach. Tuesday,

February 13, my diary says, "Thirteen is definitely my lucky number—the reviews were out of this world. The critics were so *good* to us—Richard wrote Larry that 'Mom made a *100*.'"

Little did I know then what luxury that compartment was, on the short trip from New York to Philadelphia. It was still wartime, trains were crowded and sometimes unpredictable, and just getting physically from one place to another, with all those people, was a problem. Occasionally we could get a compartment; often we settled for an upper and lower berth and Richard would climb gallantly up the ladder to the upper. I don't recall that we ever actually had to sit up all night, but it seemed to me that wherever we were going we managed to get there in the middle of the night. Often the mayor, the Boy Scouts, the Girl Scouts, the town band were waiting to greet us—all of them, poor things, absolutely exhausted and half asleep before our train pulled in. When it did, they burst into smiles and music. Once I stumbled out and told everybody how happy I was to be in Utah. Then Richard gave me a big poke in my back and I said, "I mean *Omaha*."

There were seldom any porters around, so after the official welcome we would gather up our bags and struggle off to a hotel, hoping for a little sleep before the next performance.

When we played Detroit, we ended up in the same hotel with Grace Moore, the opera singer, who was also on tour. I had met her once, and I knew she, too, was from the south, was a former Ward Belmont girl, and our birthdays were only five days apart, in December. But I was pretty impressed to find myself on the same floor with her. She had the presidential suite, complete with a grand piano. I never had seen a piano in a hotel suite before. One night she invited us to an after-show party in her suite, champagne and all. As usual, because we're all such big hams, everybody had to perform. I had the nerve to sing "One Fine Day" from *Madame Butterfly,* not knowing that it was one of Grace Moore's best arias.

I think it was in Detroit that John Boles taught me a marvelous secret about how to remove hair dye. He was forever dyeing his own hair, and it often came out a crazy sort of reddish-brown color. One day he appeared at our door to ask if I had any Bon Ami.

"Why?" I asked him.

"I've got too much dye on my hair, and I always take it off with Bon Ami," he said.

I hunted around and strangely enough there was a cake of Bon Ami in the bathroom. He just wet it and rubbed it on his hair, and off came the dye. For years afterward if I got the wrong color and didn't like it, I just rubbed a cake of Bon Ami all over my hair and presto chango, it all came out—the dye, not my hair. Believe it or not!

Everybody gets very buddy-buddy on the road, that's one of the joys. Somewhere along the line—I think that was in Detroit, too—we met Zasu Pitts, one of the greatest ladies I ever knew. Years earlier I had learned to imitate her famous fluttery hands, her squeaky voice, from watching her pictures at the Palace in Weatherford. Now I discovered how much talent she really had. That amazing woman could carry on a conversation on the telephone, entertain five or six people in her room, and at the same time make hot biscuits with crisp bacon on an electric grill in her bathroom. The grill was in there because cooking was against the rules and she had to keep the smell from getting into the hall. Fortunately she liked a shower because she could never use the bathtub—it was full of grills.

Our stage crew accomplished miracles on the road, getting the props and sets and "business" set up in city after city, in strange theaters, often with inexperienced local help. I remember only one big snafu, but that one was a beauty. My entrance in *One Touch of Venus* was on a turntable sort of thing. There was a statue of Venus in front, facing the audience. I climbed on the back, out of sight. Then when the big music and light cue came, a stagehand pulled hard on a rope, the turntable swung around, and the statue magically "came to life" as I appeared.

One night on tour, I don't even remember which city, I was standing on the turntable ready to go—and the man didn't pull the rope. The musical cue had come, and nothing happened. I whispered at him, "Hey, I'm not out there."

"Yes, you are," he whispered right back. "I can see you out there."

"But I'm not there. You'll have to take my word for it, I'm right back here with you."

The man was drunk, absolutely pie-eyed. Meanwhile the musicians, who knew something was wrong, kept playing, tre-

molo, tremolo, the lights went down again, the cue came again—
and the man suddenly pulled so hard on the rope that I went
zooming clear around, full circle, and there I was, backstage
again. It all happened so fast the audience didn't even see me going around. This happened about three times. Finally, on about
the fifth cue, the orchestra kept going and the lights came up
and there I was, half on and half off: I was on one side of the
turntable and the statue, perfectly visible to the audience, was
on the other side. Neither of us was clearly on or off stage, so
the magic of the statue coming to life didn't quite work. The
poor guy was fired that night and I was sorry. He had been with
us for ages and he never had made a mistake before.

I grew to love many of the familiar tour cities—Dallas, San
Francisco, Los Angeles, which nowadays is as big a theater town
as New York. Chicago, too, is a special place in spite of the enormous Chicago Opera House, where I played the first time I was
in Chicago. It is about seven stories high and so big you can't
see the end of it from the stage. When we played *Venus* there I
weighed about 108 pounds and the reviewer for the Chicago
Tribune, Ashton Stevens, wrote that I was "the most delightful
exclamation point" he had ever seen. That's what I looked like
to him in that vast place. Every time we said a line we could hear
an echo coming back from far away, and about three lines later
we heard the laugh that was supposed to come right after the first
line. We were playing Chicago the night President Roosevelt
died. I can still feel the shock, the silence, the sense of loss which
filled even that huge hall.

It was also in Chicago that we discovered I was pregnant.
Richard and I were thrilled. Heller was three years old and we
both wanted another baby very much. As usual, I was violently
ill during the first weeks and months, so the tour became even
more difficult. I would manage to get through one act, being
delicate and ethereal, then rush to my dressing room to lose my
last meal, and go back on again for the next act. Finally we decided we would have to stop, in Cincinnati. We took the train
to Huntington, West Virginia, where Mammy and Heller had
gone for a visit with Mammy's sister. Just the day before we
arrived, Heller was bitten badly—in the face—by a jealous family
dog. Everyone assured us that she would be all right, but the
sight of that beautiful little mouth all swollen, stitched, almost

did us both in. It was the last straw on top of my illness and the fatigue of the tour. We headed back to New York and to the Fifth Avenue apartment.

Within a few days Heller was better, I felt better, and Richard decided it would do us good to go out for one of our rather rare public appearances. Myrna Loy, who was an old friend, was very active in the Red Cross during the war. She had helped organize a huge benefit rally at the Astor Hotel, and invited us. I didn't have to perform; we were just to sit at her table, lend our names. It seemed a good idea. Richard had bought me a beautiful new broadtail coat, which Larry always called my "oxtail." I was longing to wear it, so I got dolled up and off we went.

Richard and William Dozier, who was then a literary agent but who later became a major producer, and I were sitting at the table when suddenly I felt a terrible thing beginning to happen. I whispered to Richard that I had to get out, quickly. I got up from the table but made it only as far as a huge American flag, standing against the wall behind our table. I began to lose the baby right there, behind the flag, during a patriotic song.

Richard and Bill jumped up and made a saddle seat with their hands to carry me out, through the kitchen and the fire escape. Then, while Bill stayed with me, Richard rushed off to find the manager and tell him we had to have a room, immediately, so doctors could be called to take care of me.

The manager said no. It was incredible. He said something like "She might die here, and we don't want the publicity." At this point something had to be arranged in a hurry. The men got to Myrna Loy, who dashed out of the Astor in her Red Cross uniform and drove me in her ambulance to New York Hospital. There all the rest happened.

After I lost the baby I had transfusions and everything else, and the doctors put me to sleep for the night. Richard and the doctors left because there was nothing more they could do. The resident doctor on the floor was a young man named Dr. William P. Given. I owe my life to him. He decided to look in on me one more time, late that night, and found me in a coma. Not much was known about Rh-negative blood then and hospitals didn't have a lot of it around. Dr. Given went running out to find some, only to discover that there was very little left. In the

alarm somebody even telephoned Ed Sullivan to put in his newspaper column that Mary Martin needed blood. By morning there
was a queue half down the block—men, women, children, lined
up to help me. Bless those generous donors. Through the years
since I've met people on the street who say, "Hey, you're Mary
Martin. I saved your life . . . I gave blood."

I thank them, from my heart, but I know who really saved
my life—Dr. Given. The doctors told me then that I could never
carry a baby to the end. We were never to have the little boy we
longed for and lost.

I did go on the road again, every chance I got. Our national company of *Annie Get Your Gun* played on the road, and
almost ten years later, in 1965, we did *Hello Dolly!* across the
United States and halfway around the world. My latest tour—I
won't say "last" because I shall tour again, someday—was with
Robert Preston in *I Do! I Do!* in 1968.

I always had a little trouble with geography but I did get
a firm grip on Omaha the second time around—that's where
Heller lost her first tooth, during *Annie*. And I remember Des
Moines, Iowa, because I had a friend there from Ward Belmont,
Gloria Means. We always called her "Squirrely," I don't remem-
ber why, but being greeted backstage by Squirrely Means was
one of the joys of the road. Once I walked on a stage in Kansas
City, Missouri, and told the audience how happy I was to be in
Kansas. This remark was followed by a deathly hush. During in-
termission Richard explained what a terrible thing I'd done—
mixing up Missouri and Kansas was as bad as confusing Fort
Worth and Dallas. I tried to make up for my *faux pas* later, when
I was singing "Wonderful Guy," by slipping in a line about "I'm
as corny as Kansas City MISSOURI in August."

My favorite tour of all was a musical doubleheader called
Music with Mary Martin and *Magic with Mary Martin*, in 1958
and 1959. We were making arrangements to do *The Sound of
Music* but it would be a year before everything was ready and I
didn't want to sit around for a whole year. I also had always
longed to do a series of really, literally, one-night stands. Richard
got in touch with Columbia Artists Management, Inc., to set it up.
We played eighty-seven cities in eighty-seven nights, opening in
Alaska and closing in New Haven—where most shows open. And

then finished it off by performing both shows live, back to back, on television on Easter Sunday, 1959.

Music with Mary Martin was an evening show, with a thirty-piece orchestra directed by Johnny Lesko, a marvelous ballet dancer named Dirk Sanders, whom we had seen perform with the lovely Jeanmaire, in her husband Roland Petit's ballet, and Luiz Bonfa, a Brazilian guitarist whom we had discovered at a party. All were fabulous. Luiz had a problem because he was a foreigner and not a member of the American Federation of Musicians. Richard got on the telephone to the head of the union, James Petrillo, in Chicago. He had never met Mr. Petrillo but he must have been persuasive, because Luiz Bonfa got into the union and onto the tour. Luiz is now famous as both soloist and composer.

Our afternoon show, designed especially for children, led off with the charming *Three to Make Music,* a short revue with a clown—Dirk Sanders—and audience participation. Dick and Dorothy Rodgers' talented daughters, Mary and Linda, had written it for Thomas Scherman and The Little Orchestra, based on an idea by Roger Englander. We heard it at a run-through session for The Little Orchestra's children concerts, and knew we had to have it for the tour. Then we had selections from *Cinderella,* a version Mary Rodgers had written with music by Dick and Oscar for a television musical; some jazzed-up Disney songs; and of course selections—including flying—from *Peter Pan.*

Our opening in Alaska was quite a production. We had been asked to take the show there first, for the USO, and the Army took charge of flying the whole thing, orchestra, cast, tons of equipment, all of us. We did thirteen shows in nine days, at eleven army, air force, and naval installations. We finished in Nome, I remember, but there was a whole group of soldiers off above the Arctic Circle whom we couldn't get to because of fog, bad weather. The military arranged for us to do part of our show for them via shortwave radio. The only piano we could find in Nome was in the cellar of a waterfront saloon. The cellar was so small that only Richard, Johnny Lesko, a bass fiddler, and a guitar player could get into it. We all went over, dressed in ski pants and boots, and I sang my numbers into a funny, big, round, old-fashioned microphone.

One of the numbers I did was "Daddy," which I had first

sung to some make-believe Eskimos. That day in Nome, right in the middle of "Daddy," a real Eskimo, wearing a parka, walked into the cellar of the saloon. I was thrilled—now I could sing my song to a real one at last. I looked right at him, gave it everything I had. When I finished he gave a big loud "Uggghhhhh" and walked out.

Then the Army flew us back south again, and we were on our own. Johnny, Dirk, Luiz, Peter Foy and his flying crew, the orchestra traveled from city to city by chartered bus. Richard and I traveled grandly in our first Rolls-Royce, which Richard had bought in London. Right with us, every mile of the way, went the two people who made our lives possible—Nena Smith and Ernest Adams. Nena is a beautiful Mexican-born lady whose profession is wigmaker. She was working for Max Factor, among others, when I was lucky enough to meet her during *Annie Get Your Gun*. She made all my wigs for that show and has been with me ever since as hair stylist, wardrobe mistress, adviser, friend— everything. She went everywhere with me, all over the world. Now

I met my darling Nena Smith in *Annie Get Your Gun,* and we have been together ever since.

she and her husband, Kirby, and I all live in the desert in California, and both of them still knock themselves out doing kind things for me.

Ernest was as special as Nena. He had spent half of his life with Adela Rogers St. Johns, helped raise all her children, then went to the Lunts, finally came to us. We were lucky to get him. Lynn and Alfred had given him at least seven letters of recommendation, and he auditioned every single one of his possible future employers, personally and at length. He refused to take a job until he had been clear through the Lunts' list. Bless the fates, Richard and I won, and Ernest was with us for the rest of our lives together, everywhere.

On *the* tour Nena took charge of all my wigs, costumes, props. Ernest was chauffeur, caterer, guardian angel. After each night's performance Nena packed my things while I changed. Then we'd dash for the Rolls, climb in, and awaaaaay through the night. Ernest always made cocktails and hors d'oeuvres ahead of time. Richard and I rode in the back, Nena and Ernest in the front, handing back drinks and goodies.

Not the least of Ernest's virtues was his culinary ability. He made the best fried chicken in the world. He fried it during the daytime, in our motels—we found them the most practical places to stay—or if we were in a town where he had relatives he would go to their homes to prepare it. After our cocktails we had fried chicken, potato salad, deviled eggs . . . oh, I can taste it all now. We hardly ever got to our next engagement city until about four, five o'clock in the morning. I'd go straight to bed and stay there until it was time to get ready for the next performance. No wonder I sometimes got my geography confused.

If I thought we had split-second timing on the Ford show with Ethel, it was nothing compared to that concert tour. I sang a medley of show tunes, then a sort of nightclub selection, and ended up with one song each, in costume, from six of my shows. We started with "Daddy," for which I wore the fur coat and cap. No striptease, though. There wasn't time. Under the coat I had leotards which I wore throughout the whole act; they looked like my skin. For "Daddy" I put on a pink chiffon teddy over my leotards so I could flap the coat open and shut and show the pink chiffon at the end of the number. After "Daddy" I changed quickly into the beautiful pink lace negligee Mainbocher had made for *Venus,* and sang "That's Him." Next, Chinese robes and a black wig for "Mountain High, Valley Low" from *Lute Song.* And so on through *Annie* and *Peter Pan* and *South Pacific,* for which I rushed onstage in Nellie Forbush shorts, carrying my little straw hat. The hat got to be famous. It went through I don't know how many versions and was auctioned off umpteen times as a collector's item. The real one I gave to Sister; she has the original Nellie straw today in Forth Worth.

All these changes had to be timed to a second, because before the applause for one number was finished I had to be ready to go back out for the next one. I never could have done it without Nena, who stood in the wings with all the changes, all the props. I would rush off, she'd snatch off one outfit and put me into another, plop a wig on my head, and back I'd go. How she managed to keep track of everything I will never know. She never dropped the *Annie* rifle, never misplaced the straw hat. We only missed once. Somehow I got into my entire *Lute Song* costume, wig and all, when we heard the introduction music for *Annie.* Neither has ever known just how it happened, but there was quite a flurry of arms, hands, wigs, costumes for a while. By some miracle I made my entrance on time—just before Nena and I both had a heart attack.

Matinee performances, the children's show, were even wilder, if possible. Peter Foy was on hand to supervise *Peter Pan* with a crew and flying equipment from Kirby's Flying Ballet. They had to precede us into each new town, look over the theater, rig up the flying wires, test them, be ready to go. It was on that tour that I flew clear across the IBM auditorium in Poughkeepsie. It was also on that tour that the bloody chest mike played tricks on me. We were in Philadelphia and I was sailing around, flying, singing like crazy, when all of a sudden I started picking up all sorts of train calls about "track two" and "track five." I thought I had finally gone completely balmy, but it turned out the theater was right over an underground station and some trick of the wavelength was bringing the dispatcher's announcements straight into my microphone.

A quite special problem arose when we played Atlanta, Georgia. This was before the whole black-white situation had been confronted reasonably. I refused to perform in any theater which was restricted. Partly to avoid that embarrassment, partly because we needed as big a house as we could find, the concert management reopened a theater that had been closed, locked up tight, for about thirty-five years. Peter and his crew set up; we opened on time to a full house.

I sang my Disney songs, did *Cinderella,* and got into the harness for *Peter Pan.* The music started up and I went, up, up, sixty feet into the darkness of those dusty old wings. I flew and flew and flew and there was the usual pandemonium from the audience.

Then it was over. I walked down to the footlights to blow fairy dust and I suddenly noticed that people were not just applauding, they were screaming with laughter, falling out of their seats, some of them pointing. I couldn't imagine what was so funny. After the bows I went off to the wings and there was Nena.

"What on earth happened?" I asked, but even she couldn't answer because she was laughing so hard.

When she got her breath she handed me a mirror and said, "Look at yourself. Just look at you."

I had gone up into the wings perfectly white, and I came down black as soot from all the dirt of thirty years up in the wings of that old theater. It couldn't have happened in a funnier place. *Peter Pan* integrated Atlanta in one fell swoop, on one afternoon.

XVIII
"I would like to renew my subscription."

If nobody writes it there's nothing to play;
If nobody plays it there's nothing to hear;
If nobody hears it it's plainer than day,
You just haven't got music, now isn't it clear
It takes three to make music?

Those lovely, thoughtful words come from Mary and Linda's *Three to Make Music*. I love them because they describe so beautifully the third member of the musical trio—those blessed audiences. Live audiences give to performers; they contribute far more to a show than they have any idea. Long before one hears them, one can feel them, from the dressing rooms. Their very presence starts a kind of electricity, a chemistry which comes from the give-and-take of every single performance.

No actor or actress should ever forget that the audience really *is* on our side. They are out there because they hope the show is going to be good and that they'll enjoy it. Why else would they plunk down all that money, make plans for weeks or months in advance, hire baby-sitters, come by car, bus, train, or plane, stand in line—if they didn't want to see the show?

Then when they really love it the wave of affection, of joy, that sweeps across the stage is like a glimpse of heaven with Gabriel blowing a hundred trumpets.

I remember the first time I faced an audience as a professional. It was the opening night tryout of *Leave It to Me* in New

Haven. A very wise and loving friend, Val d'Auvray, who had come from Hollywood to give me courage, asked if I was nervous. I said I really didn't know, and he gave me some wonderful advice.

"You are new and people will be curious about you. They're coming here with anticipation. They are excited, and you are excited about your first big chance. Never, never in all your life, go onstage without thinking, 'They're going to love this, because I am loving doing it.'"

I have never stopped loving doing it, and from the moment I heard Val's words I have felt that I had an ironclad contract with every member of every audience to work as hard as I could, play to the very top of my ability in every performance. Val, Irene and Doc, Mildred, all the other people who had believed in me while I was learning in Hollywood were in my thoughts as I made that first entrance—and I wasn't afraid. I couldn't wait to meet the audience. They didn't let me down, and I would never let them down if I could possibly help it. The tradition of "the show must go on" is the strongest in the theater.

I learned, of course, about the different kinds of audiences. Matinee ladies, in those days at least, were less receptive to risqué lines than, say, the Saturday-night crowd. There was a funny line in *One Touch of Venus* which I was nervous about saying and wanted to cut out. Cheryl Crawford rightly insisted that I try it. It was "Love isn't the dying moan of a distant violin; it's the triumphant twang of a bedspring." I finally said it on first matinee day, but I blurted it out as fast as I could and exited at top speed. Some ladies really didn't like it. At the evening performance I said it properly and got a howl—and this prissy lady MM loved the laugh and began to learn more about being a ham.

Then there are the benefit audiences. The ones we all look forward to are those for the Actors' Fund, which supports retired or disabled actors who need help. Each show does one actors' benefit each year of the run, and always does it on Sunday nights so other actors can come, if they want to, on their night off. The theater is full of professionals, other performers, who sit there wanting to see you at your best. Everyone onstage wants to be at his best. The electricity from an actors' benefit could light all New York.

Quite another thing are the benefits which have been bought up by some organization, usually months in advance. I have felt sorry for them. They've probably paid a hundred dollars a seat. Most likely they've gone to dinner parties before the show, with cocktails and wine, and they would really prefer to be home in their comfortable beds. Some of the men have been pressured into coming by the wives in the first place. They don't, deliberately, just sit out there and die. They simply can't help it. Sometimes I have wished that they would send their checks to the organization and then come to see the show the next night.

Somebody told me that once Zero Mostel got so mad at a sleepy audience in *A Funny Thing Happened on the Way to the Forum* that he stopped everything, went down to the footlights, and said to the people, "We're having a ball up here onstage, why don't you all come to the party?"

Henry Fonda once got so annoyed while playing *Mister Roberts* that he went down and stuck his tongue out at them. I would love to have seen that. I bet it woke them up. Once I went to another extreme: I lowered my voice almost to a whisper so everybody had to lean forward to hear what on earth I was saying.

It's a funny thing, even backstage you can kind of feel if it's going to be that kind of audience. Everybody says, "Okay, we've got one. Let's go out there and get them." I take it as a challenge. By golly, who's going to win—them or me? But on the whole they're not that bad. The only problem nowadays is that benefits often come lumped together before the big opening night, and the cast loses perspective on the show; the timing goes awry. But again, that's show biz, and if it weren't for those sold-out benefits many shows with today's exorbitant costs would never make it. The benefits saved us in *Jennie*.

Audiences on the road are special. In the first place, cities that don't have permanent, continuing theater greet a touring company as an event. The people pour in so eagerly to see something they've read about, somebody they've heard about. They are just aching to be entertained, and nobody could fail to respond. My diary from 1945, written on my first tour, has an entry which says, "House was jam-packed, and the audience so *giving*—so naturally *gave* back—what fun fun, to be a 'good ham.'" That was gushy of me, but theater is still an event for me, too.

Audiences abroad are not much different from American ones—if they can understand the words and the references. The French certainly had some trouble with *The Skin of Our Teeth*, even in simultaneous translation; and a lot of the first scenes of *Hello Dolly!* failed to receive laughter in London, because all of Dolly's scheming in dollars and cents was baffling to those who couldn't translate quickly from pounds and pence. Unless you knew exactly how much money Dolly was talking about, it wasn't funny. Military audiences, especially in war zones, just get so excited at seeing anything at all that they scream and yell the whole time. That never bothered me. If our mere presence, the costumes, the music delighted them that much I couldn't care less if they drowned out every word.

Japanese audiences are polite and warm. They make a kind of soft sound of approval which Richard once described as "like the steady glow from the fireplace after the fire has settled down and is ready to keep you happy and warm for the rest of the evening." Totally unlike the unfettered responses of a British audience. Dick Rodgers once said that the roar which came from the British on opening night of *South Pacific* was the same sound he had heard once in Yankee Stadium when Babe Ruth hit his umpty-umpth home run.

I love the London audiences. Sometimes I think they're the most exciting anywhere because they seem to want to see theater more. Especially the people in the gallery, who line up for hours for seats which are never sold until the day of the performance. We have nothing like it in the United States. London's Gallery First Nighters have even formed an organization among themselves. It is a great honor to belong to the First Nighters, and an honor to be honored by them. Bless them, they honored me twice, in *South Pacific,* and almost fifteen years later, in 1965, in *Dolly*—the biggest dinner parties you ever saw.

They are also highly vocal. They do things people would never do in the United States. If they don't like the show they holler, just yell right back at the stage. It never happened to me, thank heaven, but it happened to Noël, he told me. They would just scream "No!" if not more specific insults. If they do like it, they're just as noisy. On my closing night at the Drury Lane they yelled, "Mary, Mary, come back." They're just more demonstrative than Americans, in both directions.

Performance anywhere away from "home," or playing in anything that runs for months and months, presents a special problem: timing. There are always some gags, some songs, which go the same way each time and get a huge laugh or loud applause. Some others are a bit more tricky. For those you must sense the audience a bit, speed up or slow down so you don't lose them. Timing is the most important thing; it is the key to a successful performance. Anyone who wants to be an actor and isn't blessed with an innate sense of timing might as well forget it. It's rhythm, sense of when, at what pace. There isn't time to think about it; it must be instinctive.

I am so possessed by this idea that I used to call for rehearsals after a few months in a show just to get back the tuning, the fine timing. Shows tend to get a little longer and a little longer as the actors add a bit of business here, or begin to drag out something there. Josh Logan, Vinnie Donehue, Gower Champion were all directors who insisted on rehearsals themselves, upon redirecting the show every now and again. Some directors don't do this. They direct it, set it, then leave for other commitments. This is not good. A director's mind is the instrument needed to keep a show sharp.

Josh used to call regular rehearsals and announce firmly, "Now, we're going to take out all the 'improvements.'"

We all needed it. It was like renewal. The performance after one of those in-performance rehearsals is always brilliant. It brings back all the luster, because everybody is thinking again.

In the early days I don't remember that I had any nerves at all. I just loved it all so, couldn't wait to get out there. Later on, as I became more and more aware of my responsibility, I began to get sort of sick, and depressed, as curtain time came on. I was very calm, but sort of sad. I yawned a lot. Not from boredom. It must have been lack of oxygen, or something; I wasn't taking big deep breaths because I was numb. Then, the moment I started to make up, I stopped yawning and came to life. And how. The adrenaline would start to pump and off I'd go. I have already written about falling into orchestra pits, banging into walls, hurting myself, but at the time I truly never felt it. Richard used to say he had to tell me when I was sick, because I never noticed.

The point is, I don't think any audience should ever be aware of any problem either onstage or backstage. That's not what they paid to see. They came to be entertained, for an escape from their problems. They should never be burdened with the actors' problems, on the stage or off. I can't stand people who ad-lib or break up onstage. That isn't what the audience came to see either.

So if you are hurt, they shouldn't ever know about it. If it happens right before their very eyes, then one must reassure them that everything is really quite all right, nothing's wrong.

I must have transmitted this to Heller in her cradle, because the first time she went on with me in *Annie,* she was a trouper at age five. Just about her best friend in the world, on that tour, was a boy by the name of Charles Taylor, who played her brother, Little Jake. He was a year or so older than Heller, and the two were inseparable. Of course, they got into fights now and again; Little Jake gave her her first black eye in Richmond, Virginia. I never found out what she did to him to deserve that.

Then, in San Francisco, Heller and Little Jake and the other children who played Annie's sisters and brothers came onstage with their cart one night and I noticed that Heller wasn't looking at me. She was looking away, back into the wings. Finally she had to say a line to me. She turned around and I saw huge tears running down her face. She said her line, sang her part of the song clear as a bell, then turned away again, and I could see sobs shaking her little shoulders. I thought, "Dear God, she's sick, she has appendicitis, she's dying right here on this stage."

At the end of the act I rushed down to the children's dressing room. Heller and Charles Taylor's mother, a wonderful woman who supervised the children, assured me it was nothing, it was all over, nothing to worry about. Not until late that night did Mrs. Taylor and I find out what had happened. Heller's nanny discovered one part of the story when she gave Heller her bath; Little Jake's mother heard the rest of it as Jake said his prayers. They had been scuffling in the wings, Little Jake got mad, and he bit Heller on the shoulder. It begins to sound as if Heller spent her life being bitten, by dogs or best friends, but honestly there was only one bite each. She recovered from this one, too, and a very contrite Little Jake turned up next day with a bouquet of forget-me-nots which he had bought with his own money, for Heller.

And what was the song both those little troupers had sung onstage, through tears and regrets and childish outrage? "Doin' What Comes Natur'lly."

My first line, on my first stage, in my first show, to my first audience, was that ringing "I'd like to renew my subscription," in *Leave It to Me.*

The first night I said it in New Haven the audience, and especially the Yale boys in the boxes, laughed so hard that I stopped dead and looked down at the floor, all around me to see if anything had fallen off. Nothing had. They were laughing at my line—mainly because of what had already been said onstage before my entrance. I have seldom been so grateful in my entire life: my underpants were still on, and the audience liked me.

Thirty-four years later I got to say it again. The occasion was Richard Rodgers' seventieth birthday party, a grand and sentimental Broadway tribute in the spring of 1972. Richard and I were living happily in Brazil. I hadn't appeared on Broadway for four years. But Dick Rodgers, who wrote so many of the wonderful melodies it has been my privilege to sing, was a special, very special person in our lives. I can never say in words what Dick and Dorothy have meant in our lives. They have always been there when we needed them most. We flew back to New York for his birthday.

Long before we left our farm I had decided what I would sing to Dick, but I hadn't made up my mind what to say. Then,

It was *always* kiss, kiss, kiss with Richard Rodgers. I'm a kisser!

as I made my entrance on the stage of the Imperial Theatre, where I had played *Leave It to Me* all those years before, the right words came. I walked out and said, as loudly as I could, "I would like to renew my subscription."

That's what I would like to say, now and forever, to all the audiences everywhere.

To Maria von Trapp

XIX
The Austrian and
Texas Marias

If there was ever a triumph of audience over critics, it was *The Sound of Music*. I played in this wonderful show for more than two years, from 1959 almost into 1962. It is still playing, somewhere in the world, and it will still be playing long after everybody who worked on the original version has vanished from the earth.

From beginning to end, and all over the world—the United States, Australia, England, wherever it played—most of the critics and the intellectuals in the audience found it impossibly sweet. Some of them absolutely loathed it. But audiences loved it. No matter how critical the reviews were, they didn't keep the people out—they pulled them in.

I must admit that I agreed with the audiences rather than the critics. I adored the show. I believed in it so much that I was the principal investor in the original production. When it became such a hit, such a gold mine for us all, I had to sell my shares as capital gain. Otherwise I would have had to pay so many taxes I couldn't afford to keep playing in it.

Not that it was an easy part. Even I knew that it required perfect pitch—and I'm not talking about music now. The treatment had to be very skillful, totally controlled. It was one of the most disciplined shows I ever did. You could never do a kidding thing, never play it broadly. I had to remember the character always, keep a tight rein on my emotions and my performance.

It seems improbable that there is any living soul who

doesn't know the story of *The Sound of Music,* but in case there are a few, it was about a very lively young Catholic postulant in Austria who was sent to be governess to the seven children of a widower, Captain von Trapp. The postulant fell in love first with the children, then with the captain. She left the abbey to marry him, and in a dramatic finale the whole family climbed over the Alps to escape from Nazi invaders of Austria just before the Second World War.

It is a true story. The real live protagonists made their way to the United States, became famous as the Trapp Family Singers, and the former postulant, Maria, Baroness von Trapp, wrote a book about their experiences.

By 1956 the book had been made into a German motion picture which was an enormous hit in Europe and South America. Someone at Paramount in Hollywood decided it would also be a hit in English. They asked Vincent Donehue to direct an American version. Vinnie, who had been searching for a good property for "us" ever since *The Skin of Our Teeth,* loved the film so much that he arranged to have a print flown to New York so Richard and I could see it. We got so excited that we called Vinnie to say we wanted to do it—not as a film, but as a show. Then Richard contacted our theatrical lawyer, William Fitelson in New York, and off we went on the long, treacherous road of putting a show together. Bill Fitelson had been our theatrical legal wizard ever since *Venus.* He is something of a genius. Besides that, he represented not only us but also Leland Hayward, Vinnie, and I don't know who all. He was in a perfect position to get it all together.

Richard wanted to co-produce with Leland Hayward, and we all knew that Vinnie must direct it. He had the perfect sensitive touch for a show like this. Lindsay and Crouse would do the libretto, the book of the show, with all the dialogue. Everybody wanted Dick Rodgers and Oscar Hammerstein to do the music.

Oliver Smith was chosen to do the sets. Mainbocher would do my clothes; the talented Lucinda Ballard would design the other costumes and also my last one, the dirndl I wore when I sang in Austrian costume with the captain and the children. Joe Layton, whom I had first met on the road in the concert tour, choreographed "Do-Re-Mi" and some other numbers.

Mainbocher's beautiful bridal gown
for *The Sound of Music.*

All negotiations, all of the decisions, were difficult and time-consuming. Leland Hayward and Bill Fitelson made umpteen trips from New York to Germany to work out property rights and details. We all had endless conferences and conversations about treatment. It was three full years from the time Vinnie, Richard, and I first saw the German film until *The Sound of Music* opened at the Lunt-Fontanne Theatre on November 16, 1959.

We were all preoccupied with the problem of how to do this very touching story without being oversentimental in the scenes with the children, or melodramatic in the scenes of the decision to leave Austria and escape over the mountains. It was a problem never solved completely for the critics.

But oh, the music, the joy! I remember the first time I heard the song "Do-Re-Mi," in which Maria taught the children the musical scale: "Doe, a deer, a female deer. . . ." I heard it with Dick playing the melody, Oscar singing the simple, beautiful, rhymed lyrics he had written. It was a revelation. Here, I thought, is perfect communication, the perfect way to teach children the scale. It communicated so well that it turned out to be an international success.

Then along came "Climb Ev'ry Mountain," "Edelweiss," "The Lonely Goatherd," "Sixteen Going on Seventeen" . . . and most of all that haunting melody, the soaring words, of "The hills are alive with the sound of music." That song almost compensated for the fact that I never got my banister in our production.

In the German movie, Maria the postulant appears in her first scene sliding down a long, long banister. She is always late to her classes, always going as fast as she can, dashing madly to get places on time. So off she goes down the banister and lands with a nice clunk—right at the feet of the Mother Superior. I couldn't wait to do that. All through rehearsals I kept asking, "Where's my banister?"

I never got it. There were just too many sets, too many other things to think about. In our version I first appeared on a tree—*on* it, at the very top, gazing at the Alpine scenery and singing, "The hills are alive with the sound of music. . . ." The tree and I swept forward, from the back of the stage toward the front, as the curtains opened. I was never madly comfortable. Not until I saw my friend Florence Henderson play Maria did I really understand how effective that entrance was. I had always felt like someone's version of a saint being swept along, teetering a little, in a procession.

Two marvelous women helped teach me how to play the postulant. One was the original Maria, Baroness von Trapp. She not only had climbed her mountain, she was also living on one—in Vermont. Two weeks before rehearsals started I went up to meet her, to study with her. Within about two hours she looked

The Texas Maria with the real Maria, the Baroness Maria von Trapp, in Vermont.

at me and said, "Mary, you were born in Texas and I was born in Austria, but underneath we are the same Maria."

After I learned to know her, I could see what she meant. We both have the same drive, utter determination. We are alike. Rather quickly I came to the conclusion that perhaps the family didn't just climb that mountain to escape. She pushed them, all the way up. Because she had such will, such love for her family.

While I was in Vermont, Maria taught me how to kneel properly, how to cross myself, how to play a guitar. And I taught her how to yodel. It was a kind of Texas yodel, I'll admit, something I had learned at the Crazy Hotel in Mineral Wells. Lots of good old corny country-and-western singers can yodel as well as the Austrians, even though they have to learn it without an Alp to bounce back the sound.

After our show opened, the real Maria, who had traveled all over the world singing with her family, was much in demand for lecture tours. Once, she told me, she was at an airport to catch a flight for her next engagement. The planes were full, there was some mix-up about her reservation, and there was no seat for her.

"Perhaps you don't understand," she said to the reservation-counter people. "I am Baroness Maria von Trapp and I have a speaking engagement. I must get there on time."

They were sorry, but they said there was no space. She went and sat down, waited, saw other people picking up reservations, and finally she went back to the counter.

"You don't understand," she told them this time. "I am Mary Martin in *The Sound of Music*. I must get on the plane."

She said they put her on, and that "Now you are playing me and I am playing you." Of course, I don't believe a word of this. I think with her marvelous sense of fun she made it up to please me. She added that she was grateful. Even if that farfetched story is true, she couldn't be as grateful as this Texas Maria is to the Austrian Maria.

My other counselor, adviser, friend, was Sister Gregory, from Rosary College in Chicago. We had first met during *South Pacific*. At that time she was head of the drama department at Rosary, and every summer during school holiday she came to New York with one or two other nuns to see the shows. After she saw *South Pacific* she wrote us a letter about the performance, the show's message of tolerance, how much she had enjoyed it. It was one of the most beautiful letters we ever received. Sister Gregory writes like an angel. Richard answered her; we all read her letters, and before long Josh Logan, Dick and Oscar, Mainbocher, everybody was reading her correspondence and replying to it.

The next year she wrote that she was coming back to New York, so we invited her backstage. We couldn't wait to meet her. Everybody was lined and shined up in my dressing room when the stage manager knocked and announced "Sister Gregory" and Sister somebody else. In they came. One was tiny and ethereal, just as we had imagined Sister Gregory. The other was tall, strong, vital. She came straight in and boomed, "Mary . . ." in the kind of voice you would expect from—well, me, but not from a nun. This, of course, was Sister Gregory.

She didn't act like a nun, or the way we poor ignorant souls thought nuns acted. She was bouncy, enthusiastic, with an am-

Sister Gregory holding Heller's first son, Timothy Weir.

bling walk like a good baseball player. She also had beautiful, clear skin and sparkling, snapping brown eyes. We all fell in love with her.

She became a lifelong friend of Richard and me. When we decided to do *The Sound of Music* everyone concerned agreed that we needed Sister Gregory's advice. Dick and Oscar wrote many letters back and forth, always receiving in reply her clear-thinking, "technical" answers to their questions. Vinnie, whom she had never met, flew out to Chicago to get acquainted before he started rehearsals. We all asked her to come to New York on her summer trip to help us with the show.

She was the inspiration for those joyous songs "My Favorite Things" and "Maria," because she told us what fun nuns have, all the happy times inside the convent or an abbey. I can still hear her saying, "Don't make nuns sanctimonious!"

She went with me to some of my fittings with Mainbocher and they got along like a house afire. Main was such a perfectionist that he wanted each robe to be correct, authentic. Sister Gregory showed us all sorts of fascinating tricks about how nuns' inner sleeves are attached and how you can take them out and roll up the outer ones to scrub floors. She showed us how you tuck up long skirts if you want to run, or play games.

Whenever she was around, life took on more brilliance. Her personality, her presence, not only helped me feel the part but also helped me feel more natural and relaxed with the hundreds of priests, nuns, Catholic prelates who came to see the show and then came backstage afterward.

They came in droves. I was given many gold medals during *Sound of Music,* was blessed twice by monsignors, kissed by priests, and even received a special blessing from Pope John in Rome.

All this led to one very funny episode. I had received a note from some nuns asking if they could see me for a moment backstage between matinee and evening performances. I never left the theater between shows, and I was pleased that they wanted to see me, so of course I said yes. I waited and waited that day, and they never turned up. That night the stage manager came to me and said, "Mary, I don't know what to say. I don't know how to explain this. You were expecting some nuns, right?"

I said yes, and he told me the whole story. He had found "my" nuns backstage, downstairs in the hallway, and he thought they belonged to our production. He rushed up and, not really looking closely at them, started shouting, "Get, get, you know you're not supposed to be out here in the hall in your costumes. Back to your dressing rooms and get those clothes off. Right this minute."

The nuns kept protesting, "But, but . . ." and he never let them finish. All he said was "Out! Out! Back to your dressing rooms!"

This went on for about fifteen minutes, until our stage nuns came out of the dressing rooms into the hall, dressed for dinner. They said to the poor frustrated stage manager, "These are for real, let them alone," but by that time the real nuns were so tickled, and so frustrated, that they just left. Walked out and never tried to see me again.

It was not only nuns, or Catholics, who found a message in *The Sound of Music*. My own religious belief turned out not to be a formal, organized sort of "go to this church" kind, but rather a belief that there is Someone there, within me, and all I have to do is call on Him. I have never prayed for anything except the wisdom to solve my own problems, but that has never failed. I do believe all those things about "Let your conscience be your guide"—Mother said it so much to me all my life that it has become a curse; every time I go against it I regret it. And I have always believed in work, hard work, and the discipline it involves. I don't think anyone can get anything important—or keep it—without work.

We used to talk about these things, in the cast and with

Sister Gregory. Perhaps it was the discipline of a postulant's life which appealed to me, I don't know.

Audiences, too, kept finding a message in the show. They became quite passionate about it. People brought their children, reserved blocks of seats weeks in advance. Some saw it over and over again; that was one reason there was never an empty seat.

They demonstrated their devotion one night when we had a power failure in New York. It wasn't the big one of 1965, but a sort of preview of it, in the summer of 1960. All the lights went out before curtain time. We were frantic because people were standing in line outside, waiting to come in. They were told that there were no lights, that we couldn't see to put on costumes or makeup, that we would have to play on an empty stage because the sets weren't up. Nobody budged. They had come to see *The Sound of Music* and they were going to stay there until they saw it.

Richard sent all the stagehands out to buy flashlights, every flashlight they could find. I have no idea how many they came back with, one hundred or more; it was some of the quickest thinking I have ever seen. The whole cast was willing to perform, but we weren't sure how the musicians and stagehands would react. They caught the spirit, too, however, said they would do their best, and away we went. The audience came in by flashlight. I went out in front of the curtain to explain again that we had a real problem but we would carry on if they wanted us to. They did.

I sang my opening number wearing my dressing gown and sitting on a stepladder instead of up in the tree, holding a flashlight to my face. Those darling children, in the wings, watched me doing it, and when they came on they, too, held flashlights to their faces so the audience could see them, see their mouths, understand the lyrics better. We had had no time to rehearse what we were going to do; those children simply watched me and every single one, so quickly, did the same thing. What pros they were! And what a roar came back from the audience—the sound of music to our ears!

About half an hour into the show the lights came back on—bang. We must have looked pretty funny up there in dressing gowns or street clothes, but there was wild applause from the audience. We stopped, everything stopped, and I walked down to the footlights and asked if they would like to wait a few minutes while we put on costumes and set the stage. They called back that they would wait, but I think it was almost a letdown. We were having so much fun; the audience had never experienced anything like it; they felt as if they were part of the show, part of backstage. But we rang down the curtain, rushed into our costumes—we never did put on makeup that night—and went back out and finished it. I still think most of the audience would have loved to see the performance by flashlight, then come back another night to see it the real way.

For the whole first year of *Sound of Music* I was almost as blind as if the lights had been out. I wasn't even aware of it. I knew all the children by their sizes and the color of their hair, and I knew Theodore Bikel, who played Captain von Trapp, by his comfortable presence and his marvelous voice. Then I became painfully aware that I always had headaches on Thursdays and Sundays. I went to a doctor who examined me and explained that it was because I strained my eyes so much doing two performances on Wednesdays and Saturdays. He suggested that I wear contact lenses, beginning a few minutes at a time and then working up to full time.

The first time I wore them was at a matinee. I had put them in, in my dressing room, then I couldn't manage to get them out in time for my entrance. I went on wearing them. It was a scene in which I entered alone, with my back to the captain. His line, very stern, was "What is your name?" I was supposed to reply, "Maria Rainer." That day I went on, turned around, and saw Theo—really *saw* him—for the first time. He was so handsome, but much larger than I had thought before. I blurted out, "Luise Rainer."

Luise Rainer? I couldn't believe my ears. Theo couldn't believe his, either. He said, "What?" and I got so completely out of my Austrian character that I drawled in Texas, "Oh, Ah mean . . . Ah mean, my name is *Maria* Rainer."

I really saw the show for the first time that day, all the children's faces, the Mother Superior, everybody. I never was able to tolerate plastic contacts, but the new soft lenses are heaven, one of the greatest inventions in the world. If I could choose an achievement to be proud of forever, it would be to have invented either Scotch tape, Kleenex, or the soft contact lens.

The Sound of Music was not a demanding show physically, except for the sheer distance I had to cover. The theater was built on two stories and we had a two-story set. My main dressing room was on the second floor of the theater itself, but I also had a quick-change room on the second story of the set, and two other quick-change rooms on either side of the stage itself, in the wings. Just for fun Richard, who loved statistics, put a pedometer on me once and we found that I walked—ran—three miles at each performance, six miles on Wednesdays and Saturdays. So did Nena and another dresser, who had to meet me in every room to help with my many changes.

I never hurt myself in this show, either, except for the time I slammed into the wall during the 1960 *Peter Pan* television rehearsals and then had to go on the same night as Maria. In the first act it didn't matter much. As the postulant my arms were folded meekly most of the time, and the audiences I don't believe ever noticed the sling which held my broken arm. We had slings in the color and material of every other costume in the show. They embarrassed me only in the scene in which I was supposed to play the guitar and perform the *Ländler,* an Austrian folk dance. I stuck the guitar between my sling and my left side and pretended to strum with my right hand while a man in the orchestra pit filled in the guitar music. Theo Bikel did his part of the dance with even more than his usual enthusiasm, waving his arms like mad, and nobody seemed to notice that I was waving only one arm.

It struck me funny, because I had learned the *Ländler* in the first place from Maria von Trapp in Vermont, and she taught it to me with one of her arms in a cast. It happened the first time I went to see her. Toni Frissell went with me because *Life* wanted a story of our meeting, wanted Toni's fabulous pictures. Maria led us clear to the top of her mountain and kept saying to me, "Go on, Maria, up, up, a little higher. . . ." As I went up she went back, directing Toni and me, and suddenly she was *gone.* Gone down toward the bottom. Horrors. We reached her as soon as we could unclimb the mountain, but nothing could stop that woman. Within hours she was back, her arm in a cast, having her picture taken and teaching me the dance.

In my whole two-year run in *Sound of Music* I missed only one performance. That is not counting the time I almost missed the whole theater. Ernest was driving me one matinee day when our car broke down. I had to get out and run for a taxi. I got into the first one that came along. The driver said, "Where do you want to go?" And I didn't know. I never knew addresses, never could remember the names of theaters. I just trusted Ernest or Richard to get me there.

So I said, "Well, uh, wherever *Sound of Music* is performing, do you know where that is?"

He didn't. I couldn't confess that I'd been playing in it for two years and I didn't know where the theater was, so I just said, "Let me out, please." I jumped out and luckily got another taxi. This time before I got in I asked the driver if he knew where the show was playing. He did, so in I got and he delivered me there on time.

For the life of me I can't remember why it was that I was unable to go on for one performance. Something must have been sprained. I do remember that my marvelous standby, Renee Guerin, who had been a friend ever since she was my understudy for the second production of *Annie,* went on for me. She was so excited to get to play Maria at last that she said, "I want you to hear it." The stage manager arranged to turn all the speakers up high and leave the telephone off the hook near the stage. I picked up my telephone at my home, miserably in bed, and heard it all. She was just great. Later she played Maria in an Australian production of the show, stayed there for a while, and married her stage manager.

The Sound of Music also brought me face to face—and almost alone—with the Duke of Windsor. I had done a benefit performance with the children, singing "Do-Re-Mi" for a luncheon at the Waldorf-Astoria Hotel. When it was over I got into the elevator to go home and on one floor in walked the duke. He started the conversation by telling me how he and the duchess had seen *South Pacific* three times, how much both of them had enjoyed *The Sound of Music.* The elevator man stopped at the duke's floor, we bade good day to each other, and then the operator turned to me and said, "Oh, Miss Martin, General Charles de Gaulle is coming in on the bottom floor, you'll see him."

All I needed after the excitement of seeing the Duke of Windsor was to have to speak my one line of French. I begged, "Please take me to the basement. I can't take all this in one afternoon." So I never met General de Gaulle. But there was my Richard, who had come to take me home.

I had a funny experience with Bernard Baruch one matinee. I had known this wonderful man for years—he and I are the godparents of Tex and Jinx McCrary's second son, Kevin. Mr. Baruch always came to see any show I was in. I remember that he was very annoyed in *The Skin of Our Teeth* because Mr. Antrobus in one scene slapped Sabina—me—on the fanny. Mr. Baruch didn't think it should happen to such a nice girl. He adored the theater but he was quite deaf so he always had to sit in the front row to hear anything. Then, if he liked it, he turned his hearing aid up LOUD. He almost broke up our performance one afternoon at *Music*. He was right in the front, beaming from ear to ear, beating the time with his right hand while the children and I did the "Do-Re-Mi" number. I'd sing "Do" and back would come "Do . . . Do . . . Do. . . ." I felt as if I were singing five shows at once, in a canyon. I looked around, tapped my head to clear my ears, and then I realized that it was Bernard Baruch's hearing aid. He had turned it up so high that I was getting a feedback from the footlight microphones. Hurriedly I got a message to the stage manager, who found Richard, who tiptoed out to ask Mr. Baruch to please turn it down a bit.

I think *Music* was perhaps his favorite show. How much it meant to him! To Renee Guerin, whom it made a star. To Julie Andrews, who played the movie version. Nobody by this time bothered to ask me about making the movie, because they knew how I felt about films. But Julie, who was so brilliant as Mary Poppins, may be even better remembered as Maria von Trapp. What a role, what a show, what a joy to millions and millions of people all over the world!

One person to whom it was not an utter joy was my old friend Bessie Mae Sue Ella Yaeger Austin from Texas. We have remained friends all through the years. When I first went to Hollywood I tried to get her name into each movie. Sometimes I could be called Bessie, or Mae, or Sue Ella. If it couldn't be my name I slipped it into somebody else's. Bessie Mae always got a kick out of it. I never managed to get her into *Venus* or *Lute Song*, but when it came time for *South Pacific* I asked if I could get her into the show-within-a-show, when I did "Honey Bun." I thought it would be great if the announcement could be "The barrel rolls will now be done by Lieutenant j.g. Bessie Mae Sue Ella Yaeger."

Josh, Dick, Oscar all looked startled and said, "By whom?"

I explained that she was my best Texas friend and that her name had always been in my pictures. They were as mad for her name as I was, couldn't wait to put it in. So every night I announced, "The barrel rolls will be done . . . by Bessie Mae" etc., and everybody would clap and clap.

I sent her flowers to Dallas for her opening night. She was pleased. During the second year of *South Pacific* she and her husband, Jac Austin, came to New York to see the show. They had our seats, in the fourth row, and that night when it came to her announcement she got straight up out of her seat, turned around, and started bowing to the audience.

The people out front couldn't imagine what was going wrong with this crazy lady, but we onstage were convulsed because we all knew she was there. Finally I had to stop and announce that the crazy lady was "the original Bessie Mae Sue Ella Yaeger." Everybody clapped some more and I don't think Bessie Mae really wanted to sit down, ever.

Then came time for *The Sound of Music*. We were in Boston for tryouts when Oscar came to me and said, "What are we going to do without Bessie Mae? We don't have her in the show. We can't open without her, we might fold."

Bessie Mae is kind of a hard name to work into Austrian terms. I fooled around for a while trying to put her in the yodel number, but it didn't really work. In the end, Oscar solved it. Renee Guerin, my standby, isn't the kind of girl who likes just waiting around every performance wanting to go on. She wants to *do* something. There was a crossover just before my wedding scene with Theo, the captain, and she always made it, walking across in a postulant's costume. The program said, "Postulant played by Renee Guerin." Oscar got the idea that we should leave Renee's name in the credits, as "standby for Mary Martin," but change the program to read, "Postulant played by Bessie Mae Sue Ella Yaeger."

Renee was happy with this, I was happy, everybody was happy. We had our good-luck charm. I sent Bessie Mae flowers on opening night, and a message: "You're now a postulant. No more barrel rolls. God's in his heaven, all's right with the world."

About two years later I got a letter from Bessie Mae, a nice chatty gossipy letter. At the end of it, she wrote, "Now I know you're a darling girl, and I'm your best Texas friend, but you've got to help me. I keep getting letters from the government saying I haven't paid my income tax all these years. I keep writing and telling them that I'm not really in *Sound of Music*. . . ."

Some computer had picked her up. Some crazy computer, and heaven knows how much money it thought she had earned, being a postulant in such a hit. It took months, all of us working away, to unravel the whole story and get Bessie Mae out of the clutches of the computer and the Internal Revenue Service.

XX
Dream in the Jungle

For eighteen years Richard and I loved a wild, beautiful patch of earth in the jungles of Brazil. It is difficult to explain precisely how and why we fell in love with it and how much it meant to us to have it. We dreamed of it when we were away, returned to it for refreshment, for restoration of ourselves, as often as we could.

There is a singular, recognizable cadence to every style of life. Much as both of us adored the quick beat of Broadway, we often could hardly wait to fly back to the rich red earth of Brazil, the bright blue skies and billowing white clouds, birdsong at dawn and sunset, peace.

Our friends used to refer to it as "getting away from it all," but that wasn't the point. There was a problem to solve every day —but the problems were different from those in New York. We were never idle. Richard became a busy *fazendeiro,* or farmer; I ended up having a boutique in the nearby town of Anápolis; our simple little country house kept growing and growing until it looked like a small *cidade,* or village. We could be together for hours every day watching everything grow—the gardens, the house, all our plans. Richard, who had hardly been on a horse since Will Rogers put him on one at age five, learned to ride. I, who had loved horses as a little girl, found the joy of galloping at full speed up hills and down valleys. Workmen cut roads through our own bit of jungle, with machetes, so I could ride there.

One of the miracles of Brazil is the expansiveness of it, the horizon. The world really looks *round* there; you can see the curve on the edges where the earth meets the sky. David Warshaw, our financial lawyer, miracle manager of our lives, and close family friend for more than twenty years, came to visit us once and told me that it was all a trick of perspective, of the light, of the space. From our farm, on top of a hill, we could see one hundred miles in all directions and the horizon seemed really to curve. Sunsets were spectacular, and at night the stars so huge and so close one felt the desire to reach out and pick them. Sunset and star watching were a nightly ritual on our verandah.

And the gardens. There is a saying there that if one plants something he should jump quickly out of the way, things grow so fast and so luxuriantly. This exciting country stimulated my husband's endless imagination. Once he asked what flowers I would like in the house garden and I said roses. Richard planted three hundred bushes, all colors. He was 6 feet tall and the bushes were higher than his head in a year. It takes several days to cut the blossoms from three hundred rosebushes.

Richard was such a perfectionist, such a designer, and in Brazil he had the biggest set in the world to work with. He made three lakes and seven waterfalls, and gave me the most unusual birthday present a gal could have—my own Japanese bridge. I always wanted one, but who thinks such a crazy dream will come true? Only Richard. He designed, and had made in Anápolis, a wrought-iron red-lacquered bridge. I saw it come to the farm in two pieces on a huge truck, the morning of my birthday. I couldn't imagine what on earth it was until he had it assembled and set up to stretch completely across one little lake. It was the most exciting birthday present I ever had.

Among many crazy things about our passionate affair with Brazil is the fact that we never chose it as a place to visit, let alone to live. We decided in 1955 to go to Greece; then we got a little off course. I had just finished the long run of *Peter Pan* and had done the first television version. We were all tired, so Richard and Heller and I packed up for a freighter trip to Greece.

Our trunks were aboard; we were supposed to leave from Hoboken on a Monday morning. On Saturday, Richard went to look over the freighter and our accommodations. To his horror he discovered that it was not leaving. It wasn't going anywhere. He

My most exciting birthday present.

telephoned me to break the news, and I said, "Why don't you go to the next berth and find out if there's another freighter going somewhere, anywhere?"

There was one, leaving on Monday for South America. Neither of us had ever thought of going to South America, but what the heck? We were all packed, we had some precious free time. Why not go?

"Our" freighter was Norwegian, brand-new and beautiful. We were the only passengers. It was like having a private yacht for three glorious months. We didn't even see land for two weeks, then we sailed into Rio de Janeiro, one of the most beautiful harbors in the world. From there we went to Uruguay, to Argentina, and then back to Santos, Brazil. This time a little put-put boat came out to meet us and an English-speaking Brazilian lady came aboard to ask, "Are you Richard Halliday and Mary Martin? I have a letter for you."

Talk about circles. The letter was from Janet Gaynor and

Adrian, asking if we could come visit them to see their new Brazilian house. We knew they had property there but we didn't know just where. When we set forth on our freighter Hedda Hopper had mentioned it in her column, and added that she knew Janet and Adrian "would love to know where in South America the Hallidays are. . . ." Janet's mother saw the item, clipped it, and mailed it to her, and Janet and Adrian had promptly written to us. They had no idea where to send the letter so they entrusted it to their friend, Janet Homer, who lived in Santos, the lady who finally delivered it. She had been meeting boats in the harbor for two months, so the letter was a little tired by the time she finally delivered it.

By this time we had only a day and a night before our freighter set sail again, and the trip to Janet and Adrian's house involved almost a thousand miles of travel. Richard and I were both insane enough to want to do it, but Heller was scandalized. She kept saying. "That's the most expensive dinner I ever heard of, to go that far."

We took a small plane from São Paulo, one of those up-and-down affairs which landed about every fifty miles to take on freight, mail, nursing mothers, everything else. Finally we arrived in Anápolis and there were Janet, Adrian, a station wagon, and a woman whom we were to get to know very well, an American resident of Brazil whom everyone called Dona Joanna. Off we all went for another hour, bouncing along tracks through the trees to their fabulous house. Adrian had designed it in Moorish style, set three thousand feet in the hills above the red desert, or *campo,* at the beginning of the great valleys with mountains in the distance. It was glorious, unreal, deep in the jungle.

They were just beginning to uncrate their furniture, which had been shipped from California to the new home. Their king-size bed, the first thing they unpacked, was big enough for the four of us to dine on. We were served dinner by a French couple they had found in Brazil, and we sat there and ate and talked all night long. As we left in the dawn, Richard spotted a big green hill across the valley from their house. He said, "If that's ever for sale, let me know."

I thought he was out of his mind. We didn't know anything about farming; we didn't speak Portuguese; even getting to this remote corner of the world was a major project. But I, too, was wildly excited by the countryside. It was our first glimpse of a magic, larger-than-life world.

Then back to the station wagon, the airplane, the freighter, New York, and rehearsals for *The Skin of Our Teeth*. With all that going on, there were days and weeks in which Brazil never even entered our heads. But practically the first night we were back from Paris, in the hotel in Washington, the phone rang from Brazil. Janet and Adrian had flown almost a thousand miles to São Paulo to find a telephone and inform us that the hill was for sale.

I shouted, "Buy it, buy it." Unfortunately, ever since I had my first twenty-five dollars, which is about the largest sum of money I can really understand, I have had a tendency to say, "Buy it."

We couldn't leave the show to rush off to Brazil to handle the purchase ourselves, so we turned everything over to the American lady, Dona Joanna. She had helped Janet and Adrian buy their farm, and they thought she had done a brilliant job of getting their house built. We gave her our power of attorney, sent money, and in due course got back the most impressive set of papers we had ever seen—all gold lettering, positively dripping with official-looking seals, all written in Portuguese, no word of which we could read. But we had nary a qualm: Dona Joanna had, after all, found the Adrians' Valhalla.

Janet and Adrian had fallen for Brazil as suddenly, as unexpectedly, as we had. They had flown down for a film festival in Rio and decided they liked the country. Everyone raved so about the beauties of the high country in the jungle that they wanted to see it. A Brazilian acquaintance advised them to fly to Anápolis and look up Dona Joanna. She was something of a celebrity there, a pioneer and a very colorful woman. Her full name was Joan Lowell Bowen. As Joan Lowell she had written a marvelous book, *Cradle of the Deep,* which purported to be the story of her mother, a proper Bostonian who fell in love with a barge captain. Her parents disapproved and disinherited her when she married her captain. Then she died in childbirth and Joan, the daughter, was raised on the barge by her father. The book caused quite a stir; it was the Book-of-the-Month Club selection for March, 1929. I remember reading it as a girl in Texas and loving it. It was a very exciting adventure story.

Later it developed that the whole tale was not entirely true. There were exposé stories about "hoax" and Joan hopped on a boat to Brazil and never went back to the United States. She made the story almost come true, however, by falling in love with a ship's captain herself, a man named Bowen. She waited for him in Brazil, and when he retired they were married and began to carve out a life together. They truly were pioneers, hacking out jungle, making roads, with their bare hands and machetes. Dona Joanna became a booster and promoter for opening the country. Every American visitor who expressed an interest in land was sent to her. Janet and Adrian were no different from the others—they had to to find her.

When they reached Anápolis they hired a car and made straight for the Bowens' little adobe house. When they arrived there was no one at home except an ancient housekeeper, who invited them to come inside and wait. Dona Joanna was out on a rice truck, the housekeeper said, and nobody knew when she would be back. In those days everybody traveled on the big, lumbering rice trucks because there was no other form of transport in the area.

Janet and Adrian settled down to wait—and waited almost a week. Finally Dona Joanna returned, a lithe, sun-tanned figure in blue jeans, with her long hair pulled up into a dramatic knot on top. She took them all over the place to look at farms. They chose one, left money to buy it, and went home happy. Later they got word that the owner had changed his mind, but Dona Joanna found another place. Adrian flew down to look, approved, and left money and plans to begin the house. There was to be far more to the story, but nobody knew it then.

When finally *The Skin of Our Teeth* closed, we couldn't wait to rush off to Brazil to see our new property. We moved in with Janet and Adrian, where we intended to stay while we built our own little house on our own green hill. The very first morning we rode off on horseback with a picnic lunch to eat on our hill. We tramped for hours, deciding where to put the house, where to dig a well, where to make the garden. While we were eating our picnic we heard funny noises—*pssseeeeeeuh, psssseeeuuuh*—which sounded extraordinarily like bullets whistling through the air, but we couldn't conceive of such a thing. It was so calm on the hill; there was nobody around but us. We thought we'd all been seeing too much television, though heaven knows there was no TV within thousands of miles of where we were sitting.

That night, back at the Adrians', a man with a shotgun which looked about eight feet long appeared at the door. He engaged the French cook in a conversation which the Frenchman had some difficulty understanding, because it was in quite vigorous Portuguese. He reported to us that, to the best of his understanding, the man with the gun said that today was "just a warning." But that if we ever trespassed upon his property again he might shoot for real.

This was the first hint of what turned out to be the truth— we did not own that hill. We lived for another six weeks thinking we did, however. Every day Dona Joanna turned up with another exciting, titillating story about our new property. First she said that the man with the gun was the former owner, a man so illiterate that he had made only an "X" on the bill of sale. He didn't really understand about property rights, she said. He had our money all right, buried under his bed in a little shack he owned just below the hill itself. Our beribboned and gold-printed documents didn't reveal anything that looked like an "X," but we ignored that slight defect for the moment.

Next we were told that the man did understand, but that he had some cattle on the hill. Either he had to keep them on high ground for a time, or he had to leave them there until they had finished the corn, or they were still eating the beans—the story changed from day to day. However, the advice remained constant: "Get up early in the morning and watch," Joanna said. "When you see him driving the cattle away, you'll know it is the end. He will take the money out from under the bed, leave, and the land is yours."

We got up solemnly at the crack of dawn every day to see the cattle being driven away. We never saw them.

The next revelation from our spinner of tales was that "our" land was absolutely full of minerals—oil, gold, uranium, you name it and we had it. Once we got our hands on it, we were sure to be rich. Shortly after that, Joanna told us that an herb grew on our land which could be applied to our faces to rejuvenate the skin. If we could find a way to bottle it, it would revolutionize the entire feminine beauty business. By this time we were beginning to believe that everything in the whole world existed on our land —everything, that is, except us.

It seems incredible now that we could have been so gullible for so long. On the first two trips I didn't really connect "Dona Joanna" with the Joan Lowell of the book hoax, but it was obvious that her powers of imagination and description had improved, if anything, with the years. Her stories were so complex, so fabulous, they were like the unfolding plot of a Republic movie.

Finally, irrevocably, it became clear that we didn't own the hill and never would. Joanna had taken our money to buy hundreds of acres farther off in the jungle, up toward the Amazon. She had heard that several rich Texas cattlemen were planning to start ranches in Brazil. One Texan did actually turn up, but he didn't stay very long and I don't think he bought anything. Then nobody else came. She was stuck with her unsold acres and we were stuck *without* ours.

It began to dawn on all of us that our new friend had been less than honest, or at least had overextended herself. Janet and Adrian's lovely house had been built with green wood, which began to shrink and split as it aged and settled. Dona Joanna gave Richard and me a check on a bank in Anápolis to repay our purchase price. When we tried to cash it, the bankers explained politely that she had no funds in that bank. Quickly she wrote another check on another bank, but it was the same story.

We were all embarrassed and upset. Adrian, who had contracted a low fever, was so horrified by it all that he became sicker. The Brazilians in Anápolis were even more upset than we were. They felt that the honor of Brazil was at stake, despite the fact that it was another American who had gotten us into our difficulties. Our wonderful Jibran, a businessman to whom the Adrians had introduced us, decided to take action. He and friends—a banker, a lawyer, a doctor—came out to call on us and offered to find another property and put up the money so we could buy it. It would take us years, they said, to recover our money from Dona Joanna but that they could manage it more quickly. She owned hundreds of acres, coffee plantations, filling stations, heaven knows what all, and she transacted all her business in Anápolis.

Richard and I resisted at first. We felt it was too much

responsibility for them, too generous. But we reckoned without the resolution of Jibran, a man of great persistence and our closest Brazilian friend to this day. He and his friends stood firm; we had already spent six weeks with Janet and Adrian; some decision had to be made quickly. We agreed to go look at other farms, and we found one we loved for exactly the same amount of money we had paid for the hill. The group of men bought it for us, and I'm happy to say within a year they got their money back.

There are many strange sequels, or nonsequels, to the story. Joanna wrote at least one more book, *Promised Land,* about her life in Brazil and I heard that Joan Crawford at one time bought movie rights to it. It was never made into a film, however. She, Joanna, sold land deeds to Cary Grant, to Claudette Colbert, I don't know who all. The last time I saw Cary Grant he asked me how his property was in Brazil. "Haven't you ever seen it?" I asked him, and he said, "I've never even *heard* anything about it since I sent my down payment."

I don't think Dona Joanna was a bad woman, or that she intended to cheat anyone. She was simply a wild dreamer with an imagination which got out of control now and then. She had her troubles; at one point she went to Anápolis and asked to be locked up in the town jail to save her from "enemies." Brazilians can get pretty excited when they are angry. She's dead now, poor woman, but the Brazilians will never forget her, and neither will we.

After all that drama we finally owned a farm, and a modest adobe house we could begin to fix up. As often as we could, maybe once a year, we rushed to Nossa Fazenda, "our farm." Richard worked like a demon on every trip, renovating our house, making plans, planting crops.

After a few years we decided perhaps we were crazy to own a place so far from New York, so difficult to get to. Darling Janet didn't live in Brazil anymore because Adrian had died, suddenly, of a cerebral hemorrhage in 1959. They had always spent part of the year in the United States, and when he died Adrian was in California, busily designing the costumes for the Broadway production of *Camelot.* Janet was in New York, at Adrian's insistence, doing preliminary work on a play, the first she had ever agreed to perform in. Janet and Adrian had never been separated before. She always has thought that Adrian had some premonition; that he sent her away. She was in New York when it happened, and she couldn't get back to California until too late.

Our lives had changed, too. Our Heller was married and no longer free to go sailing or flying off to Brazil with us. After she had lived the upside-down theater life for almost nine years, sleeping in the morning to be ready for matinees and studying at night after the evening performance, she went to a Quaker school in Pennsylvania. She was fourteen, and before she was fifteen we were sure she was going to get married any minute. We lived through the *Perils of Pauline* while she got engaged and unengaged to a series of young men. After her first year of college, in 1962, she married Anthony Weir. Richard and I had planned a huge formal wedding for them, had addressed about five hundred invitations, Mainbocher had made her a gorgeous wedding dress. Then Heller and Tony—after having asked us to go with them—decided to elope. They thought the money would be more practical than the wedding. In the end Tony's family and friends, our family and friends, friends of friends all joined the cavalcade—seven cars of mad elopers. We drove around for three days and nights, from Delaware to Washington, D.C., to Maryland before we finally found a place that didn't require a long wait—Leesburg, Virginia. What started as a quiet little elopement ended up costing much more than any wedding would have—the story of our lives.

Still, Heller was settled—we thought—and in the United States. By 1963, when we went back to Brazil, we had made up our minds that this would be the final visit, the Decision. Probably we should sell it. We didn't. That time we were able to stay for several months and we found ourselves hopelessly hooked. We even bought more land.

Our very first nonfamily guest in Brazil was just the man to fill the gap left by Heller and Janet. Jean Baptiste Tad Adoue III —what a name. Tad has been a special person in our lives for more than thirty years. He's a displaced Texan from Dallas and I like to think I knew him when I was a child, but I didn't. We didn't meet until New York during the war, when he turned up at our Fifth Avenue apartment in navy uniform with the boy from Weatherford whom I adored, Ralph Kindel, Jr., and my old beau Gus Cranz's college roommate, Elmo Coon from Millsap, Texas. Richard and I loved Tad Adoue at sight.

We were all the same age bracket, but Tad seemed like a

son to us. When we went to London for the Noël Coward play in 1946, we wanted him to go with us. Visas were difficult in those days because of all kinds of shortages in England, so Richard decided we should take Tad as our secretary. He cabled Noël's office for help with a visa, but Tad's name so baffled the British that we got a cable back asking a) if this person was male or female, and b) if he or she was an American citizen. Quickly we cabled back that he was male and American, and Richard added, "Certain you realize unusual personal relationship secretary in this business Tad only second congenial personality we discovered in seven years." I honestly don't know, now, whom Richard considered the *other* congenial personality.

We never got a visa for Tad, but we never lost Tad. He has been somewhere nearby ever since, ready to rush to us when we need him. Over the years he has telephoned, sent mountains of clippings from New York and trade papers to keep us in touch with the world. He has flown to meet us everywhere from Rome to Sicily to Cuba to Brazil. His most spectacular sudden appearance was in a hotel bar in Taormina, Sicily, in 1952. Richard and Heller and I had been wanting Tad to come to London to visit during the run of *South Pacific* but he never got there. Then we decided to take a little vacation, and we told him we were going to Sicily. The first night we were there, Richard and I got Heller to bed and went down to the bar. I was talking to Richard and all of a sudden I looked to my right and there was Tad, sitting there quiet as a mouse.

"Tad!" I yelled. "What, how on earth, when . . . ?"

All he said was "Well, you said you were coming here. I thought I'd just come along and surprise you."

When he turned up in Brazil, this shy man with the Will Rogers smile who never asks anything, who only wants to give, Richard and I felt that part of our family had come home.

All the rest of the family visited us in Brazil, one time or another. My sister and her husband, Bob, Richard's sister, Didi, Larry and my fabulous daughter-in-law, Maj, my granddaughter Heidi and grandson Preston, Heller, my grandsons Timothy and Matt, David Warshaw, Dr. Edward Biggs (a wonderful diagnostician who saved my life) and his wife, Sister Gregory, Dorothy Hammerstein—a constant warm stream of friends, kin, producers, playwrights, songwriters.

They were our special joy and diversion, apart from the countryside itself. Getting living space ready for them—and for ourselves—was something else again.

When Richard and I first tried to live there we really were camping out. He instantly decided to expand our adobe house and civilize it a bit. Within days there were fifty people milling around the place, including the wives of the workmen. One day Richard and I tried to have a light lunch sitting on the sill of a nonexistent window when suddenly up above the sill, on the outside, popped the heads of four of our workmen—all Japanese, all brothers, all cross-eyed. It was hard to keep a straight face. I'm afraid we giggled a bit, and all four of them broke into gales of laughter at us. We never found out what was so funny, but everywhere we moved inside our little house they followed us, peered in again, and died laughing. We finally decided to give the whole thing up. We couldn't eat another bite.

The workmen were everywhere, and the only privacy was a tiny little bathroom so cramped that you had to sit on the john to put your shoes on. One day I was in there, having showered and put on bra and panties, when one entire adobe wall of the bathroom fell down. Just fell flat, out into the air. I paused for a moment in the effort to put on my boots, looked up and over my shoulder, and there was a Brazilian workman on top of a tall ladder, leaning on a beam of the roof above the collapsed wall.

He wasn't startled in the slightest. He beamed a Brazilian smile and said, *"Bom dia."*

"Bom dia," I said back to him, and then I screeched for Richard. "Tell him to put back that wall. How can I ever get dressed?"

Somehow they got up a canvas covering; Richard told the man to go away and fix the wall later. Then he forgot all about it. The last time I looked, the man was still sitting under a tree in the shade, waiting to be summoned to fix the adobe wall. They can knock one down in five minutes, put it up again in an hour.

When we finished the first stage our house had only one bedroom—ours—but I had a huge second-floor studio and Richard had a big office. Both had couches for guests. We had no electricity, but candles and kerosene lamps were lovely. Then we added a guesthouse with its own kitchen, bedroom, bath, living room. When that overflowed we built another one, and added *sala* after *sala* to the main house, each in a different color and decor. We never stopped building. Every year we seemed to need more farmers and that meant more houses for them. Richard designed them all. Our farmers were people who had had very little in their lives. Richard made them family homes with bathrooms, cement floors, eventually even hot-water systems.

They all became part of our family. I was either "Dona Maria" at our farm or, later, at my boutique, "Mary March," the strange pronounciation they managed when they tried to say "Mary Martin."

Eventually we added a chicken farm—seven thousand chickens—and had a fantastic egg production. We raised all kinds of fruit and vegetables. Right on our own land we could produce everything we needed except salt, electricity, and telephones. We did finally get electricity but we still kept our candles and our beloved old refrigerator, which ran on kerosene. It worked beautifully except that occasionally it got an air lock in its pipes. Then we had to turn it upside down for an hour and whack it, like burping a baby, until it got going again.

We never did get a telephone, because Richard couldn't abide telephones in that lovely countryside. They interrupted our dream in the jungle.

XXI
From "Mary March" to "Dorry-san"

If I had once looked like an exclamation point on the stage of the cavernous Chicago Opera House, I must have looked like a thumbtack to several thousand soldiers, sailors, air-force men and marines in the vast hangars and outdoor stages of Vietnam and Korea. When I played *Hello Dolly!* for the troops I was not as skinny as I had been in *Venus,* but I came on crowned with a towering white feather hat about 3 feet wide.

I can think of no other role—except perhaps my beloved Peter Pan—which could have coaxed me away from Brazil in 1965. Richard and I were blissful at the farm. But then along came an invitation we couldn't resist, to do a show I was mad about, to play a different type of character than I had ever played, to work with a new director whom I admired tremendously, and to be able to say yes, at last, to a producer who for ten years had been tirelessly bringing me shows for consideration—David Merrick.

On one of our quick trips back to New York, Richard and I saw Carol Channing knock Manhattan on its left ear as Dolly Levi. It was one of the most exciting experiences of our lives, watching this darling clown girl, whom we had known from her first Broadway show, become the brilliant Dolly, bright and glittering as a diamond on the stage. We couldn't wait to tell her how marvelous she was, to meet director Gower Champion, who had thought up all those stairs and all those waiters so Dolly could make *the* entrance of all time into Harmonia Gardens. And who had produced

this marvel? The man who never took no for a final answer,
Mr. Merrick.

Carol, bless her show-biz heart, agreed to come to supper at
our apartment after a Saturday-night performance. She and her
husband, Charles Lowe, brought Gower Champion and his wife,
Marge, into our lives. It was a love feast. Things can get pretty
lovey and feasty with a bunch of stimulated hams, so of course it
ended up with our inviting everybody to come visit us in Brazil.
Gower and Marge in due time really arrived there, bringing with
them all sorts of exciting prospects. First, David Merrick would
like me to play Dolly in the Soviet Union for the State Department. Second, he had an exciting property called *I Do! I Do!*
which he would like me to think about after Dolly.

This was my fourth opportunity to play a part written for
or made famous by other people: first Annie, then Peter Pan, then
Sabina, now Dolly. I was delighted when Richard said yes, he
would love to see my characterization of Dolly. Did I have any
ideas?

I certainly did. I would play her like Sister.

My sister, Jerry Martin Andrews, loves everybody, just like
Dolly Levi, and she is also the con woman of all time. She gets
people together, she gets them engaged, she gets them married, and
all the time they think that *they* thought of it. And they all love
her forever. She's quite a dame, my sister, and me playing *her,* as
Dolly, was one of the high spots of my career.

We began rehearsals in New York in March, 1965. In April
we opened in Minneapolis and did a short tour of the United
States and Canada. When we were in Toronto we received word
of the death of Larry's father. Ben and Juanita and their son,
Gary, always came to see my shows, but Ben wasn't with us anymore when *Hello Dolly!* got to Texas.

Sister came to Dallas to watch me play *her,* and Larry and
Maj, Heller and Tony, and all the grandchildren—only three then
—flew to Dallas to surprise Richard and me on our twenty-fifth
wedding anniversary.

In the autumn, the entire *Hello Dolly!* company flew off to
the Orient. We landed briefly in Hawaii, which pleased me because I had never been there. In Honolulu we were met by official
greeters, a Hawaiian band, the assembled press of the islands, and
an astonishing lady with a big hat and a flowing muumuu, abso-

Here I am playing Sister, in *Hello Dolly!*

lutely covered with leis. She darted toward the plane, bowing and sashaying along, headed straight for me. She started draping leis all over me—two, ten, a couple of dozen—until I could hardly stand up. I thought she must be the queen of the islands. Then she snatched off her hat. It was Bea Lillie.

I couldn't believe it. She was visiting friends on Oahu, about seventy-five miles away, but she made the trip to perform one of her best Lillie pranks. Of course, she was invited into the lounge for interviews with all the rest of us, and the press interviewed her the whole time. She had us on the floor with laughter. I decided right then and there that I would never put my foot on the same stage with that upstaging woman.

From Hawaii we flew to Tokyo and one of the warmest, most lovely experiences of my life. It seems close as yesterday. It began at our first press conference when we arrived. There must have been a hundred people there, all so polite, so eager for us to enjoy their country. Those were the days of the simple silk shirtwaist dress, and half of my offstage wardrobe was versions of this,

The Queen of the Island—
Bea Lillie.

in all colors. Richard had the idea of having an extra one made up which I could give to someone in each of the countries to which we were going. I gave away the first one in Tokyo, and the Japanese loved it. They replied by giving me an entire Japanese outfit—kimono, obi, geta, the works.

The Tokyo audiences got the dollar-and-cents jokes better than the British did in *Dolly,* perhaps because they'd had more intimate experience in the past few years. I had to make a curtain speech almost every night, and even after that the audience waited outside for thirty minutes, an hour, to call out *arrigato,* "thank you." Having become accustomed to being "Mary March" in Brazil, I learned to recognize myself as "Dorry-san" in Japanese, their pronunciation of "Dolly" plus the charming honorific "san."

I had tried to learn a little Japanese long before we went there. While we were in Toronto, Richard found a woman who worked for the Japanese embassy who was willing to help me. I wrote out some words I wanted to sing to the tune of "Hello Dolly," about "Hello, Tokyo, I'm so glad to be here in your town. . . ." And I asked to have the words taped for me in Japanese. After the embassy lady taped them, I listened carefully for hours, and wrote them out in my own phonetic language so I could reproduce the sounds. It took me a long, long time to learn them, and the Japanese lady thought my written phonetic Japanese was the funniest thing she had ever seen. The only people who laughed harder than she did were the press-conference people and the audiences when they heard it. Weeks later I found out that the lady had translated and taped my words into formal, classical Japanese. So when I marched out and sang my song with a slightly Texas accent in the equivalent of Shakespearean Japanese, they nearly died laughing. Politely, of course.

There was some trouble with gestures, too. Our normal ordinary wave, with both palm and fingers outward toward the person, is very like a gesture which means "come here" to the Japanese. And our casual "hi" sounds just like their *hai*—"yes." For the first few nights when we left the theater I would wave from the car, saying "Hi"—and dozens of Japanese tried to get into the car. No wonder. To them it looked as if I were saying, "Yes, come on in."

Every single day at the theater they brought me tea and little hot scented towels while I was making up. Delicious, delicate tea in those fragile, lovely bowls, served on a lacquer tray on the tatami-mat floor. I yearned to do my makeup on my knees, right on the floor the way the Japanese do it, but by the time I got there they had moved in a huge American dressing table and mirror. Nena and I hadn't the heart to tell them we would have preferred to do it their way. They had gone to so much trouble.

We played Tokyo long enough for me to see the famous Kabuki theater and meet some of its stars. We were presented to the empress of Japan, to the crown prince and his family. The United States ambassador, Edwin O. Reischauer, and his lovely Japanese wife gave an embassy dinner I will never forget. Our official host and hostess in Japan were the son of Mikimoto the pearl king and his wife, who arranged for us to see the great shrine city of Kyoto, the ancient capital of Japan and the original home of the Mikimoto family. We saw the shrines, the geisha school, pearl divers at work. We fell in love with the charming, efficient people of Japan.

On one memorable afternoon I went to visit a Salvation Army orphanage in Tokyo and was greeted by a chorus of children, each one of whom looked like a tiny porcelain doll. They greeted me by singing "Do-Re-Mi" from *The Sound of Music*. I *knew* that song would be an international anthem for all children.

Tokyo even staged a combination earthquake-typhoon for my enlightenment. Richard and I stayed up for hours listening to the noise of the storm, looking out the hotel windows. I remember shouting, "Look, the top of that tree almost touched the ground." And then, "Good heavens, that one *did* touch the ground." The furniture started jumping around, mirrors swung from side to side, and as Richard and I clung to each other half from fear and half from excitement suddenly on the Armed Forces Network radio came the voice of Ethel Merman, singing "Blow Gabriel Blow." Bless that girl, she was louder than the typhoon.

On closing night in Tokyo I not only sang my best Shakespearean Japanese to them, I also surprised the company by doing a quick change into my Japanese costume, complete with an elaborate headdress—a present from the Kabuki theater company—and a parasol, and doing a long, very formal Japanese bow to the audience. Usually I went out on the ramp at the end of the show in the last Dolly costume, with the big white hat. Not that night! I practiced the quick change into Japanese costume for days, to be sure I could make it right. Everybody was astonished. I will never know who enjoyed it more: the audience, the company, or Dorry-san. In return, the audience absolutely pelted us with flowers, tied into little paper parasols which sailed right onto the stage. I have never seen anything like it, the air full of bright oiled-paper parasols with every kind of flower in the world.

I left Japan with an awful lot of souvenirs, but a big part of my heart stayed there.

Next stop for Dolly and me—Vietnam.

Next stop—no, not the Soviet Union. Russia wasn't ready for *Hello Dolly!* yet. They canceled us, with no explanation so far as I know. That cancellation, of the engagement which had been the main purpose of the tour when it began, threw everything into confusion. It also involved me in the only political-ideological controversy of my life, and the only hostile press conference of my career.

First, David Merrick had to go back to the United States and confer with the State Department about our next move. Then President Lyndon Johnson asked David to take the show to Vietnam. No full-scale show with orchestra, sets, costumes, and a large company had ever played out there, and we all knew there would be logistical problems. David agreed to try, however, and I, coming from Texas, knew the President and wanted to be of help.

Richard wanted to know the feasibility of such a big move before he agreed. After many overseas telephone calls with David Merrick, Richard made arrangements with the military to fly to Saigon, together with our chief electrician, carpenter, sound man, to make sure the whole project could be done.

Before his first flight there he made me promise not to worry, not even to awaken when he tiptoed out, about 3 A.M., to catch his military plane. I promised, but I also woke up, and I'll never forget the sight of him walking as quietly as he could down that long, long corridor, turning every few steps to wave to me. The official designation of where he was going was "difficult country," but I knew it was a war.

He made three trips to Vietnam to oversee preparations. The rest of us kept on performing in Tokyo. One night the cast met and voted not to go to Vietnam, because they disapproved of the war. Two people were willing to go, but the majority refused. At this moment Richard was in Saigon and I, having had no experience in handling a situation like this, could think of nothing except to ask for another meeting. I told them that I, too, disapproved of the war. But that didn't mean disapproval of all the Americans who had been sent there. Our President and State Department had asked us to go, our producer had agreed. I felt we had a commitment to the President and to the American troops. I felt dreadful about all of it, but I told them if nobody else would go, I would.

There were tense moments while the discussions lasted, but

in the end everyone agreed to go. I thought the crisis had passed, but it came up again at our first press conference in Saigon. The correspondents present were mostly American, some French, a few other nationalities. They didn't smile at us. They were cold, and they asked me bluntly, "Why did you come here?"

They asked if I knew how dangerous it was. I was forced to admit that I did not, because I had had no experience of the war. I got up enough courage to ask those cold faces if they were afraid. They said they were, because they knew what could happen at any time. So I said, "Well, if you can stand it, I can stand it. I'm here to perform, and I'm ready to do it anytime, anywhere."

At the time I couldn't understand their attitude toward our being there. But looking back, through all the tortuous years of the war, I think they resented our lightness in the face of very serious business. Life and death. Also, no one was prepared for such a big project as our full show. Certainly later I questioned my own impulsive "Yes, I'll go." Our happy company was at odds; I never had felt before any antagonism with either a company or with the press. I questioned my own presence there.

Still, we were there, and we had work to do. Whatever the problem was with the press, it passed. Many of them traveled with us later, and they couldn't have been nicer. As for the company, almost all of them ended up by saying it was one of the great experiences of their entire lives.

Certainly it was for me. I had never been anywhere near a battlefront. My World War II contribution had been mainly singing "The Star-Spangled Banner" at patriotic rallies. On one occasion, when I came to "And the rockets' red glare," I sang "and the robin's red breasssssttt." I didn't really notice what I had sung until I got to "the bombs bursting in air."

"Air?" That didn't rhyme at all. Then I knew what I had done.

Fortunately, nobody asked me to sing the national anthem in Vietnam, and our cast quickly became number two on the Vietnam hit parade. Ambassador Henry Cabot Lodge was number one. He gave a welcoming party, though less than twenty-four hours before the party the Vietcong had attacked the embassy and blown a huge hole right where the reception line was supposed to be.

Anything I write about our days there will sound horribly

Here I am entertaining those wonderful boys in Vietnam.

naïve to the men who fought there. I must risk that to say something about their dignity, their courage, their resourcefulness
when we intruders from another world needed their help. They
put up a whole new two-story building to house our company, in
the middle of Saigon, and they brought up trucks with generators
to give us light, water, everything we needed.

When we went to outlying bases, the military sent us by
helicopter. They were enormous things, wide open, no doors, full
of boys who looked about seventeen or eighteen, holding machine

guns. Very serious, very polite. I leaned back on what I thought were sandbags, and asked questions.

"What are these?"

"Hand grenades, ma'am," replied the very sober young man.

We flew low, with both air and helicopter full of noise. Engine noise, that funny flapping noise which helicopters make, and explosions. Dust.

"What was that?" I asked.

"An incident, ma'am."

Bombs blowing up, houses, people, around us, below us, everywhere. Nothing but incidents.

After one performance General William Westmoreland came to my tent dressing room to ask if I would accompany him to a military hospital in Saigon. He said to change from my costume, if I wanted, but to leave my makeup on because we must hurry. It was about 120 in the shade but the general looked cool, crisp, calm. He said the men of the 173rd Airborne Brigade had been trapped about two hundred miles away by Vietcong at a place called the Iron Triangle. Many had been killed.

At the hospital there were stretchers, stretchers, stretchers, corridors full of them. This was a scene I had never seen. I looked at General Westmoreland for courage, gritted my teeth, and walked with him and with Richard down the corridors and into the wards. The general was magnificent. He strode from bed to bed, with a quick look at each man's name from the chart at the foot. Then he stopped to shake hands, talk, call each man by his name.

As we were leaving, we walked past a boy on a stretcher who opened his eyes as we passed. He looked up and said, "Mary Martin? You're here? I saw you just three days ago, in Bien Hoa."

Three days ago a laughing boy sitting on a sandbag with his fatigue hat in his hands. Now here. He didn't live. Things like that kept happening, unbelievable, horrible things.

All through the tour we had a television crew from NBC doing a documentary produced by Lucy Jarvis. They asked us to walk through Saigon streets and talk to the people. Next day the whole street where we walked was blown up. The kids in the cast went out to dinner one night and got safely home, thank heaven, but the next day the spot where they had eaten was obliterated.

We arranged to give one performance in Saigon for the civilians. They were almost afraid to come into the theater for fear it would be destroyed while they were inside. It was a tiny theater, and our scenery was so scrunched that I got caught in it at one point, between the sets and the wall, and they had to ring down the curtain for several seconds while somebody extracted me.

To my regret I was unable to adapt "Hello Dolly" to their language so I could sing my own version of it to them as I did in Japan. The Vietnamese language, like Chinese, has many meanings for a single word, depending upon delicacies of pronunciation and voice pitch. I never dared to try. Like so many other things in Vietnam, the language was so complicated that the best will in the world could not cope with it.

There were many beautiful things there: the sight of a sea of close-cropped soldiers' heads, tier after tier, sitting on sandbags; the sound of their laughter; the beauty of the landscape, marred and scarred as it was; the starched, bashful courtesy of young men faced with a touch of home. There was a special moment when one of our young dancers, working in her first stage show, was reunited with the boy she had fallen in love with back home. The military found him for her in Vietnam; David Merrick brought him into my dressing room; I called the girl in. Seeing them there together . . . oh, the drama of it.

I provided some drama of my own, very much against my will, by becoming allergic to penicillin. This after having used penicillin almost since it was invented! When we arrived in Saigon I had a terrible cold. My temperature shot way up, and I was terrified that after all these miles and this trauma I wouldn't be able to perform. Richard asked for a doctor and in came the most darling navy man, so young that I blurted out, "Are you a doctor?"

"Yes, ma'am," he said. Then he questioned me severely about penicillin and whether or not I was allergic to it.

I said, "Absolutely not, give me the biggest shot you can." Then I went straight to bed. I awakened a few hours later with my entire body blown up to twice its normal size. My face was bloated like a cream puff, my eyes swollen shut. Richard raced out like a madman, and the next thing I knew I was surrounded by doctors giving me shots to counteract the penicillin.

Somebody said, as he put in a needle, "This might make you shake, but don't worry."

Ten minutes later I was shaking like those trees in the Tokyo typhoon. Uncontrollably. The next four or five hours are a blank, except for shots every forty minutes or so, and more shaking. I don't know what shock treatments are like, but maybe they're something like the sudden highs and lows, the up-down-up-down of those hours.

Somehow they got me onto the stage. Nena started to dress me. The swelling had gone down enough so that I could at least fit into my costumes, and use my hands.

"Miss Martin, can you hear me?" Nena asked. "Do you know what I'm saying?"

She read lines to me, other people's lines, and I responded automatically. I walked onstage like an automaton. The men didn't seem to notice. I remember noise. Airplanes going over, roaring. Men yelling, applauding, screaming. Pandemonium. We probably could have performed the alphabet that day, in costume, and it wouldn't have mattered to them.

By the second act, after more shots, I began to realize where I was and what I was doing. We finished the show and after the bows General Westmoreland brought Marshal Ky to the stage to say a few words and present me with an impressive plaque which told the history of Vietnam. Ky spoke beautiful English. He handed me the plaque, which looked about as big as a bed. I smiled and took hold of it. He then let go and I went boom, straight down on my knees, my white feather hat waving in the breeze. I couldn't get up.

The two men hoisted me by both elbows. Somebody took away the plaque, I straightened my hat and rendered some well-chosen words which I neither chose nor recall, and that performance was finished. I still have the plaque, and I swear it is so heavy that I would have fallen down with it even if I had been in good health that day in Saigon.

From Vietnam our company went to Okinawa and Korea. We dispersed back in Tokyo. Richard and I took a trip to Hong Kong, Bombay, Beirut, and Rome before going to London, where we joined the principals to start rehearsals with the English cast and with Gower Champion for the London run of *Hello Dolly!*

We opened in London on December 2, 1965, right back at the dear familiar Drury Lane Theatre Royal. For a week before the official opening we played benefit performances for the favorite charities of the Royal Family. One night was for the Queen Mother, one night for Queen Elizabeth's favorite charity, one night for Princess Margaret and Lord Snowden, and so on. On December 1, I got a message between acts asking if I would please stay onstage because somebody wanted to come wish me happy birthday.

Now nobody knew it was my birthday except Richard and me, but when the curtain came down that royal footman appeared again—I don't know if he was the same one, but he had the same wig and knee breeches—carrying a tray and a bottle of champagne. Behind him was a beautiful lady carrying two glasses. It was Lady Mountbatten. She smiled and said, "It's your birthday, let's drink a toast."

Bless her, she remembered. There has been a bond between us ever since *Pacific 1860*, when Noël Coward introduced us. Lady Mountbatten, Noël, and I were all Sagittarians, born within a week of each other in late November and early December. We had celebrated "our" birthdays twice before together, in 1946 and 1951, but I never dreamed that she would still remember in 1965. She did, and we drank our toasts right there on the stage.

On the night of the Queen Mother's benefit, we were advised that she wanted to come back to meet the entire company. When we finished our bows we all stood at attention behind the curtain. I could see the royal entourage coming into the wings, and then someone beckoned me over. I rushed, curtsied, and that lovely lady said she wanted to see me alone just for a moment before she met the others. "This is a special occasion for me," she said. "Do you remember the last time we met?"

"Yes, ma'am." I said. "Almost fifteen years ago."

Then she said, "*South Pacific* was the last thing my husband and I saw together."

I was deeply touched.

It was the next night, I think, that Queen Elizabeth II came to *Hello Dolly!* and she, too, asked to greet the cast onstage. I went down the line and presented all the Americans, so nervous I could hardly remember their names.

Seeing these people I admired so much, being in the London I loved, kept me going. Underneath I was deeply tired and I didn't know it. The drug cortisone masks many things. It took

Richard and I meet the lovely Queen Mother Elizabeth once again during *Hello Dolly!* in London in 1965.

over and worked for my adrenal gland, which had become almost dormant. I never felt either pain or fatigue as long as I took the cortisone pills, which had been prescribed to counter my penicillin allergy. When Richard and I traveled, with no deadlines to meet, I was fine. The moment I had to go back to work my eyes would begin to swell up so horribly that I could not see. So I went back to cortisone, and from one show to another. I was on this corrective, supportive drug for the next two or three years.

Perhaps we should have been warned. Richard and I knew many doctors all over the world, and we had had an amusing experience when we did *South Pacific* in London fifteen years before *Dolly*. That was the end of a rigorous three years of performing, and that time I *knew* I was tired. My personal doctor, a friend, came to our flat and made a series of tests to determine the source of my fatigue. He placed a false name, "Miss X," I presume, over the results and sent them to British laboratories and consultants. The laboratory technicians gave Miss X the works, and came up with a chart.

"We've never seen anything like this," they told my doctor. "Miss X is about as active as a hibernating bear early in the morning on Monday, Tuesday, Thursday, and Friday. All the chart measurements—blood pressure, reflexes, adrenaline, energy—are at the bottom, the lowest level to exist and still be alive. Then about four or five o'clock Miss X comes to life like a bear in spring. Everything goes up, up, up, and comes to a peak about midnight."

Perhaps, they indicated tactfully, Miss X was just a strange kind of lady. Except that on Wednesdays and Saturdays her whole pattern changed. On those days the energy started to build at about 11 A.M., went up and stayed up until two o'clock in the morning.

I was impressed. Not that I understood any of the tests, but I certainly recognized my own pattern. On ordinary days, after breakfast about 1 P.M., I started getting up for the show, but I didn't actually get out of bed until about four in the afternoon. On Wednesdays and Saturdays I had to get up about eleven or I would never be ready for the matinee. Also on those days, bodily alertness couldn't fall off because there wasn't time between the matinee and the evening performance. So the old adrenaline had to keep pumping away until a late dinner after the show.

Richard and I asked the doctor what could be done about it.

"Nothing," he said, "so long as you live the life you live. You're on the track like a greyhound—the dog, not the bus—and you can be dormant until it's time to run. But when that time comes, well . . ."

There have been times when I wanted to stop running, but not many times. After *Dolly* closed might have been a good time to stop. Except that I was signed to do another irresistible show. It coaxed me along like the racing greyhound chasing the mechanical rabbit. The rabbit was *I Do! I Do!*

XXII
I Do! I Do! I Do! I Do! I Do!

This show was like fate. It was meant to be in my life. When Gower Champion first talked to me about it in Brazil, Richard and I were discussing a lot of future projects, including *Mame* and *Walking Happy*. In the end there was no choice: I had to play *I Do! I Do!,* the story of a marriage.

Our musical version was based on Jan de Hartog's play *The Fourposter,* taking a couple from their wedding day until fifty years later with all the big events and little irritations of any marriage: children being born, growing up, a husband's wandering eye at that certain age, the wife's fury, reconciliation, growing older more or less gracefully, and in the end moving out of "this house" which they had shared and which had seen so much of love and life and laughter.

It seemed a culmination to me. I couldn't wait to play the aging woman at the end, because Richard and I were approaching that part of our lives together. Two very talented Texans, Harvey Schmidt and Tom Jones, who were then best known for *The Fantasticks,* did the music, lyrics, and libretto. From the moment I heard them their songs went straight to my heart. They were touching, funny, wry, bittersweet. I was moved each time I sang them, at every performance. They are still so perfect that it is difficult for me to play the record of *I Do! I Do!* Particularly the last song, "This House," and about my last words in the show, "Marriage is a very good thing, though it's far from easy. Still, it's filled this

Richard and me

house with life and love. . . ." I knew what I was talking about. Richard's house and mine had been filled with challenge, ups and downs, but always with the excitement of life and love. In our business marriage and career seldom work. Ours worked because we worked at it, because we had complete confidence in each other and respect for each other.

Just as the subject matter of *I Do! I Do!* was a culmination of my life, so the challenge of performing it was to my career. This was a very demanding musical, two full hours with just two people onstage. No supporting cast, no big production numbers, no chance to vamp while somebody else took over. Both roles required the stamina of boxers. Boxers with enough strength to go fifteen rounds.

Everybody concerned—David Merrick, Gower, the writers—knew the man they needed to play Michael to my Agnes. Robert Preston. Robert and I had made a couple of movies together, years before, when we were both under contract to Paramount. I also knew his wife, Catherine Craig, a beautiful actress who captured her Robert about the same time I captured Richard.

Bob Preston has the strength, the presence, the total professionalism needed for *I Do! I Do!* The show could benefit from his way with a song and a dance, the talent he demonstrated so brilliantly in *The Music Man*. First Bob said yes, then there was a horrible moment when he said no. He had just finished performing in *A Lion in Winter,* and he wasn't at all sure he wanted to take on another production right away. Richard and I, having just closed *Dolly* in London, were in Brazil when Bob said no. David Merrick asked us to fly to New York for one day and night to hear another actor. This man could act, he had a beautiful voice, but there just wasn't the special astringent quality of Bob.

After the audition, Gower, Richard, and I went back to our hotel. We were pretty glum. Gower asked me how badly I really wanted to do the show. I said very badly indeed, but only with Bob. We were all sitting around as at a wake when all of a sudden David Merrick walked in and said, "I've got Bob Preston."

To this day I don't know how he did it, and neither Bob nor David is telling. All I know is that David is a Sagittarian, as I am, and we don't give up easily. We are born under a sign which makes us go straight to the target.

Richard and I were so happy we could have flown back to Brazil without a plane that night. And just to make one of the show's songs, "My Cup Runneth Over," come true, we knew that Sister Gregory was waiting for us at Nossa Fazenda. She had come down for her first visit and we had to abandon her there, for a day and a night, to cope with the casting crisis in New York.

Back home in Brazil the fun began. All my life before I do a show I go into spartan training. I vocalize for hours every day, do ballet to limber up, take exercises. I didn't actually work out with a punching bag for *I Do! I Do!,* as my singing teacher, William Herman, had me do before *Sound of Music,* but I did everything else.

Sister Gregory helped me rehearse. After I had finished my puffing and panting we would retire somewhere so as not to disturb Richard, and she would cue me, Sister Gregory being Michael and I learning Agnes. It was a dream time. I can still see her in her long black robes walking among the trees in the garden, reflected in the lakes on the farm. She walked early each morning.

Then we worked. Each evening we all gathered on the verandah to watch the sun safely down and the moon safely up. Sister Gregory always wore white at night, as white as the high clouds which lit up the deep-purple and red sky.

One of the funniest songs in *I Do! I Do!* was "Flaming Agnes." This comes in the second act after Michael has announced that Agnes has begun to go to pot with age. Agnes, of course, is livid, and she proclaims that if what he says is true then "this pot is gonna be hot." She scrambles around to find a bird-of-paradise hat which she has kept hidden from Michael for years, claps it on her head, and in her most raucous voice sings about how hot Agnes can really be. While I was learning this number I remembered a crazy dance step that a Texas friend of mine used to perform after she had had one more mint julep than was absolutely necessary. It involved extending both arms with the wrists drooping and prancing slowly from one toe to the other with a little knee bend in between. It fitted the cadence of the song, and it sure looked funny.

Sister Gregory was enchanted. "That's the number I would like to do," she said, and then she hiked up her skirts and did the dance around the room with me. With that seal of approval, I couldn't wait to show it to Gower. He liked it, too, and added many embellishments, such as having me wear Michael's huge bedroom slippers while I did it. Gower's mind is so inventive, and so *on key*.

It is certainly no secret that sudden improvisations, born of memories of personal experiences or funny scenes, provide the human touches audiences love. Because this show was about marriage, just about everybody involved in it had plenty of experience. While Harvey and Tom were writing the song "Nobody's Perfect" they kept asking everyone for examples of irritating little husbandly or wifely tricks. One whom they asked was Tom Jones's wife, Elinor, a very successful writer herself. Elinor thought for a minute and then said to Tom, "You chew in your sleep."

"I do *what?*" Tom asked. Then he put the line into the song and it always brought down the house.

During one rehearsal, just to liven things up or work off some surplus energy, I climbed onto one of the children's tricycles and rode it wildly around the stage. Gower watched for a moment and then said, "Great. Leave it in. Do it every night."

It was his idea that after the wedding scene I should stop

my mad movement for a moment—Bob and I were always running, through the whole show—and pause, and throw my bouquet
into the audience. It was the first time I had thrown anything into
the audience on purpose since I beaned the lady in the glasses with
the prop bracelet in Detroit. This time it turned out better. Because I always threw the bouquet from the same spot, with the
same gesture, the flowers landed in practically the same place every
night. By chance, the area I hit happened to be our own house
seats, though I didn't know it. People kept coming backstage to
thank me for throwing the bouquet right to them, not knowing
that I couldn't see far enough into the dark to aim at anybody.

Our entire rehearsal time was like a three-way tennis game,
a love match. Bob would suddenly do something which Gower and
I loved. Gower would think up something we couldn't wait to try.
I stayed awake nights dreaming up things to please them. I can't
ever remember having such concentrated fun while working. In
the end it was the truth of the show, its honest little touches which
made its appeal.

Compared to the book and score of other shows, this one
was changed hardly at all. Tom and Harvey had written such tight,
true words and music that there were almost no changes. There
were a few in the second act, and from one of them came one of the
funniest scenes in the show, when Robert and I played a very off-
key duet on violin and saxophone. Harvey and Tom had originally
written a lovely number called "Thousands of Flowers" but it was
too lyrical for that spot in the show. We needed a big pickup number. They came up with "When the Kids Get Married," in a knee-
slapper hillbilly style. Just what we needed, but Gower thought it
should have some special business.

"Can you two do anything besides sing and dance and act
a bit?" he asked.

"I can play the violin," I said. After all, I still had Mother's
violin and Queen Mary's music stand.

"I can play the saxophone," said Bob.

"You can't!"

"We can."

That's how that terrible sound of music and beautiful bit
of business got into the show. It also gave me a chance to include
Bessie Mae in *I Do! I Do!* While I warmed up with the bow and

the violin I sang a little "Bessie Mae, uh . . . a-Bessie Mae Sue Ella," tapping my foot in the fuzzy bedroom slippers, before I let fly with "When the Kids Get Married."

I Do! I Do! opened at the Forty-sixth Street Theatre in New York on December 6, 1966, with one of the smallest casts in Broadway history, and played to absolutely capacity houses for more than a year. They laughed, they cried, they came back to see it again. Bob and I had no standbys, no understudies. This has seldom been done before. Usually there were understudies or a swing company, but David felt that if people paid to see just the two of us, then that's all the people they should see. Before rehearsals began, he agreed to cut out the Wednesday matinees. We had a gentlemen's agreement to do Saturday matinees as long as we were physically able. Bob and I did them for the first six months of the Broadway run, then we had to stop. I missed one performance during the Boston tryouts, when I had such a painful swelling in the joint of my big right toe that I had to be hospitalized. While we played New York I think Bob and I missed only one performance each. On those rare nights, the show was canceled and the audience got rain checks.

Though we had no other actors to help, we did have a big orchestra, hidden behind a scrim at the back of the stage so we could get closer to the audience. And we had The Bed.

The Bed was a huge four-poster, the center of every scene, the symbol of our marriage. It was the only thing which never changed throughout the performance. Sometimes we felt it was playing against us instead of with us: it was so solid, so enduring. It could never catch cold or sprain its ankle; it never had to hail a taxi in a blizzard to get to the theater on time.

It was occasionally forced to move, or twirl, and once it even managed to stab me. During one bit of "Flaming Agnes" I had to slide down the back of the bed and one night a nail or tack or something scraped straight down my back. I bled through the whole scene but didn't know it, and neither did the audience because my costume for that number was blood red.

The bed also bucked on cue and twirled. We twirled it. Its wildest gyrations were in the first act. Bob and I had come home as newlyweds. We climbed into bed and sang "Good Night" to each other, with a refrain about "go to sleep." Then, after a dis-

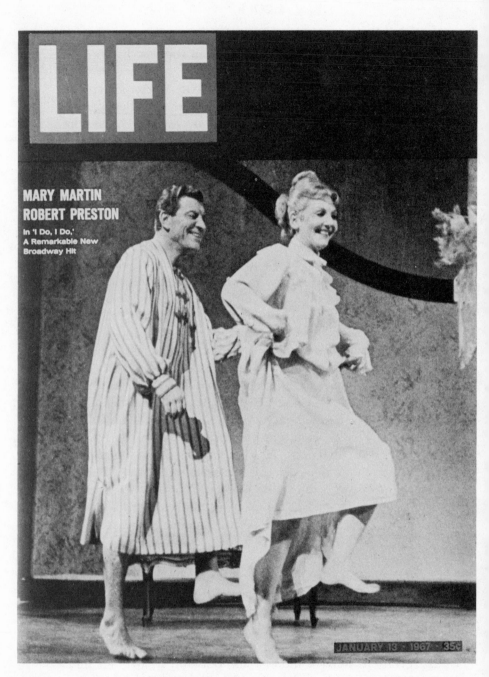

This one speaks for itself.

creet interval of connubial bliss and a short snooze, Bob got up to dance around, twirl the bed, and sing "I Love My Wife." Of course he woke me up twirling the bed. So then I got up and we danced a soft shoe together, barefooted, he in his nightshirt and I in my nightgown. It was a dear number, and we both gave the bed a push or two while we did it.

It seems to me I was always pushing that darn bed, shoving it forward, bringing it back. Not only that, I had to bring on all the props. Gower was a demon; he loved to see me carry props. Naturally, with only the two of us onstage and only one small break between acts, the stagehands couldn't possibly walk out and place things. They could only hand them to us—mostly to me—in the wings. Once I asked why Bob couldn't carry some of the props and Gower simply said, "He has his part and you have yours." Then, with a gleeful gleam in his eye, he spelled it out: "In this scene, Mary, you bring on the baskets, the children's toys, the hats." Or "Now, Mary, the clothesline, the clothespins, the baby's wash . . . and when you walk off don't forget to take the books, the tricycles. . . ."

Gower plotted the production like a wartime invasion— every moment, every prop, every second. One of us, Bob or I, had to be onstage the entire time, singing or talking, while the other ran off to make necessary costume changes. I had fifteen costumes and five wigs, so I had to hustle my bustle. The moment I went off, Nena and two assistants swarmed all over me, changing wigs, clothes, shoes. Bob would continue to speak his lines to me, or sing, from the stage as I answered him, on a microphone, while dressing. Then I would rush back on and Bob went off. This sort of thing takes not only stamina but also choreography. Gower is a master of that. Every move, every change, was made on a beat of the music.

At one point early in the show Bob had to disrobe completely in front of the audience, going from his full-dress wedding suit and top hat down to his long johns, which we in Texas used to call a union suit. While he is doing all this, he thinks he hears his bride, Agnes, coming back to the bedroom, so he races to get his nightshirt on over the union suit, pop on a nightcap, and hop into bed. Bob's timing on this mad quick-change was a high spot of the show. It may have looked easy but it took hours and hours of work. All through rehearsals Bob and his dresser, Jimmy, stayed late at the theater to work on it. I have seldom seen anyone work so hard for just a few seconds onstage, but all the hours paid off in a show-stopping performance.

He was handsomely considerate of me, too. We both love garlic and Bob is particularly partial to Italian food loaded with it. Unfortunately it makes me ill when I work, but because we had to kiss about every fifteen seconds through the entire performance, Bob always brought me a tiny taste of his Italian dinner before we went on. Hence no problem while kissing. I call that consideration. It became part of the show, part of the stage marriage, part of the truth of *I Do! I Do!*

Bob also brought himself. He remained strong enough for a year on Broadway to carry me to our bridal bed in the first act, then bounce off through the door with Agnes in his arms at the end of the second act as sprightly as "fifty years before."

Then we closed on Broadway, and I had to go to the hospital for the first major surgery of my life, a hysterectomy. We had already promised to take *I Do! I Do!* on the road for twelve to fourteen months, so I tried to recuperate as fast as possible and go back to work. Now that I look back on it, I realize that having a hysterectomy sort of "between shows" is unwise, but a commitment is a commitment.

Off we went, Richard and I, Bob and his Cathy, and we had a marvelous time all over the country both on and off stage. Bob and I were both coming apart at the seams, but we didn't know it. Bob began catching colds which he never acknowledged, and having troubles with his voice. I had diverticulitis and didn't know it—the cortisone I was still taking masked it. We were all spared the sight of a burst abscess right on stage at the theater in Detroit by the fact that I woke up one Saturday morning absolutely unable to move. Dr. Edward Biggs of Chicago flew up to Detroit to diagnose my problem. "If you want to live," he said, "and we hope without a major operation, then my word is law. Stop working."

We stopped. We went out in a blaze of love and laughter on a Friday-night performance in Detroit, and that was the end. Except for the book. All through *I Do! I Do!* Richard and I had worked like beavers on a needlepoint book. It was mostly about how we got interested in needlepoint, and how to do it, but it also included some of our experiences, some funny stories. I talked my version into a tape recorder, and Richard wrote his, at night. Then we'd put the two together. They were almost always identical.

We wrote, rewrote, and finished the book, and it was published in 1969.

It gave us a huge, happy laugh when later we saw the book in a display window of a bookstore near our apartment. In the big city of New York there was a handwritten sign on the top of a stack of copies.

The sign said, "Neighborhood girl makes good."

XXIII
With This Card
I Thee Pledge

Toward the end of the run of *I Do! I Do!,* I wrote The Contract on a crazy card for Richard's birthday, in April, 1969. We had lived with contracts all our lives, but this was the first one *I* had written and it was special. It said, "This is for two years in Brazil. For you to be the greatest *fazendeiro* that ever was. No matter what comes up—shows, television, pictures—we will not come back."

Richard opened the card, read the contract, looked surprised, and then—so quickly, I cannot tell you—he signed it, too.

We fulfilled it, and the two years of The Contract went by so fast that we stayed on in Brazil. Those were the happiest years of our lives. If only they could have lasted ten instead of almost four.

Many people who knew that I was ill at the end of the run of *I Do! I Do!* assumed that The Contract was made to give me time to rest. That isn't true. The Contract was for Richard. I wrote it while I felt strong and healthy, because I wanted him to be in the place he loved more than any other, living the life he loved. He had given so much to me; now was our chance to be together with no outside interests, no interruptions except pleasant ones.

He and I had stresses and strains in our years together which we tried desperately to hide, not only from the world but also from ourselves. Unfortunately it seems true that any life, however full it is, however generously rewarded, is pulled this way and that by

the very things which are most desired—love itself, success, friends—
and the constant necessity to compromise one thing to fulfill another.

Richard spent years trying to live both his life and mine.
He got up early to take care of all the complex details of our career, correspondence, home, financial affairs. He surrounded me
with protection and silence while I slept to be ready for the next
performance. Then he took me to the theater, did more office work
in our New York apartment while I performed, saw me safely home
again. Endless days and nights of this exhausted him physically and
emotionally. There were years in which he drank too much. He
never had been a drinker. When we were married, and for years
after, he would have maybe a beer or one glass of wine—rarely.
Then a doctor in California told him that a cocktail before dinner
would relieve his strain, enable him to relax. That's how it started.
Neither of us knew that Richard was hypoglycemic, susceptible to
alcohol. The condition is the opposite of diabetes; people who
have it cannot, must not, drink. Because we didn't know, because
the doctor had prescribed cocktails, Richard drank. There were
times when he would drink until oblivion and not remember what
he had said or done. It was devastating to watch this man destroy
himself. Finally, because of his love and concern for me, he com-
mitted himself to a hospital for treatment. I wasn't allowed to see
him for months. I was in constant contact with his doctors, but I
have never felt so alone in all my life. I learned that life without
Richard meant very little to me.

I cannot say enough for those wonderful doctors who
helped Richard find his way back from utter despair. But the
desire had to come from him, and he won. All through that
period I, too, was headed for a physical collapse, though I knew
it no more than Richard knew he was hypoglycemic. I was terrified that perhaps my own energy, my need to work, had pushed
Richard toward his crisis. Mine didn't come until the end of
the New York run of *I Do! I Do!*, when I had the hysterectomy.
When it was all over I alarmed the doctors by being so *up*, so
on, so eager to sit straight up in bed and entertain all comers.
Dr. William Given, the same man who had saved my life when
I lost our baby boy, came into my room one day and asked, "Why
are you so unhappy?"

"But I am not unhappy," I said. Then I burst into tears.

Dr. Given told Richard that my behavior was not normal after major surgery. He asked our permission to call a psychiatrist. We agreed. When the psychiatrist walked in I started having uncontrollable giggles. The man's so gentle, so considerate manner, something even about the way he looked, his eyes, was exactly like Vinnie Donehue. My Vinnie a psychiatrist? I couldn't stop laughing. Then I broke down again.

"I am caged," I told him. "Caged, caged. I live in a beautiful apartment. I have a beautiful home in Brazil. I have a beautiful life. But all I do is perform, sleep, rehearse, get ready for the next show, then perform again." I complained that other people could go to Paris, take cruises, window-shop in peace and quiet. I couldn't. At that point I don't think I had been inside a store for ten years. If I needed something it was brought to me. I never went to it.

My problems poured out in such a flood that I couldn't believe my own voice: never in my adult life had I been able to catch cold, like other people, and go to bed. I couldn't have a headache, or get tired, or feel out of sorts. I had to go out there and *perforrrrrrrm.*

Even at the height of my self-pity, I knew it was nobody's fault but my own. Nobody made me do it. It was the life I had chosen. I was raging at a life I had made, but in my heart I was blaming my husband, who had always tried so hard to make everything perfect for me. How often we put the blame on those closest to us!

I know my outburst hurt Richard, but he forgave me. We shared our two crises together. They are agonizing things to remember, painful things to tell. I recount them only because we survived them, because this is what the word *marriage* means to me. When we took the vow "in sickness and in health . . . till death do us part" we meant it, and we lived it.

Ours was a happy ending. Richard came out with flying colors, I began to feel better, and we went happily away to our beautiful Brazilian interlude.

During our first months back at Nossa Fazenda I rested, rode horses, consumed several tons of fruit and bacon and eggs for breakfast. Breakfast is my favorite meal of any day. We both got up at dawn, went to bed about nine in the evening. We got tanned, healthy, peaceful. I still didn't have my customary vitality, but at the end of the road tour of *I Do! I Do!,* and six weeks in a Chicago hospital, I had learned from Dr. Biggs that it would be six months before I could shake all the aftereffects of cortisone and rely upon my own adrenaline supply again.

One day I walked into Richard's office at the farm and said, "I would like to start a little needlepoint shop."

"You'd like to do what?" he asked.

I explained that he was busy farming all day, dealing with the staff, planning new houses and waterfalls, crops, and gardens. I thought it would be fun to teach needlepoint, design pillows, rugs, and bags, and have a little shop in nearby Anápolis.

Richard, who was always fascinated by dates and statistics, stared at me for a moment, then looked at his calendar.

"It's six months!" he announced. "To the day."

He encouraged me to go right ahead but said he didn't want to get involved. He already had too many things on his mind. By then I had two close Brazilian friends, Jalma Wilding and Marielys Bueno, whose husbands were leading doctors in Anápolis. They agreed to help me. I knew exactly what I wanted —a little house in a garden, in the center of town. We found just that on a tiny street called Maria, which seemed an omen. The house was small, with a huge water tank on top, three palm trees in the garden, and a field of waving corn next door. It belonged to a dentist who was busy drilling a woman's teeth when Jalma located him. The dentist put down his drill and the patient was patient for half an hour while Jalma explained that we wanted to rent his house.

The dentist wanted to sell, not rent. After Richard's approval, I hired a contractor to knock out a partition to make the house functional as a shop. Brazilians are very efficient at knocking things out, but I didn't intend for the contractor to knock the whole thing down. That's what happened. The house beams had been so eaten by termites that when one partition went, the weight of the water tank collapsed the entire thing. Now I owned quite a bit of corn, three palm trees, and a heap of termite wood.

I was nervous about describing this disaster to Richard, but as always he was magnificent. He remarked quietly that he guessed I would have to build a new shop on the land. I begged him to make at least a sketch for a new building for me. Of course he got fascinated and designed the whole thing. It was terribly chic, with an upswept roof which made it look very Oriental, red lacquer hand-carved doors, and decorative tiles outside.

As a general color scheme we used the colors of the dust jacket of my needlepoint book—red, green, white, and black. Nossa Loja, "our shop," was Chinese red with black and white tiles outside. I decorated the inside with masses of green hanging ferns, huge display tables, wicker furniture which was made in Anápolis. The wicker man became so expert that he even covered our upright piano at home in white wicker. I spent months with an ironmonger and a sink maker, figuring out how to make a tip-back chair for shampoo sinks. When it was finished, and it worked, I felt like Thomas Edison.

The sinks were for the beauty parlor. My Brazilian friends and I had decided that neeedlepoint wouldn't be enough to keep us going. Brazilian ladies would first have to learn about do-it-yourself projects, and that might take time. One of the doctor husbands remarked that most women seemed to live in beauty parlors, so we designed one for Nossa Loja. I went to Anápolis' most successful hairdressing establishment and asked if the four sisters there—all named Martins—would like to move to our new building. They were delighted. When they asked what the rent would be I had no idea. "Oh, whatever you're paying here," I said. A businesswoman I am not.

When the Loja opened—right on time, a miracle in a Latin country—I introduced the, ahem, Mary Martin collection. I had been having a ball using the fabulous, colorful Brazilian materials to whip up caftans for myself and my friends, or dresses made like Persian pajamas upside down. Mine were simple, loose things with only two seams, because two seams were all I ever understood.

Dema, the wife of Zico, our farm manager, made the first ones. She had an ancient pedal sewing machine which she operated barefoot, but she was a wizard with it. I never learned to draw or design properly so every single garment had to be fitted on me, with me giving directions in sign language. Eventually I learned how to say "longer," "shorter," and "tighter" in Portuguese but that was about all.

Marielys painted beautifully, so I was able to teach her how to paint canvas for needlepoint. Jalma the jewel turned out to have unbelievable powers of organization. She pulled everything together.

Somehow we managed to get fifty models ready for my first collection and my first customers. More than a thousand people came to the opening, flying in from Rio and São Paulo, driving from Brasilia and surrounding cities. For entertainment we had a four-man combo of young Mormon missionaries who had formed their own group and volunteered to play and sing for us. Richard and I dressed up Nedje, one of Dema and Zico's nine children, in a Vietnamese national costume which I still had in my wardrobe from the *Hello Dolly!* tour. Nedje in costume was official greeter at the opening, looking like a toy Liat in *South Pacific*.

Nossa Loja was an immediate hit. The building itself, all on one floor but with rooms the height of two stories, brought a new style to the entire town. Lots of people came just to see "the Chinese building those crazy Americans put up in Anápolis." *Women's Wear Daily* sent a writer and photographer, Hector Arce and Frank Diernhammer, all the way down to do an article on the Loja and my fashions.

Jack Paar came down twice to do specials for his television show on the farm, the Loja, our life there. The first time, I think it was 1965, he brought his wife, Miriam, and Randy, their daughter. They are an intensely close family, and I think at first we attracted them because Richard, Heller, and I were as close as they were. We had never met before that first visit but we all became fast friends. Jack and Miriam came back for another show in 1971.

Eventually the Loja was so successful that I had ten seamstresses at work in their homes all over Anápolis. Dema would make the first dress, the model, and I would take it down the line to the others to copy. They were busy as bees and old Mary March was busier than anyone, dashing from one house to another, acting as tailor's dummy. We also branched out into hats, bags, jewelry. We flew ten thousand miles all over Brazil to choose something from each of the states—hammocks, ceramics, jewelry, whatever was the specialty of the state, for the Loja.

On our second Christmas there Richard and I learned that Heller and her family would not come down for the holidays. They were having marital difficulties which eventually led to divorce. Christmas Eve without Heller and the little boys would be just too lonely, so we decided to open the Loja for the evening and have a Christmas party there for the staff, Dema and Zico and the children, the cook, the maid, the brothers and sisters—about twenty-five or thirty people. Dema had never seen the store, after having made all those dresses, and a lot of the others hadn't seen Anápolis at night with the Christmas decorations up. It was quite an expedition with our car and the big Ford truck loaded to the gills. We had records of Christmas carols in Portuguese, champagne, flowers, and one of my "Silent Night" recordings. But there was nothing silent about that night.

In the middle of it all there was a Brazilian downpour, the kind which has to be seen to be believed. Then Dema's feet began to hurt because she had put on shoes for the occasion. But we had fun, and when the rain quieted down a little everybody went out to see the sights, leaving Richard and Nedje and me at the Loja just in case any customers came in.

Sure enough, one did. A car pulled up and out got a man, his wife, the wife's mother, and a baby in arms. They were all 5 by 5. The wife wanted a pants suit and her husband made me understand that she should have the best, whatever she wanted, expense was no matter. Nedje, who by this time had been promoted to head *vendeuse,* thought it would be fun to let me be the saleslady. Well, everything in the shop was a bit too tight for this lady. I was getting out pants, jackets, everything, like crazy, trying to find something that would fit. Piles of clothes everywhere, fittings, rushing around, while Richard entertained the mother, the husband, and the baby.

I was getting more and more desperate. By this time we had started buying a few clothes in addition to the ones I was making. Some of them were kind of tacky and I had them stashed in a back room. Somehow the lady and I got back there, too, and she hauled out one model and said that's what she wanted. I couldn't stand it on her; it looked awful. She kept looking at herself in it, and I kept saying, "Wait a minute." Finally in all the bedlam I spotted a suit which looked as if it would fit, and put it on her. It was perfect. The lady kept saying, "No, no," and I kept saying, "Yes, yes, come out here and show your husband and mother how great you look."

The poor lady was in tears, but she walked out—and then

they all started having hysterics. The whole family was laughing fit to kill, Nedje was laughing, everybody was jabbering in Portuguese, and finally Nedje said, "Dona Maria, *you've sold the lady her own suit!*"

By this time I was so embarrassed I let her have the one she wanted. Richard went out into the rain to try to find Dema somewhere in the town to come to the Loja and start opening seams and making adjustments. They both came back dripping wet. There was one final crisis: the shop had an electric sewing machine and Dema had never used one before. Nedje had to get it going and explain to her mother how it worked; and then at last, whew, we sent our Christmas Eve customer away happy. We laughed all the way home.

During the Loja years Janet often came back to her beloved Brazil to be our guest, with her husband, Paul Gregory. Paul had been a friend of all of ours for years, and he and Janet married five years after Adrian's death. Paul is a dynamic, larger-than-life man who has done theater, films, television, been agent, director, producer. His productions are always exciting—including the ones in the kitchen. He is a great gourmet cook.

At one point in his career he was with MCA and was Ralph Edwards' agent. Years later Ralph, who had been impressed by Paul's innovative mind, asked him to produce some of the *This Is Your Life* television shows. Paul's first great idea was to do some of the shows outside the United States, in exotic parts of the world. Ralph loved it and said yes to the first specific suggestion—my life in Brazil.

Paul and Janet set everything up with Richard, in an exchange of cables all of which got wildly garbled as the Brazilian cable offices tried to cope with the mysterious English language. Even if I had seen some of those strange messages I might not have understood them, but I didn't. The whole point was to surprise me. And believe me, that it did!

I thought absolutely nothing about it—except to feel joy—when Janet and Paul came for a visit and Janet said she would like to go off into the jungle to look at some land she and Adrian owned. I couldn't wait to go with her. She and Jibran and I took the Jeep and were away for eighteen hours, way up in the jungle. When we got back, Richard and Paul told us that a man had called from a television station in Rio. He wanted to come up and photograph the Loja, televise me showing people the shop. Of course, I agreed, and Janet and I went to the Loja beauty shop to get all done up for Brazilian television.

We were almost finished when a crew of men with lights, cameras, microphones, all the paraphernalia TV people use all over the world, started setting up at the entrance of the Loja. They told us to stand by, near the red front door, until they gave us a cue, then walk out and greet some people they had brought for the occasion. We got our cue and walked out, and coming toward us were a man and his wife. As we met, the wife shyly stood back and the man, looking very *"chic-ie"* (that's the way the Brazilians always pronounced it) in a colorful shirt, a Brazilian-style straw hat, and a snazzy moustache, started talking a mile a minute. In Portuguese. But was it? I am not the right person to question this language, having never completely mastered it, but his pronunciation *was* odd.

Janet said, "That doesn't sound quite like Portuguese to me."

At this point the man whipped off his straw hat, peeled off his moustache, and said, "I'm Ralph Edwards. This is your life!"

I went into shock—right on camera!—and then delight. I had known both Ralph and his wife, Barbara—the lovely shy lady standing outside the Loja door—many years ago.

Janet, Ralph, and I were bundled into a horse-drawn buggy for a short sequence of "riding off to the farm." Because it was so far we got out and went most of the way by car, then got into the buggy again to ride down the bamboo-shaded road to the house itself. All the way Ralph and Janet looked pleased as punch, explained how they had fooled me. But there was much more in store for me.

As I stood on our verandah, out came my sister, Jerry, Heller wearing a sarong and such a deep tan that I didn't recognize her at first; Bessie Mae Sue Ella and her husband, Jac Austin, whom I also didn't recognize because he had grown so much hair and moustache that he looked like a cross between Mark Twain and Buffalo Bill. Well, screams, kissing, joy. Then came another surprise, a chorus of children singing "Do-Re-Mi" —in English. Jalma had spent a week teaching the words phonetically to her children and friends' children. When they fin-

Sister visits me in Brazil.

ished the song out marched, from the hidden back row, my grandsons Timothy and Matthew. What emotion!

Ralph Edwards had flown them all out to Brasilia a few days ahead of time and hidden them in hotels. While Janet lured me off into the jungle everyone ran around like crazy at the farm making final arrangements. While Janet and I were safely at the beauty parlor, the cast of characters assembled in the house.

It was fabulous, but the most wonderful thing of all—and I shall be grateful to Ralph, Paul, and Janet all my life—was to see my husband standing on our terrace when we arrived, facing a camera and a mike for the first time. Richard absolutely loathed having his picture taken and would *not* do a voice recording. He was thin most of his life and he thought he looked dreadful. He said no to all photographers, would turn away, put his hands in front of his face, anything.

He also felt deeply that one star in the family was enough. He always wanted to be in the background. Consequently I have very few good photographs of him. But now, because of Ralph Edwards' thrilling show, I have a filmed record of my Richard, family, friends, and Brazil.

For months and months I absolutely loved the Loja. Then it began to take its toll. Jalma and Marielys had families to look after. Our Nedje at age eighteen had graduated from greeter to manager, and she even kept the books. But still Jalma and Marielys and I realized we weren't running the Loja, it was running us. I had to spend more time away from home, which was not the point of Brazil. Jalma was just too good and kind ever to tell the tiniest white lie, so when people came from Rio or São Paulo or Brasilia, insisting they wanted to buy *the* dress or *the* needlepoint from me, she would hop into her car and come rushing out seventeen kilometers to tell me somebody wanted my attention.

I decided there was no reason to exhaust all concerned, so in the second year, just before my birthday, when Richard asked if there was anything I particularly desired, I said, "Yes, I want to close the Loja." I had tried it, loved it, seen it succeed. Now it was finished. Just like a show.

We had no thought then that another closing was coming, the closing of the happiest chapter of the thirty-three years of our life.

It happened in March, 1973. Janet and Paul again were with us on the farm and the four of us had had the most marvelous time working on an idea we had for a "talking cookbook," on tape. We had been sitting around giggling, talking our recipes, until almost sunset. Richard had been ill with a cold and was sleeping in one of the guesthouses. All our married life he refused to stay in our room if he had a cold, he was so afraid I would catch it. That evening we all thought he was much better. I urged him to come back to our room. He said he would stay away one more night, not to take a chance. We all retired about ten o'clock.

Next morning Richard, who was always an early riser, hadn't appeared by eight o'clock. I walked to the guesthouse and found him lying on the bathroom floor in agony. He had been there all night, in too much pain to move, unable to call for help. Frantically I drove to Anápolis to get Jalma's husband,

Dr. Joe. Richard hated hospitals and he fought us all because he
didn't want to leave the farm. Finally we persuaded him to go
to Anápolis. All that day and all night Dr. Joe and the staff did
X rays, trying to find out what was wrong with him. Facilities
weren't elaborate, and Richard had to keep getting up, in that
horrible pain, and going for X rays and tests. The X rays showed
an enormous block in the intestine, but the doctors couldn't
determine what it was. They advised that we fly him to Brasilia
to a larger hospital.

Our friend Jibran made the hospital arrangements. Everyone, including the American ambassador, William Rountree, and
his wife, Susan, and a new friend, the Netherlands ambassador
Leopold van Ufford, helped us. All except Richard, that is. He
just wanted to go back home. Dr. Joe found a light missionary
plane to take him from Anápolis to Brasilia. I wanted desperately
to go, but there was room only for Richard, Dr. Joe, the pilot,
and an oxygen tank. They flew and I drove, for two hours, with
Zico. Janet and Paul followed us in another car. By the time I
got to the hospital Richard was in shock, surrounded by a dozen
doctors, including a heart specialist, lung specialist, surgeons. He
didn't know me.

The decision to operate had to be made quickly. When
it was over the young surgeon and the other doctors came out
looking relieved. The operation was successful; the blockage
wasn't a blood clot of the main artery, as they had feared, but
adhesions from a double-hernia operation years before. I stayed
in the room we had reserved for Richard, but he never got there.
They took him straight to intensive care, where I could not go.
As I had neither slept nor eaten for two days the doctors sent
me to our hotel with Janet and Paul, and promised to call me if
there was any change. There was no call.

Early in the morning Jibran came to my room to say
the outlook was not good. His son-in-law, who had performed
the operation and had never left Richard's side during the whole
agonizing time, had called to say that Richard's lungs were filling.

The doctors wanted him to cough, but none of them
spoke English. They decided to break all the rules and admit me
to the intensive care unit to plead with him to cooperate. He
recognized me, but with all the pain, the drugs, the shock, he
was wild with fury and in no mood to cooperate. He kept saying

there was nothing wrong with him; who were all these people, why didn't they speak English? I stayed with him, pleaded with him. But this dear man who used to cough so he could be heard all over the farm now couldn't make a sound. It hurt too much.

I had to watch my love fill with poison, watch the doctors try everything—draining the lungs, performing a tracheotomy—in vain. In the end it was pneumonia that took him away. Everything stopped functioning, his lungs, kidneys, his brilliant brain. But not his heart. His beautiful giving heart still belonged to me for a little while. As I held his hand, clasped tightly in mine, as our hands had been clasped for thirty-three years, Richard left me. When he needed me most, I couldn't help him. How could he ever know the depth of my love?

Richard and I both had put in our wills that we wanted to be cremated. On that ghastly March morning I learned that it wasn't possible in Brazil. Dear God, what a decision. I had either to take Richard away from the place he loved or go against what I knew to be his firm wish for cremation.

Once again friends came to the rescue. Bob Jacobs of Florida found a solution. He could arrange to fly us to Miami, have a quick service, have Richard's body cremated, and get us out again quickly, spending only one night in the United States. I couldn't bear the thought of staying longer. I had to do what Richard wanted done, then go home to our farm. Heller, who had flown to Brazil as soon as she knew Richard was desperately ill, Janet, and our friend and lawyer David Warshaw made that awful trip with me from Brasilia to Guatemala to Miami. There faithful Tad met us, and Heller's fiancé Bromley DeMeritt, whom I had not met before. Didi, who had just made the long trip from New York, stayed at the farm with Paul Gregory to help her through the awful hours.

Everything in Miami was mercifully quick, quiet, dignified. I had no strength for even one more decision, so David Warshaw took Richard's ashes back to New York with him. The rest of us flew back to Brazil, hours and hours through the night, to that very silent farm.

As soon as possible I went away, as far as I could get from the memories. I ran to Sister and her comfort in Fort Worth. Didi went with me and there was another circle . . . our clasped-hands ring had been made, to Richard's design, by a man named

Paul Flato in California. Afterward he moved to Mexico City and he wrote us that he would love to see us again sometime, see the ring again. I had no intention of ever going there, so I forgot about it. The best air connections Didi and I could make from Brazil to Fort Worth were through Mexico City. We found ourselves there resting for a day or two on the way back. One day we walked out of the hotel, and just across the boulevard was Paul Flato's shop and his sign. I walked past it two or three times, but I couldn't face going in, or face Paul Flato. I didn't even have the ring then, because a month before Richard's illness it had broken in two and dropped off my hand. After Miami I had given it to Heller to take back to New York and have mended.

For weeks, with Sister and Bob in Fort Worth, I couldn't bear to leave the house, see anyone, talk to anyone except Heller and my Larry, who had been in London making a picture at the time of Richard's death.

While I was in Fort Worth, and even now when I have the long nights, when I question my innermost self about our life, my guilts, my regrets for many things, I wonder if I ever really knew my husband. Does anyone ever completely know a person even after three decades together? Richard was a very private person. Yet he had the glorious faculty of making each day exciting and sharing his excitement. Whether it was work or play, producing in the theater or producing on a farm, dictating a letter, reading a play aloud, watching a sunset, he made each day brighter.

Among my many questions was a practical one, a decision one. Where should I put Richard's ashes? Oddly enough, we had never discussed where we wanted to be buried. We decided on cremation, and never thought beyond that.

I have never believed that the real person, the spirit within, is under the ground. Only the ashes or the body is there. The spirit of Richard remains forever with all who knew and loved him. It will be reflected, echoed, immortal, in Heller and her children and her children's children.

Still there should be a place, a specific spot, to which these bearers of the spirit can go and say, "This was my father . . . my grandfather . . . my grandmother." Memories are stronger with a focus, a place of continuity.

So I began to think backward. What if I had gone first? I knew that Richard would have taken me back to Weatherford, to the family plot with Mother and Daddy and my brother, Preston, who lived only one day. Slowly the conviction came that my hometown was *our* place. In my heart I knew I would not live in Brazil again, not without Richard.

Sister went with me to the cemetery. It was easier than I had expected—simple, peaceful. I remembered the beautiful marble clasped hands which hung on the terrace of our New York apartment. Nancy Hayward found them for us in Europe, and Richard and I once had remarked that they would be suitable one day for our mutual marker stone.

I telephoned Ben Washer in New York, who had been our friend and theater colleague for ages. I asked him to see if the hands were still there, if he could ship them to me. Ben called back that they were there; he would take care of sending them. Several days went by. Then Ben called back.

"Mary," he said, "I don't know how to tell you this. After we talked there was a terrific rain and wind storm. When I went to get the hands I found they had crashed to the terrace floor during the night. They are smashed to bits."

In the end I used some smaller, bisque clasped hands, another present from friends. They are there, with Richard's name and the dates.

I think I was moving, without knowing it, into the future. I was putting Richard back into what had been my life before I met him, into what my life was to become after him. So that I could link him even more strongly to me.

That circle is closed, that door is shut.

XXIV
A Door Closes,
Windows Open

Heller brought me back into the wide warm world with a joyous announcement: she was to marry Bromley DeMeritt in summer, 1973. I was so happy for them both, so touched when Heller said she wanted Tad to stand in for her father at the wedding. I knew how pleased Richard would have been. I came back to life enough to join Heller in a phone call to Tad.

That summer I took a house on Martha's Vineyard, close to my friends Kit Cornell and Nancy Hamilton. I wanted to restore my soul, and the ocean has always helped. Nena Smith went with me and we walked for miles on the beach in the cold brisk air without talking. We never had to. Suddenly one day Ernest Adams appeared, saying quietly, "Madam, I'm here to help with the wedding." Such friendships are rare, precious.

It was a garden wedding with beautiful blue skies, roses on stone walls, the ceremony under a grape arbor. It was Mexican in theme, Quaker in service, officiated by a distinguished Congregational minister, Dr. Eldon H. Mills, celebrated on Bastille Day, July 14.

My family came, Richard's sister, Bromley's family, whom I met for the first time and loved, Bessie Mae and her family, friends and friends and friends. Dearest Kit, who had been so ill, came, and with that fabulous life force which saw her through her brilliant career she walked—for the first time in many months—across the garden on the wedding day.

As I looked around at my children and grandchildren, the old friends, my handsome new son-in-law, I could almost feel my heart opening, expanding. I had loved them always, but how many of these family occasions I had missed, over the years!

How wonderful it is to be the age I am! What a lovely time of life!

I often have felt that I cheated my children a little. I was never so totally *theirs* as most mothers are. I gave to audiences what belonged to my children, got back from audiences the love my children longed to give to me. There in the wedding sunshine I felt I had been given a very valuable present which I could unwrap slowly in the days and weeks and years ahead, savoring each moment, each discovery of the contents of my special present.

I got to baby-sit for a full week with Timothy and Matthew. They let me sing to them when they went to bed. I took them to my favorite places—shooting galleries, popcorn stands. I don't know who was the proudest of the gold ring we won on the carrousel.

With my closest friend, Janet Gaynor,
in my new life in the desert.

In all the months since then, Heller has found the happiness she longed for. Bromley understands her perfectly, as Richard did me. He gives her so much rope—but with such authority. He is so gentle in his great strength.

Now at last I have time both on the clock and in my heart to be with them all. Because of Janet and Paul, who live there, I bought a house I love in Palm Springs, California. There are palm trees and peace, beautiful skies, a view almost as wide as Brazil. I have friends, guesthouses, and Richard's and my clasped hands. This pair I designed myself, and had them made of wrought iron to serve as the latch on the gate to my new paradise.

I also have total privacy when I choose to have it. I can ride a bike to shop and to take my toy poodle for her daily bike ride in a basket on the front. I can shop in peace; nobody stops me to ask for an autograph or to take my picture. I am near enough to Malibu so Larry can bring Maj, Heidi, and Preston for surprise visits. They usually arrive unannounced, in a United Parcels van which they have converted into the most luxurious

My California family: Preston, Larry, Maj, and Heidi Hagman.

bit of rolling stock since Cornelius Vanderbilt's private railway carriage. It has a Plexiglas bubble top, hi-fi, a king-size divan, champagne on ice, and a license plate which says WING IT.

Preston submerges himself in a four-foot diving bell in my swimming pool and doesn't come up for hours, perhaps to insulate himself from my endless discussions with Maj about dresses, fabrics, gardens; I adore being with Maj and having girl talk.

Larry fills the house with his booming laugh, his ideas for me, his criticisms, which are always right. The one thing I'd love most to do would be work with him in another show, either playing with him or being directed by him. When he isn't around, I can usually catch one of his television series such as *I Dream of Jeannie* or one of his movies. It is fun being identified in Malibu as "Larry Hagman's mother."

Then there is Heidi. When she was born, Larry and Maj asked me to help think of a name for her. I decided that "Heidi" sounded Swedish, which fitted both her parents' backgrounds, and I admit that I also visualized it on a marquee somewhere: "Heidi Hagman." It looked right in my mind's eye. When she was only five years old the two of us were walking down Fifth Avenue one day when she suddenly turned to me and said, "Gan, I've decided what I want to do. I'll be in the theater, in musical comedy. If you're good, I'll let you be in my show."

"Thank you, Heidi," I told her. "It takes one to know one."

She once wrote me a letter in Brazil in which she signed her name three or four different ways. She said she was experimenting with signatures so "When I am famous I will know which way I want to write Heidi Hagman."

Chickens coming home to roost! Or circles. When I was about her age in Weatherford, I spent hours experimenting with different ways of writing Mary Martin. For when *I* became famous.

Heidi, also like her grandma, is mad about dancing. She studies ballet, modern, *t'ai chi*, and after she saw the film *That's Entertainment* she asked if I would teach her to tap-dance. If I had suggested such a thing a week earlier she would have given me a withering stare. I went straight out and bought tap shoes for both of us.

When she wanted to make enough money to pay her way to Europe, she took up catering. She and a girl friend make all the food in Maj's kitchen, with Heidi cooking while the friend reads the recipes they have collected or made up. They cater television and movie sets, and last summer they were such a smash hit at a catered luncheon for seventy-five people at their neighbors', the Burgess Merediths, that *The New York Times* ran a story and a picture and Heidi got a firm offer from a publisher to write a cookbook. Perhaps because she has discovered that one of my favorite late-night suppers is a combination of cold baked beans, pickled pigs' feet, and ice cream, Heidi has offered to cater my next party. I can't wait to be the first on my block to hire the now famous Heidi Hagman, the Barefoot Cateress of Malibu.

Heller and Bromley, who live in New York, help me support the telephone company with long, lovely calls back and forth. Bromley takes wonderful pictures of Timothy and Matthew as they grow, and now he has an exciting new subject, the baby girl. Mary Devon DeMeritt will be called "Devon" but she is the third Mary: Mary Virginia, me; Mary Heller, her mother; and now Mary Devon. Devon DeMeritt would look great on a marquee, too.

My New York family: Heller, Bromley, Timothy, Matthew, and the third Mary—Mary Devon DeMeritt.

Three generations of daughters: Juanita and Mar
Virginia, Mary Virginia and Mary Heller, and Mar
Heller and Mary Devon.

Heller and I have a wonderful new relationship now. She tries to look after me, watch over me. She's becoming the mother. I did this with my own mother, I remember.

Timothy at present is the shy artist of the family. But the girls his age, eleven, are not shy—such phone calls he gets! Matthew is the actor and playwright, and will probably grow up to direct and produce. A regular Noël Coward, yet. He wrote a play when he was seven which brought compliments from his teacher. Heller suggested that maybe *Vovó* would like to see it, and she offered to make a Xerox to send me. Matthew thought this over and said, "No, I'd like *Vovó* to have the original. I'll keep the Xerox."

In intervals between family visits, guests, bicycle rides, and moonlight swims, I move furniture, change draperies, reupholster things. I never can leave well enough alone, not even in my own home. I have also taken up painting again. I am much better at painting pianos and antiquing furniture than I am at painting canvases, but I love it. Like needlepoint, it is both absorbing and distracting. I've done it for years but I still have to paint people from the back because I can't do faces.

One of my special pleasures is to visit Janet Gaynor and paint with her. Or, more accurately, to watch her paint. She has such concentration, talks so quietly, creates such beauty while painting. Janet is having a whole new career as an artist. In early 1975 she had a show at a gallery in Chicago and sold the whole thing, about fifty paintings, in two days.

I learn a lot from watching Janet, but, most important, I have learned a new point of view about life from this very wise woman. I was always so busy living it that I didn't have much time to think about it. I learned about other things—my work—but I don't remember having a mature thought on any other subject until I was about thirty years old. Sometimes I think everybody should be born thirty and start out from there. We *can* learn, I am sure, until the day we die, and I for one am looking forward to each day, each new thought.

From the outside world comes a stream of scripts, ideas for a Las Vegas appearance, shows to be written. I am considering them, and my girl friend Ethel Merman is terribly tempting with her idea for a concert series. What fun the two of us could have singing together again, two ole bags "doin' what comes natur'lly!"

My adrenaline is back. There are only so many pianos and glass-topped tables to be moved, so many bicycle rides, so many oil paintings from the back and needlepoint cushions from the front.

I have been blessed by a second chance to know my children and their children, to have time with Sister, Didi, friends. My heart belongs to them.

It also belongs to Nellie, Dolly, Maria, Annie, Peter Pan. To audiences, to Richard, whose concentrated devotion to me as his wife, to our career, would have been in vain if I don't continue to work.

I want to work, and I will. Who knows? Maybe when I come back through my new window in my new life I'll bring not the Lost Boys but children and grandchildren.

It *does* run in the family.

XXV
What a Window

It was almost ten years ago that I wrote that last paragraph: "I want to work, and I will. . . . Maybe when I come back through the new window in my new life I'll bring not the Lost Boys but children and grandchildren. . . ."

Well, that window was the largest that I have ever flown through. And the most rewarding. I have never been so happily busy in my life. I have six grandchildren now, to fly with me through the many exciting windows of our lives. The oldest, Heidi Kristina, was married October 29, 1983, and I look forward to one day becoming a *great* grandmother. The youngest is Geoffrey De-Meritt, four, who manages to be as busy all the time as his father, Bromley, is and his grandfather, Richard, used to be. It seemed to me that Richard was always up cleaning the roof when we had dinner guests. Bromley's like that, and Geoffrey, too. He's the only one of my grandchildren I didn't get to name, because I didn't get there on time. I wanted to call him Duke DeMeritt. Because I couldn't, I can't seem to remember his name. I call him Gregory, which confuses him a bit.

In many ways the past ten years of my life have been like a roller coaster—big, big highs and then deep, deep lows, like the automobile accident that took away my beloved friend Ben Washer and left my Janet, Janet Gaynor, so hurt and ill. Partly because of that, partly because of all I learned being cohost of the television program *Over Easy,* I am now into causes. If once upon a

time I was Audition Mary, now I am Benefit Mary, going everywhere, meeting people, singing and talking for causes.

Then the joy of seeing my Baby Boy become an international star, big bad J.R. on *Dallas*. I used to say it was fun being
"Larry Hagman's mother" when he was the star of *I Dream of
Jeannie*. But I certainly never expected the commotion of being
"J.R.'s mother." I love it. I've been signing autographs for his fans
as his mother for years, but now they ask me to sign "J.R.'s *real*
mother" so as not to be confused with Barbara Bel Geddes. Every-
time there is a big crowd in front of me, or behind me, I always
think it must be because J.R. is there. It's unbelievable, that
show—viewed, I am told, in ninety-one countries, and such a hit in
England.

My big, bad, baby boy, J.R.

What is so exciting to me about Larry's success is to see the same commitment to his profession and his audience that I have. He's been a top television star for five years, and each performance is still important to him. He's also done it all by himself, even though he generously says I helped him. When he was younger, he wanted no part of it. So it's a wonderful experience for me, and our closeness reaches out to the whole family.

In 1981 Larry and I performed together in England for the eightieth birthday of that dear lady the Queen Mother. That was quite an evening altogether. Because Larry had made a country rock record, he was invited to sing for her at the Palladium. He decided that I should come, too, as a total surprise. His wife, Maj, and I sneaked into London, almost in disguise, and hid. On the big night I was tucked into his dressing room, and he was out there singing up a storm when all of a sudden he forgot his words. Just forgot. Three times. He was winging it and singing, in perfect rhythm, "I've forgotten the words." Finally he just stopped and said, "I'm sorry, Mom, I blew it."

The audience thought he might be saying that to the Queen Mother, because they call her "Mum," but he was saying it to me, hiding back in the dressing room. Then he said something about "I know another song . . ." and he told the audience about how he had sung in London when he was seventeen years old with some corny lady named Nellie Forbush. Then he went into "There is nothing like *this* dame" . . . and I came on in my baggy pants, singing "Honey Bun" at the top of my lungs and stopping once to look up at my big Baby Boy—"Get a load of Honey Bun tonight." We had a ball. We even did "The Eyes of Texas." After the show, when we were presented to the Queen Mother, even she couldn't resist saying to Larry, "I hardly dare ask who . . ." and before she could even say, "shot J.R.," Larry gave her that big, wide Texas smile and said, "Even for you, ma'am, I can't tell." After the Queen Mother had spoken to us, Prince Charles came along and looked Larry straight in the eyes and asked, "How does it feel to bomb onstage?" I remember being scared to death that Larry would reply something like "How does it feel to fall off a horse?" But he didn't. He was very polite, but afterward he said to me, "I'll never do that again, never try to sing alone." But he will. He's a natural at that, too. (We later found out that in British slang, a "bomb" means a "smash" or a "hit," and we both felt much better.)

That night at the Palladium was one of the big highs on my roller coaster, as was singing for Queen Elizabeth II and Prince Philip in San Francisco the next year, 1982, with Tony Bennett. A brilliant young San Francisco producer, Steve Silvers, organized the whole show, including his company with costumes from his show *Beach Blanket Babylon.* Among the special effects were some huge hats with models of Big Ben, the Tower of London, and I don't know what all on top. The queen looked a bit surprised, but Prince Phillip seemed to love it. There were about one hundred young people in a symphony orchestra, several choirs and bands, about six hundred people altogether. I sang "Getting to Know You," and then the voices of the children's choir came up behind me and there wasn't a dry eye in the house. Tony Bennett sang "I Left My Heart in San Francisco," as only he can sing it! The queen had never been to California before. It had rained and stormed the whole time she had been on the West Coast, but I'm told that just before she and Prince Phillip arrived for our show the sun broke through and blazed on them for a minute. It must have been an omen.

There was another thrill later that year when John Raitt and I performed in the gardens of the White House, with that marvelous violinist and man Itzhak Perlman as master of ceremonies. The occasion was a televised special called Young Performers at the White House. The Reagans have been hosting this event every year as their contribution to the careers of new talent in the entertainment world. Most of the performers John and I introduced were already performing in New York or Los Angeles, and I really think they have big careers, big futures, before them.

It was a special joy for me to participate because I'd never before performed at the White House. And also because I've known Nancy Davis Reagan since she was a young girl. Her mother, whose name was Edith but people called her Dede, was an actress and had been in vaudeville. Dede's second husband, Nancy's stepfather, was Dr. Loyal Davis, a renowned brain surgeon. I had met them first in Chicago when we went on the road in *One Touch of Venus,* and over the years I had seen them again and again.

Nancy Davis was a lovely young woman who wanted to be an actress. She went to New York, auditioned, and got a part playing a handmaiden to Helen Craig's Princess in *Lute Song,* which I did after *One Touch of Venus*. It wasn't a large part, but, by golly, it was Broadway, and there she was every night and she was lovely. Nancy and I had one moment together onstage in a song called "Monkey See, Monkey Do."

Out of that show she got a contract to go to Metro-Goldwyn-Mayer in Hollywood, and eventually she met Ronnie. The first time I went to the White House after he became President, he called me Mary and so naturally I called him Ronnie. Ben said, "You can't do that, it's not protocol. You have to call him Mr. President." I now try very hard to remember, but it's difficult, because I've known him such a long time. Since *I* was in Hollywood, and that's a very long time.

In 1976, the first time he ran, I sort of stayed away. I have stayed out of politics as much as I could, throughout the years. But after the campaign Nancy called me and said, "Well, we lost, but we're having a twenty-fifth anniversary party. Would you come to *that*?" Of course I said yes, and Larry escorted Dorothy Hammerstein and me to the party. Then, after they won, in 1980, Nancy and I talked on the phone sometimes, especially after the President was nearly killed. In 1982, I had a special request from Nancy to come to a White House dinner for the president of Brazil and his wife. That was my first official visit to the Reagan White House, and it was all because of my long love affair with Brazil, and our home there.

It felt strange, because the last time I had been in Washington specifically *because* of Brazil was in 1979 when Janet Gaynor and I were invited to the Brazilian Embassy to be given a very special medal by Ambassador Pinhiero—such an honor from the government of our adopted country! It started out to be such a joyous occasion for all of us who made the trip—Janet; her husband, Paul Gregory; Ben Washer; and me. Then it turned into a sad time for me. On the plane going to Washington I dozed off and heard someone call my name. "Mary . . . Mary . . ." I woke up and asked Janet and Ben if they had called me. They both said no.

Later, in the hotel, I heard Ben on the telephone saying, "Thank you, I'll be in touch." I asked if there were a message from Sister. He said no, but she kept coming back into my mind. I said, "There's something. I feel very strange about Sister. Is there a message?" Finally he told me that she had had a heart attack and was in a hospital in Texas. It was very odd that the voice had said,

"Mary," because Sister never called me that. She always called me Baby. Sister left during the night. But the next day we had to go to the Brazilian Embassy to appear on a show that was being transmitted to Brazil and then attend a reception and dinner. The following morning Ben and I flew to Texas.

I had never been to anyone's funeral except for Richard's. I hadn't been able to get to Mother's or Daddy's. But even though I was there for hers, I still can't really believe that Sister is gone. So many of the ones I knew and loved so much, just gone, gone. I know it's because that's the age I am, and the time of our lives, but that doesn't make it easier. I'm almost afraid to buy the newspaper, and I keep remembering Noël Coward saying, "Just try to get through dinner, my dear . . . all we try to do is get through dinn*ah*."

On the other hand some wonderful *new* people have come flying in through that window. One thing has led to another, and I'm so busy that the past few years are turning into as much of a blur as all those audiences used to in my stage days.

It's funny, but I can truly say, now, that I don't miss the stage. I adored it, just adored it all those years. I can sit in the audience and adore it still, but I have a whole new life, and I don't miss the old one. This new phase began, I guess, with the first edition of this book in 1976. I went on talk shows, and autographed copies in bookstores and talked to people who were buying copies. It was a new and exciting experience. After the book came out, the Dallas Women's Club asked me to come down and make a speech. I was overwhelmed. I said, "I can't talk, not just talk to all those women." Larry said, "Yes, you can, Mother. You talk all the time, you just don't know it." He told me to get out some slides, remember some stories about my life and career, and he promised to help me rehearse. So that's what we did. I "performed" for four days in Dallas, and, bless their hearts, my audiences liked it. I've been talking in public ever since.

After that, I was approached by Fieldcrest Mills and asked if I would design sheets and towels for their coming season. They thought of me, I guess, because of my needlepoint book, which had come out in 1969, and because I had designed dresses and hats, handbags, needlepoint rugs and pillows, all sorts of things for my shop in Brazil. I agreed, and we selected three patterns: "Some Enchanted Evening," which turned out looking Oriental with muted flowers; "Needlepoint," which included family mementoes I had worked in needlepoint—Heller's little jacket, Larry's guitar, and Janet's hydrangeas; then there was "Flying." I didn't think you could sleep on Peter Pan, so we did a design with hot-air balloons.

I toured ten or twelve cities twice a year for Fieldcrest, talking and appearing on TV and in department stores. It was another form of show business, but this was bringing me really close to people. Before, I had missed the closeness in my life. Theater audiences are close in their appreciation, their graciousness, their applause. But they aren't physically close. This was another new experience. As was the different work schedule. In the theater I never got to bed until the wee hours and I didn't stir out of it until afternoon. Well, for Fieldcrest I was getting up at six in the morning, doing my makeup and hair, which takes me about two hours, and changing clothes three or four times a day for television interviews and newspapers. Then there were luncheons, appearances in three or four stores, dinners with department store executives and their wives and friends. Everyone was wonderful to me. It was exciting, but my adrenaline had to stay at high peak until the tour was over.

At the Kapiolani Children's Medical Center, I was touched beyond words when eleven-year-old Brian Wofford whispered to me, "I love you."

What started out to be a two-year contract lasted for five years. After the accident, in fact, I owed Fieldcrest one more performance. And so in September 1983, I performed in Hawaii to benefit Kapiolani Children's Medical Center. There was so much love in those children—it was the kind of appearance I most loved to do for Fieldcrest.

In about the middle of my Fieldcrest activities, about four years ago, Hugh Downs telephoned and asked if he and the crew of *Over Easy* could come to Malibu and tape a half-hour show, interviewing Larry and me. *Over Easy*, a program for older people, was already an institution on the Public Broadcasting System, and I liked it. Hugh said it would be an interesting show because Larry and I would be together for the first time since *Dallas* had made him an international TV star. I told him yes, but only if Larry agreed. He did, and the whole *Over Easy* crew came down from San Francisco. Larry, of course, put on one of his crazy hats—he owns about a thousand of them. He chose an Indian headdress and sat there looking like Chief Sitting Pretty. Everybody had such a good time that we taped another half-hour show, and for the second one I wore a silly hat, too. Hams!

Later, Jules Power and Richard Rector, the originators and producers of *Over Easy*, asked if I would come to San Francisco and be a cohost on the show. Well! For years San Francisco had been one of the places I wanted to live, and I just couldn't believe it when the offer came. Jules said Hugh Downs was going to New York to do the *20/20* show and he, Jules, wanted to find the perfect cohost for me. He did, too. I couldn't have been more pleased when he said, "Jim Hartz," whom I had met on the *Today* show and just adored. Now, he's like another son to me.

Over Easy became a circle that embraced all the other circles. My children joined me on it; my grandchildren, old friends, new and exciting friends who were doctors, lawyers, psychiatrists, and, of course, our famous chef, Narsai, who was on every show. For the first year we performed to—at?—maybe *at* a live audience, and I just learned so much, and received so much. People who've seen the show on TV come up to me on the street now and ask how I am and what is going on. They're different from theater fans. These people have us in their living rooms and they feel closer. They feel they know *Mary Martin,* not Nellie Forbush or Maria von Trapp or Peter Pan, but Mary. I feel I know her better now, too. One thing I've noticed is that the farther I get from my stage life, the more Texan I become. I just sound more like Weatherford every day.

Speaking of Weatherford, I finally *did* get top billing in my hometown. I went back there when the majority leader of the Texas House of Representatives, Jim Wright, unveiled a statue of me as Peter Pan. Right in my beloved Weatherford, right in sight of the new library. The statue was done by Ronald Thomason, a famous Texas artist, who came to visit me to measure everything, get everything right. I kept saying, "Couldn't you make my nose a little smaller?" but he ignored that. And I want you to know that the nose on the statue is *my* nose. My backside, too; you sure can tell who it is from the rear. But the funniest moment of the ceremony was due to my grandchild Mary Devon, who was in my arms when the statue was unveiled. She and all the grandchildren, when they were little, always have gone straight for this nose of mine. It is, after all, the most prominent part of my face. Well, I was holding Mary Devon, and all of a sudden she bit the bronze nose of the statue. Just bit it, right there in front of everybody. I thought, "That does it. It's really me; that statue looks like me."

To Uncle Ben

XXVI
Southern Comfort
with a Gent

Perhaps it's time to tell about the accident. For Janet Gaynor; for her husband, Paul Gregory; for me; but most of all for Ben Washer, because it took him away from us. My husband Richard and I had known Ben Washer for almost thirty years. Richard knew him first because he and Ben had been young journalists together in New York. Beginning with *The Sound of Music,* Ben became our press representative. When I was performing in *One Touch of Venus,* he was out of the country, at war, being Irving Berlin's pressman for *This Is the Army.* He always forgot to include on my résumés that I was in *Venus* because he wasn't there for that one, and anything he didn't see he didn't believe.

When my Richard left and I had to start a new life, I asked my lawyer if I could afford to have Ben Washer as my manager-companion. With a deep sigh of relief, my lawyer said yes. I think he was afraid he would have to leave his own family and teach me the practicalities of life, like where the bank is and how you write a check, and how you pay the supermarket and where the airport is.

Ben arrived in Palm Springs on a hot August day and did not leave my "presence"—his word—for the next ten years. His favorite comment when somebody asked him what his duties were was, "Baby-sitter for the oldest baby in captivity." He did everything, and with such humor. I once heard him talk to a reporter for a national magazine. The reporter said, "Tell me, sir, I understand you're living with Mary Martin. Is this an affair?" And Ben said, "Sorry, old boy, you're barking up the wrong tree." He did everything and never refused.

Things did get a little tense about eight years ago when I had almost simultaneous operations for a node in my throat and another on an ovary. I used to tell Richard that if I ever wrote a book I would call it, "If It Isn't One End It's the Other." Because it seemed to me that for all my life either my throat was busted, or my foot was, or something. Richard always said, "No, Mary, that's not your image." Maybe it wasn't my image, but it was the God's truth. I've always had trouble with my throat, from stripping all the gears singing. There finally came a time in 1976 when it really bothered me. I was hoarse, couldn't sing, could hardly talk. So I went to Chicago to see my dear Dr. Paul Hollinger, who told me thirty years ago I was going to ruin my voice if I didn't stop belting high C sharp. Well, he found a node on a vocal cord and took it off. (After the operation I wrote on a piece of paper, "Was it C#?" "No," he wrote, "the whole scale.")

Thank heaven his hospital is the kind where they give you a total physical examination no matter what you come in for. During the physical they found something wrong on my ovaries. So Dr. Edward Biggs, who had saved my life twenty years before by taking me off cortisone and telling me to stop working, assigned a surgeon to perform another operation. By this time I couldn't talk because of the throat, and I couldn't move because of the other end. Ben and I were living at the Drake Hotel, and I had to write notes to him. Because he was a little bit deaf, he bought me a police whistle so I could summon him from anywhere. I would whistle, and he would walk in very solemnly and ask, "Did you blow, madame?"

The doctors had told me I could go home, if I had a tight, firm panty girdle to hold me together. I blew for Ben and wrote that he should go to Bonwit Teller and buy me a panty girdle. Ben, a confirmed bachelor all his life, really didn't want to know about women's things at all. But I had to have the girdle, so I gave him my credit card and wrote down which department to go to, the size, and all. That poor embarrassed man did it, but he pretended to be deaf and dumb. He went into the store and stood there, handed the saleslady the piece of paper, and wouldn't mumble a word.

He wasn't "Uncle Ben" at first; he was just Ben. "Uncle"

came later and was one of the most marvelous gifts of my new life. When Heller and Bromley's first baby, Mary Devon, was born, Heller asked if Ben would be her godfather. I wasn't sure he'd agree. He couldn't abide children, he had said, and he had proclaimed that all of them should be shut up in closets until they were twenty. But after he held this beautiful little baby girl in his arms, he said yes. Yes, he would be her godfather. He wrote her wonderful, wry, funny letters and just loved her to death. Gradually he deigned to look at, and eventually love, the others. They all started to call him Uncle Ben and so did I, though usually he called me Madame. He even started a fund for Mary Devon's education, to make sure she would go to college. He wanted her to go to Wellesley or Smith. I told him nobody in my family had finished college. Whereupon he replied, "But this one will." And I believe him.

All the family, including me, loved Uncle Ben, an elegant, kind Southern gentleman who is deeply missed.

We lost him in San Francisco the night of the accident, in September 1982. I suppose all accidents are ironic because you always think, "If . . . if . . . if . . ." That night, for example, we could have eaten at home. We could have accepted an invitation to a friend's house. But we all wanted to go to a new place in Chinatown, and for Chinatown you must go in a taxi because there's no place to park. The accident happened, I'm told, only about two and a half minutes from my house. Paul Gregory and the taxi driver know at what intersection we were hit, but neither Janet nor I knows. I don't ever want to know; I might have to cross it another time.

We had telephoned for the taxi, and Ben had given the driver the address when we got in. Janet is little and doesn't like to slide across a big backseat, so I told her I'd get in first and slide through; Janet got in next to me. Ben, the perfect gentleman, always opened and shut all car doors and thus was the last one in, sitting on the right side of the cab. Paul got in front with the driver because he is so tall. It was still light, about seven-thirty in the evening.

I looked to the front seat and noticed that the driver had on a hat and rather long hair, and I thought this was the first time I'd had a lady driver. But then the driver turned around and I saw he was a man. The last thing I can remember is thinking, "If only I had my scissors, I'd sure cut that hair." That's absolutely the last thing I remember. I don't remember starting off, don't remember driving even a short distance.

Later, I learned that there was a man driving a van very fast. They say he went through a stoplight and straight toward us, hard. Ben was killed instantly. Paul had serious whiplash, broken ribs, and a bruised kidney. Janet caught the impact of both my body and Ben's, and she was smashed up inside. My pelvis was broken in three places, and I had two broken ribs and a punctured lung.

They say I got out and was sort of standing by the cab, all of which I know nothing about. The first thing I remember was seeing Heller, Larry, and Maj there, and I thought, "How nice. Is it Christmas? Is everybody home?"

Finally they had to tell me, so very gently, "You've had an accident. You're in a hospital."

"When?" I asked them, bewildered.

"It's been a little while."

"With whom?"

"Janet, Paul and Ben," they reminded me.

"Are they all right?" I needed to know.

"Ben's gone," Larry said sadly.

"And Janet?"

Larry told me she was fine—he couldn't bear to tell me any more just then.

It seemed to me that my family kept coming back and standing in a yellow light like the sun. Every time I saw them I thought it was another day. Later, I found out it was a yellow light in the hall of the intensive care unit.

I don't really know how long I was there, but I was eventually moved to a private room. I am just so grateful that help came soon after the accident and that we were taken to the Trauma Center at San Francisco General Hospital. The prompt and expert care of the center saved Janet's life and mine, I am absolutely sure. Still, after two weeks, I was very eager to get back to work, to get home, to get off medications, and I requested a nurse who could leave the hospital with me.

In came Bea Kilgore, whom I've known since she was born, because she's the daughter of dear friends, Dr. Eugene Kilgore, a famous hand surgeon, and his wife, Mimi. Bea is a trauma nurse at

San Francisco General, but the night of the accident she wasn't on duty because she had a bad cold. As soon as she was well again, and I was beginning to come out of my fog, she took a leave of absence and looked after me for ten weeks, never leaving my side. The pain was pretty dreadful at first, but I kept being distracted because my head itched so badly. Bea listened to me complaining, and even before we left the hospital she said, "I'll fix it." She got everything together and gave me a shampoo in bed. When she had finished, she said, "Look, Mary. Just look." The bottom of the basin was filled with bits of pulverized glass. I must have hit that cab window and demolished it. Nobody ever talked to me about concussion, but I wonder.

Recovery was difficult. It was almost impossible to stand up straight in the beginning, leaning on a walker. But Bea never let me off the hook. She made me do it even if it hurt and hurt and hurt some more. I pushed myself day by day until I was able to walk down to the intensive care unit to see Janet.

When I first saw her, I was shocked, because she was absolutely blown up out of proportion because of all the poisons in her system. Her bladder had been injured very badly. She had four operations while she was in intensive care, and has had two more at the Desert Hospital in Palm Springs. While she was in intensive care, I visited her every day, even though she didn't know me. Finally, right before I left the hospital, she did recognize me.

I have tried to make myself remember my stay at the hospital, just force myself to remember, but I can't. It is still a blur in my mind—people coming and going, flowers, telephone calls, letters. I answered five thousand letters myself, but they just kept coming. My friends from *Over Easy*—Jules and Dottie Power, and Jim and Alexandra Hartz—were at the hospital almost immediately. And my children. I felt hurt, but I sure felt loved. Immediately, I started talking to Jules and Jim about when I could come back to the show. I wanted to do it from inside the hospital, or from home, or from anywhere.

The day I left the hospital, they had a wheelchair for me, but I wanted to go out on my walker, to prove to everybody, including myself, that I could do it. I was going slowly out the door toward the limousine when suddenly there was all this noise. I looked up and the doctors and nurses were all hanging out the windows on the top floor—*crowing*. They all knew the *er-er-er-*

errrrrrrh; they were Peter Pan people. You can imagine what that did to me: I turned around and blew kisses because I was too emotional to say a word.

They told me in the hospital that I'd be on the walker for two and a half months. I thought, "There's no way I'm going to be on it that long." When I got to my San Francisco home, I had to climb four flights of steps to my bedroom, but I could sit down on my fanny and scoot up one step at a time, while Bea lifted the walker. She encouraged me to walk and keep walking, and finally one day just before she left me she said, "Look how you're using that walker." I was carrying the thing! I don't know how long I'd been doing that. If you're determined, and stubborn, you can do all kinds of things people say you can't.

I wanted to go right back to work and I did, on my walker and with my children, on *Over Easy* in October 1982. By then I had a message: If it could happen to me, it could happen to you. It could happen to anybody, and you just have to cope with it.

It has given me great joy to see Janet's recuperation. A miracle has happened through Janet's tenacity—her belief that she will recover—the prayers of millions of people all over the world, and the devoted care of her husband. Right now, Janet and Paul are looking toward the future and considering building a new home in the desert.

The last thing I was able to carry out for Ben was to make sure his wish to be cremated and have his ashes scattered in the sea was fulfilled. This was done by his brother, Jim; his sister-in-love Mary; and loved friends.

In December 1982, Ben gave me his last gift—my birthday party. I've had more birthdays than I want to remember, but this one was important because Ben had planned it all. He had known that we would be back in Palm Springs by December, and he had set the whole birthday party up with my dear neighbors Nelda Linsk and Margo Spinner, Roger Taylor and David Smith. (Roger and David had catered fabulous parties in Palm Springs for years, and I was fortunate enough to have them with me in San Francisco during my three months' stay for *Over Easy.* Both young men made my stay in San Francisco very pleasant and comfortable. On the night of the accident, Roger was the one who answered the phone when the hospital called.)

I didn't know a thing about the party—didn't suspect anything. The day of the party, everybody was trying to get me out of the house. Hal Broderich and Cal Van Der Woude took me off to Cal's new art gallery and then loitered all the way home. I was pretty tired and anxious to go to bed, but when we finally opened my front door, there were about eighty-five people inside. That's a lot of people for my new home. It was the most unbelievable surprise party: Walter Annenberg and his wife, Lee, were there; Jinx Falkenburg McCrary, Dolores Hope, my brother-in-love Bob, Judy Thomas, Ruth Zuckerman, Alice Faye, the Richard Taylors . . . oh, so many other friends. And they were all singing, "Hellooooo, Mary, well, hellooooo, Mary," like *Dolly*. I was so flabbergasted that I lost my voice, couldn't utter a sound for about thirty minutes. People had come from San Francisco and Texas and all over, even Bob and Ray came out from New York. Bob and Ray aren't the ones you remember from radio and TV, but Bob Landson and Ray Jones from San Francisco, my summer landlords and old friends. It was fabulous. I stayed up until after midnight and even got up on my aching bones and did a little dance routine with Alice Faye. The message is: It can be done.

Uncle Ben knew it, and he was very much with us there that night, for my birthday.

XXVII
Getting to Know You

I've been singing "Getting To Know You" for years, but it never meant so much to me as it did on that wonderful television program *Over Easy*. From 1981 to 1983, *Over Easy* was the only regularly scheduled program which dealt with issues affecting the lives of older people, helping them help themselves. I never did really figure out how Jules Power decided to put that young Jim Hartz and me together. One day in my shower, which is where I do all my deep thinking, it came to me that I'm *Over*, and Jim is *Easy*. I told that to Jim just before we went on. He said, "You've got to tell it to the audience." So I did. *They believed me!*

I really did get to know *them:* the fans, the live audience, all the people who watched that show. I wasn't very good on it, at first. Jim was terrific, so professional; he'd been working in television since he was nineteen years old, and he was, I think, forty-one when we started together. In the beginning I didn't know anything about cameras. Whenever I had performed, cameras had followed me; I didn't even know where they were. Now, all of a sudden I was in this huge studio in San Francisco and there were four cameras looking at me and they all had these red lights. So I just stood there. Jim was mouthing things at me, and the crew and the audience were having hysterics, but I was mute. Silent. Finally I mouthed back at Jim, "I can't start, the lights are red."

He said, "That's the way we do it." Well, not where I come from. You go on the green, you sure don't go on the red. You'll get hit or arrested! Well, that's how we started our first show. Eventually, of course, we had to stop that show and begin all over. I finally learned. But on the last show taped in 1982, that dear crew painted the camera lights green for me, for fun.

For a long time I didn't look at myself on the show. I never have been a fan of mine; I don't like to look at myself. Finally I did look at a tape of *Over Easy* and I was just appalled. For some reason I had thought that if the cameras were on the guests, they'd be on me, too, because we were sitting so close together and I'd be sort of talking along. Well, no way. I discovered that when the cameras were on the guests I wasn't there at all, but you could hear my voice in the background saying, "Uh-huh, uh-huh," and "Oh, my." Just dreadful! After I finally watched myself and heard myself, I stopped saying all that stuff. Or tried to.

In the first year I was pretty restrained. Then I decided just to be me, and sing. My old friends came on the show with me, and I rolled with it: I got to sing along with Ethel Merman and Florence Henderson and Pearl Bailey; Van Johnson and Maxine Andrews. Betty Ford came on the show and talked about alcoholism and was so, so good and courageous. Then my old friend Jinx Falkenburg McCrary came on and talked on the same subject— about the book she's writing and about Alcoholics Anonymous, which she says saved her life. Bob and Dolores Hope were on, and so were James Stewart and his wife. Jimmy just loves to sing. One of his numbers is "Red Red Robin." While the orchestra was batting out "bob-bob-bobbin' along," Jimmy was singing "bob . . . bob . . . bobb-in' . . . a . . . looong," and it went on forever. Because *Over Easy* was only a half-hour show, there just wasn't time—oh, such a disappointment. Jimmy's so warm and funny—and dear!

We taped two half-hour shows a day, four days a week, sixty-five tapes in three months. We had Saturday and Sunday off, and Monday, although I used that day to go to I. Magnin's and try on clothes for the show. That little chore led me to another of my new friends, Marilyn Scott, who helped me choose clothes that would photograph well and not be too "busy" for television.

All the people on the show performed for union scale, but it was a very expensive show to do. We had nationally famous doctors and experts on everything from nutrition to exercise, economics, family relationships, anything that could be important to our audience. We also had a huge research department that looked into the same problems and subjects. For a while we also had a live audience. The show brought them in by bus and, believe me, many of them were *Over*. They'd see the show and have lunch and then be taken back to their homes. It was such fun, getting to know them. As time went on we got a younger and younger following. Now, a lot of them are what I call Peter Pan people, in their forties.

Over Easy was seen by four to six million people a week, on about 250 public television stations. It became an institution, a friend. We received more than a hundred thousand letters a year from viewers.

We talked about all kinds of things. One of my favorite programs was with my grandchildren. Geoffrey, at age two, crawled all over everybody, and Heller's big boys talked about school. We all talked about grandparents. As always we had a guest expert, in this case Dr. Arthur Kornhaber, and he reminded us, "Every time a child is born, a grandparent is born." He described the special relationship between grandparents and grandchildren. It was wonderful for us, right there, but think of what it meant to all the people watching, all the grandparents out there.

Right now we doubt that the show will go on again. The federal government supported it for years, but it doesn't have the money to do it now. We have also lost one of our underwriters. Sun Oil is still with us, bless them, but we need another. It is a program I think should be kept going.

Public broadcasting is in dire straits all over the country. People send in money, of course, but they can't earmark it, can't say, "This is for *Over Easy*." I've been on a lot of fund-raising programs, and everywhere I go people come up and ask what they can do to save *Over Easy*. Perhaps if enough people wrote to PBS it would help—it couldn't hurt. If we could have commercials I know we could stay on television, but so far that's against the policy of the Public Broadcasting System.

From being on *Over Easy*, I've learned a great deal about talking with people. I've even learned about listening. Do you realize how many people don't know how to listen? I was one of them, but now I know. It's rewarding to listen. During the first year I'd sit in the middle with Jim on my right and the guest on my left. If I asked a question and didn't give the guest time to answer, which was quite often, Jim would casually put his arm around behind the chair and touch my shoulder. One tap with a finger meant "Start talking . . . or asking" and two taps meant "Stop." He got me under control that way.

Over Easy has been a fabulous experience for me. It has brought Jules and Jim and Dick Rector and their wives into my life. Those of us working on the show were like a family. On *Over Easy* I felt that sometimes I was doing a little bit of good. Trying to help people. But I think about it the way I think about everything in my life: Love it, love it, but when it's over, it's over.

I believe that I was spared in the accident because there are still things I am supposed to do. People rush up to me all the time saying, "How well you look!" One person said, "How good it is to see you *above* and well." I'm sure he really meant to say "about," but I quite like "above." I'm glad I'm *above*, too.

Perhaps because of the exposure of *Over Easy,* or perhaps because I'm *above* that accident, all these special events keep happening to me. Sometimes they are ironic. In June 1983, the Hollywood Presbyterian Medical Center gave me its first annual Heart of Hollywood award. To celebrate, Hollywood and Vine was closed and decorated with about ten thousand balloons to call attention to the building of a new Trauma Center. I accepted because of the Trauma Center, but also because I was so touched that *Hollywood* wanted to honor me. Me! I auditioned up and down its streets for two years and couldn't get a job. Couldn't even get a job in a shoe store—I auditioned there, too. I've always said that I didn't have anything to do with Hollywood, but people say, "What do you mean? You have a star in the sidewalk." Well, I do, and Larry has one right next to mine. We went together when he received his, and he said, "Who do you think gets top billing?" I said, "It all depends on which way you're walkin'." My star has been there for years, but it wasn't for movies. It was for all the shows I did at the Civic Light Opera.

There was quite a production for the closing of Hollywood and Vine, and Los Angeles Mayor Tom Bradley presented me with a beautiful Steuben glass heart which I will cherish forever. In accepting the award I said that I once wrote an article for *Reader's Digest* in which I said, "Be careful what you dream, it might come true." If anybody had told me years ago that I would receive an honor from Hollywood, or see that famous intersection closed . . . I am so proud, and so surprised, to have been chosen for that honor, and to have had a small part in launching the new

I become a Boy Scout on my seventieth birthday. Among the family at the celebration were Geoffrey and Mary Devon DeMeritt and Larry.

Hollywood Presbyterian Medical Center.

So many new things, in my sixty-ninth and seventieth years. Like being named Ms. Wonderful—how about that?—by the Thalians, who do so much good work for mental health organizations. They also work like mad for Cedars of Sinai Hospital, and *they* are absolutely wonderful. Debbie Reynolds is the president of the Thalians right now; she and they have given so much time, and talent, and energy, to help others.

Then there was my boy scout ceremony, on my seventieth birthday, December 1, 1983. I think I'm the only lady boy scout—at least that's what Jimmy Stewart told me when he made me one. For the occasion I found an old-fashioned peaked boy scout hat, khaki, in an antique store in San Francisco and bought it months ahead of the ceremony to have it ready. It was just the thing to top off a khaki-colored Oscar de la Renta dress I already had.

I don't think I'd worn that dress since Bob Hope's seventy-eighth birthday party at West Point in 1981. I've known Bob for years; he and Dolores used to feed me when I was unemployed in Hollywood. I could go to their house for lunch or dinner and they always made me feel welcome. Over the years Bob had asked me to appear with him, do something with him, but our schedules had never meshed. Finally, for West Point, I could say yes, and then I asked what we were going to do. "I'll leave that up to you," he said. In the end we did "Honey Bun."

Bob loves to dress up, and he's so funny. We got my "Honey Bun" costume out of the Museum of the City of New York, and he wore the Myron McCormick coconut bosoms and the wig and all. He was absolutely marvelous, but in the middle of our number, of course, his bosoms started to fall off and my sailor pants began to sag, so we cavorted around with my getting in front of him so he could fix his bosoms and his getting in front of me so I could hitch up my pants. It was pretty hysterical, and out on the parade grounds were all these thousands of people, all the cadets in their khaki uniforms. When it was over and I walked down off the platform in my Oscar de la Renta, a darling young cadet looked up and said, "Miss Martin, may I say something?"

"Yes, yes, dear, what do you want to say?"

"Miss Martin, this is the first time that the color khaki has ever looked attractive around here."

I thought it looked pretty well at the boy scout ceremony, too.

XXVIII
Gran, or Ganny, or *Vovó* Gets Another Chance

Until recently, the only real regret of my life was that I didn't get to spend enough time with my children. They had to be with me when they could catch me; I had that other kind of life, disciplined to the theater. Now, I'm so grateful to have this second chance. We are together, a lot, and when we aren't together we talk for hours on the telephone. We spend Christmas together, and Thanksgiving, and because our family runs around so much, we pass through each other's hometowns—Houston, Palm Springs, San Francisco, Malibu—and stop off to visit.

My grandchildren have grown like mad since I last wrote about them, but the biggest change of all, I believe, is in Preston. When we last saw him he was sort of baby fat and had blond, curly hair all over his head. He spent a lot of time at the bottom of the swimming pool in a sort of bathysphere—maybe to get away from us, I don't know. Well, to see him now! He's six feet six inches and he finally cut his hair so you can see his face. He's a licensed pilot who wants to be an astronaut one of these days. The big change came one summer when I was in Brazil and the Hagmans rented their Malibu home and lived in mine, in Palm Springs. The first thing that happened to Preston there was he got on a bike and the front wheel fell off and he broke his jaw. As if that weren't enough, he suddenly began to grow so fast that his vertebrae started to separate, so he had to be put into bed and kept there, about three months, both to ease the pain and to let his back rest.

When finally I got home and Preston got up out of his bed, he just kept getting up and up and up. On seeing how tall he was, and really seeing his face, I said, "Preston? Preston, is that you? What on earth happened?" Preston said, "I guess I've been growing, in bed."

The girls, all tens on the Bo Derek scale, just flip over him, but right now Preston is more dedicated to his schoolwork, studying for his master's degree in space and aviation engineering. He already is qualified as a multiengine commercial pilot, and is also a licensed air mechanic. This was the little boy who would never read; we didn't even know he could speak, for a while.

In 1983, in San Francisco, Preston escorted me to a dinner party given by President and Mrs. Reagan for Her Majesty Queen Elizabeth II and Prince Philip. When I called and asked if he could do it, he said, "Oh yes, Grandmother, but I will have to fly in at the last minute because of my classes." He got there just in time, rushed to shower and dress, and then he couldn't get the suspenders of his tuxedo pants attached right, and I couldn't do up my white gloves, so we buttoned each other up and off we went in all our grandeur. He looked at my red, white, and blue skirt and my blouse and said, "What's that on the blouse?" I said, "Bunnies." Bunnies designed by Michael Vollbracht, all hand printed on silk, in Italy. Later I heard he told somebody, "Do you know what my grandmother wore to see the queen? Bunnies. She's a bunny girl."

In the limousine on the way to the dinner somebody ran out and gave us an envelope from Her Royal Highness, an invitation to the dinner she and Prince Philip were giving the next night on the royal yacht for President and Mrs. Reagan's anniversary. It was addressed to me and the invitation included "an escort." Of course, I asked Preston if he'd like to go. I waited and waited for an answer, and finally Preston said, "Grandmother, I want to do it more than anything I've ever been asked to do in my life. But I have to leave at five o'clock tomorrow to get back to my classes."

I was so proud. I never would have done that—classes didn't mean that much to me, but thank the Lord they do to him. The night he was there, he had a ball. He was so tall he could see everybody in the room and was thrilled to meet Steven Spielberg, and Joe Montana, the football player, and a lot of other people. It was a fabulous, marvelous night for both of us.

Then there's his sister, Heidi, who has already had quite a

Preston and I meeting Queen Elizabeth on her California visit. This is the "bunny blouse" that so amused my escort.

life. Ten years ago she was being the Barefoot Cateress of Malibu and a big success, but then she decided she wanted to be an actress, and a dancer, and a painter, and I don't know what all. She went to New York on her own and studied acting with Uta Hagen. I saw her in a studio performance and she was so good; I was terribly impressed. She can dance, too: ballet, modern dance, you name it. She never has really learned to tap-dance, though. And one time she asked me if I would teach her ballroom dancing. For a while, the children just danced like crazy, though not *together*, but it's coming back. I taught her a few ballroom steps.

Next she started painting, quite seriously: huge oils and very delicate, very beautiful watercolors. I adore her watercolors and have a special wall of them in my new home in Rancho Mirage. Heidi has always admired Georgia O'Keefe, so she went off to Sante Fe and rented a little house and started painting full time. That's where she met the man she married last October, Brian

Blont. He's about seven years older than she is and very serious about his work, but so modest. When somebody asks what he does, he usually says, "I tear up papers." He does, too. He makes beautiful collages, tearing bits of paper which he dyes himself and gluing them to make compositions. Some of Heidi's new work has been influenced by his, she admires it so much. Brian's physique isn't like the Hagmans or the Martin men, or Heller's Timothy and Matthew. He's medium height and has delicate features like my Richard, but he's strong, so strong and gentle. He's another Southern gentleman, and he insisted on asking Larry, formally, for Heidi's hand. Bromley did that, too; years ago he came to me and very solemnly asked for Heller's hand. I like that; so unlike my own experience. I don't know what Larry and Brian said to each other in their interview, but at one point Larry asked, "Do you think you can pick up Heidi and carry her across the threshold? Because you're about the same size, you know."

I assume Brian was flabbergasted. Larry then said, "Heidi, you pick him up because you might have to." Heidi did, and Larry took pictures.

They were married October 29, 1983, at Larry and Maj's home in Malibu. It was a lovely wedding and very sentimental. I sang two songs—the first one at the beginning of the ceremony (I was out of sight) was called "The Wedding Song." Heller's four-year-old, Geoffrey, carried a needlepoint pillow that Heller had made for Heidi, and Mary Devon, who was eight, was the flower girl. At the end of the wedding, I sang "The Sweetest Sight That I Have Seen," which was written by Oscar Hammerstein as a poem for his wife, Dorothy. This was especially meaningful to me because Dorothy had stitched the poem in needlepoint and hung it on their wall. Jerome Kern had put the poem to music. When Oscar died, Dorothy Hammerstein gave the needlepoint to me. So there go the circles again . . . when I sang the song at the wedding. Of course, everybody cried. But Larry promised me he wouldn't; he seems to make a lot of noise when he cries!

Heller's two big boys, Timothy and Matthew, are as special now as when they were little and used to bring their friends home to "meet my grandmother, Peter Pan."

Timothy had a learning difficulty that was finally diagnosed by one of the wonderful doctors who came on *Over Easy*. He talked to Tim, identified the problem, prescribed some special tutoring, and Timothy has just blossomed. He graduated from prep school and is now in college.

Matthew never had to worry about his studies until lately, he is so quick and bright. I think he failed a couple of subjects just because he was sixteen-going-on-seventeen and not paying attention. There's no doubt where he got that from—*moi*. What he didn't get from *moi* was his ability to write. When he was about five, he wrote a play just for me, and it had a proper beginning, a middle, and an end. He's very talented, and I think he really will do something in the theater or in literature.

I always think that if any of the children have trouble in school, it must be my fault. I couldn't have been bothered with college, thought it a waste of time and couldn't wait to escape. Nowadays, however, I have received three honorary degrees, and one scholarship is given each year in my name. Can anybody believe it? I can't. The first degree was from my dear Sister Gregory's college, Rosary, in Chicago, where she was head of the drama department. When I received it, it was a very hot day in Chicago, and I was up on the stage when all of a sudden there was a crash like nothing you've ever heard, the loudest thunderclap in the world. I thought, "That's Daddy and Mother up there, and Richard, all saying, 'There's no way, just no way Mary could ever get a degree.'" The heavens opened and it poured like crazy. I don't think anyone heard a word I said, but I have the degree. I received another from Stonehill, a famous Catholic school outside of Boston. Another came from Redlands University in California, a wonderful place. The scholarship is at Northwood Institute, a school that specializes in the arts and business. If only I had learned about business, imagine what I could have become.

With all these degrees and placques, I feel like my beloved friend Helen Hayes, who has so many honors and who really deserves them. My grandchildren, I am sure, will earn their own degrees and not have simply honorary ones.

Next, in descending order of their ages, is Mary Devon, the one who bit me on the nose—bronze nose, that is. She's just so beautiful you want to die, very sensitive and quiet but with a mind of her own. Three years ago, when she was five, she sang with me once on stage; she was the same age as Heller when I taught her to crow in *Peter Pan*. I was doing part of a cable TV special, and they wanted something from *Sound of Music*. I thought it would be great to have eight children, all colors, creeds, and nationalities, singing "Do-Re-Mi," because that song has become international. Children everywhere sing it: Japanese children, Koreans, Norwegians, Italians, everybody. We could do it, I thought, as a kind of birthday party for all the children in the world. Mary Devon never had been on a stage and was very shy, but I taught her the song, and she learned it. When the performance came, all eight of the little ones ran onstage, and Mary Devon had to start them off. I motioned for her to sing "Do," and she belted it out like Ethel Merman, just *"Dooooo,"* so loud she almost knocked us all over. She sings very well, and she seems to have been bitten by the family bug to perform. When Heidi was about four, she announced that she was going to be a musical comedy star and would let me perform with her "if you're good." Well now, along came Mary Devon, who asked me after that first show together, "When are we going to do *Peter Pan?*"

"Well, we can't fly anymore because you're too big for me to carry in my arms," I said.

"No, I mean when are we going to do it on the stage?"

"What part are you playing?" I asked.

"Peter Pan," she said flatly.

"What am I playing?" I prodded.

You know what she replied? "Captain Hook!"

I may not have to play Captain Hook right away, because Mary Devon is into horses now—she loves them, can't think of anything else. Maybe she could play Tom Mix and I could play Tony, his horse. Mary Devon also likes her little brother, Geoffrey, very much, that busy, busy, little boy. When he was about a year old, he could shove chairs around and climb up, mountaineering around the kitchen like a little monkey. Heller and Bromley had a swimming pool, and they put up a big fence to keep him from falling in. In about two days he had learned how to climb up the outside and down the inside so that by the time he was four he could swim like a fish.

What's so wonderful about all of them, about all families, is that the thread continues. Shortly after my Richard left, Heller and Bromley were married and Mary Devon came along. Then Bromley's father left us, and little Geoffrey was born. The thread continues; the closeness makes up for those who have left us. Mary Devon told her mother, after Uncle Ben left, that she still talks to him. "I know where he is," she said, and I'm sure she does.

I am only beginning to understand the bond between the old and the young, partly because of what I learned from the experts on *Over Easy*. They taught me the importance of the continuity of a family, the role grandparents and aunts and uncles can play in the lives of children, giving them a sense of history, even if it's only family history; a feeling of "that's what I will be like when I get older"; a nonjudgmental kind of love and a "place to go" in times of trouble. As a proud and happy grandmother, I can only tell you that one of the nicest things I ever heard was from a psychologist who said, "Watch a baby in a crowd of people. His eyes light up at the sight of the older ones. There's a natural attraction."

XXIX
Where Did It Go?

On one of the nights I couldn't sleep—and we all have those nights—I thought, "Let's face it. It's a new phase, a new circle. Being in the sixties and seventies. The time when those we love must leave—Sister; Uncle Ben; Joe Linsk, my neighbor next to the "pink house" in Palm Springs. Johnny Engstead, who took so many photographs in this book. Lynn Fontanne—oh, too many." Then you think of how each and every one enriched your life.

I am so proud of my brother-in-love Robert Andrews. My sister said to me once, "I hope Bob goes before I do. He will just not be able to cope with life." Well, he has learned how. He doesn't like it. He misses her so deeply. But he works at it. I'm proud of my Nena, too, who took such good care of me in the theater, and took care of her Kirby for almost fifteen years. He performed in so many of our shows, was so close . . . and now she must learn to live without him, as I am learning to live without Uncle Ben, without my Richard. And learning to accept the fact that my dearest friends Janet Gaynor and Ethel Merman were stricken, Janet in the accident and Merman with a stroke. When I heard about Merman—I've always called her that—I felt as if someone had said, "The Statue of Liberty has fallen down." She's that kind of lady.

Merman and I had been asked to perform during the Irving Berlin tribute at the Academy Awards in April 1983. I could not do it, but Merman was going to appear and sing many of those songs she made famous. The following day she was going to leave Los Angeles and come visit me in Palm Springs. When I didn't see her on the Oscar ceremony, I became alarmed. After great trouble getting through, I found out that she had had a stroke and was in the hospital. She had been all packed—ready to go—and was on the phone calling for a car when she collapsed.

I went to see Merman in a New York hospital, and she could neither walk nor talk. But I could, and I said, "Look, Merman, I made it. I can walk and talk and so will you. Remember when we performed together on *Over Easy,* and I switched 'you' and 'I' in the wonderful song from *Annie Get Your Gun,* and sang, 'Anything I can do *you* can do better'?" She valiantly tried to do just that.

But the Lord had other plans for my loved friend.

I like to think that her next show will have these words from Psalm 13:6:

> I will sing unto the Lord,
> because he hath dealt
> bountifully with me.

My mother used to tell me that "life doesn't owe you a living," and she was right. Nowadays some people, both old and young, seem to feel that life does owe us all a living. I don't believe it. I think we owe something to life, for the privilege of living.

And that, after all these words, brings me to this: I want to sing in a bar again. I started in Hollywood that way, so why not end up that way? I'd like to sit on top of two pianos, with a bass and a drum, and just sing softly. My natural, quiet soprano has come back—sort of. I could use it, sort of, and sing to people right around me, close to me. I bet some friends I love would come and sing with me—Max Showalter, Van Johnson, Maxine Andrews, Ben Dean. Maybe even Heller and Larry and my grandchildren would guest star. Wouldn't that be some cast?

There are days when it's easy and days and days and nights when it's not.

I find the only solution is to keep as busy as possible, and I have managed to do that almost to an extreme. Sitting down to write this chapter in my life makes me face the fact that I am seventy years old now. I just can't conceive of how that happened.

My mother, my sister, my friend Bessie Mae Sue Ella, yes, but me? Where did the time go? Now I know the true meaning of Ogden Nash's lyrics from *One Touch of Venus:*

> Time is so old, and love so brief
> Love is pure gold and time a thief . . .

I was thirty when I first sang those words. Now I am seventy, and I have found that love *is* pure gold, and I have had a lot of love.

Index